MENDING A SHATTERED HEART

A Guide for Partners of Sex Addicts

Second Edition

MENDING A SHATTERED HEART

A Guide for Partners of Sex Addicts

Second Edition

©2009, 2011

Edited by
STEFANIE CARNES, PhD

Gentle Path
PRESS

Carefree, Arizona

Gentle Path
P R E S S

Gentle Path Press
P.O. Box 3172
Carefree, Arizona 85377
www.gentlepath.com

Second edition: 2011

For more information regarding our publications, please contact
Gentle Path Press at 1-800-708-1796 (toll-free U.S. only).

ISBN: 978-0-9826505-9-2

Editor's note: All the stories in this book are based on actual experiences.
The names and details have been changed to protect the privacy of the
people involved. In some cases, composites have been created.

Contents

Introduction

If you're reading this book, chances are your heart has been shattered. Your world has been turned upside down in a whirlwind of betrayal, anger, and confusion. The authors of this book want you to know that you are not alone. Hundreds of unsuspecting people wake up every day to discover their loved one, the one person whom they are supposed to trust completely, has been living a life of lies and deceit because they suffer from a disease–sex addiction.

Clinicians conservatively estimate that between 1 and 3 percent of the general population are sex addicts. Even those conservative numbers translate into more than 10 million people in the United States alone. Furthermore, sex addiction is not just an epidemic in the United States; it reaches all cultures and ethnicities spanning the globe. However, this is a disease shrouded in secrecy and shame.

Even in our progressive society, we seldom speak of sex addiction. Those afflicted tend to cautiously guard their identities, so they are not labeled and stigmatized. The general population remains uneducated or misinformed; they often equate sex addiction with sex offending or pedophilia, even though the majority of individuals with problematic sexual acting out cannot be classified into either of those categories.

Support groups, treatment centers, and literature for sex addiction have proliferated in the past twenty years. Addicts can now turn to many confidential resources for support. Yet sex addiction is a family disease because it impacts the entire family system. But, unfortunately, support is generally not available for the partners and family of sex addicts. The wreckage of pain and suffering rips through the family. Spouses or partners are devastated and angry. Children are frightened and confused. Parents of the sex addict wonder, *What did I do wrong?*

As the spouse or partner of a sex addict, you feel the responsibility to sort through this wreckage and to help your family do the same. Yet the resources for spouses and partners are few and far between.

1

You may feel like you cannot reach out for help because you want to preserve the confidentiality of the addict. Or you may feel shame, embarrassment, and worry what others might think of you. The stress generated from this experience is akin to a major medical trauma; however, people going through a major medical trauma often have a community of people providing support. You, on the other hand, are left to suffer alone.

This book is designed for the spouse or partner in the initial phases of learning about the sex addiction in their lives. During this time, you'll be flooded with questions and feel confused. Each chapter is based on frequently asked questions by partners. These questions include: *Should I stay or should I go? Is this going to get better?* and *What should I tell the kids?* At the back of the book, you will find a list of resources, such as Twelve Step meetings, inpatient treatment resources, and recommended books categorized by topic.

This book would not have been possible without the expertise of the people who contributed to it: Jennifer Schneider, Cara Tripodi, Patrick Carnes, Omar Minwalla, Mavis Humes Baird, Sonja Rudie, Barbara Levinson, Robert Weiss, Joe Kort, Caroline Smith, and Paul and Virginia Hartman. Their willingness and diligence during the writing of this book was amazing and driven by genuine compassion for the partner's struggle. The authors have collectively worked with thousands of sex addicts and their families. Families like yours have taught us about their suffering. Many of the authors have experienced sex addiction in their own lives and have been touched deeply. Here, they share some of their own personal wisdom.

The communities that support compassionate treatment for sex addicts and their families have also been instrumental in the development of this book. These organizations include the Society for the Advancement of Sexual Health, the International Institute for Trauma and Addiction Professionals, and the network of Certified Sex Addiction Therapists. During the writing of the first edition, my employer at the time, Pine Grove Behavioral Health and Addiction Services, also made this book possible. My Pine Grove colleagues' commitment to treating people with love and acceptance has been a constant inspiration; their open-mindedness, patience, and support of my work has been immeasurable. I would also like to express appreciation to Gentle Path Press, especially to Amy Campbell, Rebecca Post, Corrine Casanova, Serena Castillo, and Suzanne O'Connor for their assistance with this book. Finally, I would like to thank my father, Patrick Carnes, for his loving support, encouragement, and advice.

It is my sincere hope that this book will provide information and comfort to individuals and families struggling with sexual addiction. Many people have walked this path before you. Allow their wisdom to guide you and provide you with the answers to your questions. Know that you are not alone and you do not have to suffer silently.

— Stefanie Carnes, PhD, CSAT-S

ജ‌ങ

Part One:
For All Partners of Sex Addicts

ജ‌ര

Editor's note: Each chapter in part 1 of this book contains information that all partners of sex addicts should read. The information here is intended to support you as you begin to learn about sex addiction and what your options are as a partner of a sex addict. The Question & Answer format was used for the specific purpose of answering some of the most common questions that partners of sex addicts have.

Chapter One:
What Is Sex Addiction?

Stefanie Carnes, PhD, CSAT-S

ℰℭ

Tiffany could not believe what she just heard. After all of the sexual improprieties her husband, Jason, had engaged in, he was blaming her for his acting out. According to Jason, Tiffany was critical, blaming, non-supportive, and wasn't meeting his sexual needs. He had attempted this bait and switch before, shortly after she discovered his first affair, and she had fallen for it—hook, line, and sinker. She thought, *Maybe I have been pushing him away. I have been emotionally and physically distant in recent months.* The birth of their daughter, Amy, had placed a strain on their marriage. The love and intense connection they had in the beginning of their relationship just wasn't there anymore. Life had taken over, and it had gotten busy.

Jason rationalized to Tiffany that his affair was just a meaningless sexual fling. He told her that his affair partner had come on to him, and he had tried to resist her advances but eventually succumbed to a one-night stand. He had promised Tiffany he would immediately cut the ties with the woman, but Tiffany suspected he still had contact with her. She confronted him a few times, but he always had an explanation. Tiffany began to wonder if she was being paranoid. She ignored her gut instinct and chose instead to keep the peace and move on with life.

Two years after Amy was born, Jason lost his job. He was underperforming at work and it cost the family dearly. He was distracted in all areas of his life, including his duties parenting and helping out around the house. He even became financially irresponsible. He seemed to be living in a fantasy world that Tiffany couldn't penetrate. She found herself in the role of primary breadwinner, primary parent, housekeeper, and accountant. With all these extra burdens, Tiffany became resentful of Jason, and she didn't have much time to invest in her marriage. Admittedly, she became more critical and unsupportive of her husband. As her anger and distance increased, his neediness increased. Occasionally, their love would spark and they would reconnect. *He's such a good guy,* she would tell herself. *Soon, he's going to snap out of this depression he's been in.*

Tiffany's nightmare escalated one morning when she accidentally opened an application on Jason's iPhone. She discovered he had a profile designed for married men to find affair partners. In his in-box, she read many communications from women with which he was clearly having affairs. Suddenly, it became clear to her why he was always so possessive of his phone. Tiffany confronted Jason, who claimed it was all a joke and that he was just "playing around." Tiffany was furious. Because she had an important business meeting that morning, she placed herself on automatic pilot and went through the motions of her day. She stayed late at work that evening, not wanting to face the circumstances. When she got home, Jason had an emotional breakdown. He told her he believed he was a sex addict and needed help. He reported that what started off as curiosity progressed and he felt out of control. He was spending hours every day on the Internet looking at different women's profiles and trying to hook up with them. With tears in his eyes, he explained that he had done things that disgusted him and were degrading and meaningless. He felt worthless and hopeless, and felt entirely addicted. *I've tried to stop,* he exclaimed. *I even went to see a therapist about it. This addiction has totally consumed my life! I've given up everything that I ever cared about, and it's just getting worse.*

Tiffany knew Jason was hurting, but after his betrayal, she found it hard to empathize with him. She gave Jason the cold shoulder for weeks. Her anger and resentment colored every interaction with him. She had become a nagging, angry "mommy" figure to Jason, and she detested every minute of it. She harassed him about being unemployed and not following through on his responsibilities. She was embarrassed to tell anyone about Jason's acting out, so she confided only in her sister, who advised her to divorce Jason. She thought about the impact divorce would have on Amy. She considered taking Amy and moving in with her parents or asking Jason to move out.

Jason finally snapped under all the pressure. He told Tiffany he felt like he could never live up to her expectations and that he would never be good enough for her. He said her nagging and criticism drove him to seek solace from women who believed he was worthwhile and attractive. He told her that she was stingy with sex and even when she did agree to it, it was routine and boring.

Tiffany was astonished that he was blaming all of the dysfunction in their relationship on her. He was a master at deflecting blame and responsibility and thought the best defense was a good offense. When Tiffany thought through the situation logically, she wondered why she tolerated all of this abuse from Jason. But on an emotional level, she questioned herself: *Maybe I have been condescending. I have been pretty horrible to be around.*

As in the case of Tiffany, the betrayal experienced by most partners of sex addicts is devastating and confusing. Addicts can be masters at deflecting blame and responsibility. Discovering your partner is a sex addict is a trauma that, for many partners, causes an acute stress reaction and possibly symptoms of post-traumatic stress disorder (PTSD), such as hypervigilance and intrusive thinking about the trauma. The deception and violation of the covenant of the partnership shatters the trust in the relationship. Feelings of loss, pain, and shame can be overwhelming. Many partners find themselves overwhelmed with questions: *What is sex addiction? How did I not know this was going on? Is there any hope for this relationship? How can I protect myself in the future?* This book addresses many of these important questions.

How do I know if my partner is a sex addict?

Sex addiction is not the same thing as infidelity. It is not a moral problem or an "excuse to behave badly." Sex addiction progresses, gets out of control, becomes a compulsive pattern, and takes over the addict's life. The illness escalates, and most addicts have profound shame and despair around their behavior. According to a clinical definition that is often used, it is an unhealthy relationship to any sexual experience (thoughts, fantasies, activities, etc.) that a person continues to engage in despite adverse consequences. As with other addictions, many sex addicts report feelings of withdrawal, such as irritability or restlessness when unable to act out sexually. Furthermore, some report a tolerance to sexual behaviors, where their sexual behaviors escalate over time, increasing in intensity. For example, someone with an addiction to pornography may find themselves needing more and more stimulation to achieve the original effect.

Following are ten key criteria for sex addiction. If someone meets three or more of these ten criteria, he or she would be considered a sex addict. These criteria need to be present over a prolonged period of time (e.g., six months) and not be part of a major mood swing, such as in bipolar disorder.

1. Recurrent failure to resist sexual impulses in order to engage in specific sexual behaviors

2. Frequently engaging in those behaviors to a greater extent or over a longer period of time than intended

3. Persistent desire or unsuccessful efforts to stop, reduce, or control those behaviors

4. Inordinate amounts of time spent in obtaining sex, being sexual, or recovering from sexual experiences

5. Preoccupation with sexual behavior or preparatory activities

6. Frequent engaging in the behavior when expected to fulfill occupational, academic, domestic, or social obligations

7. Continuation of the behavior despite knowledge of having a persistent or recurrent social, financial, psychological, or physical problem that is caused or exacerbated by the behavior

8. The need to increase the intensity, frequency, number, or risk level of behaviors in order to achieve the desired effect; or diminished effect with continued behaviors at the same level of intensity, frequency, number, or risk

9. Giving up or limiting social, occupational, or recreational activities because of the behavior

10. Distress, anxiety, restlessness, or irritability if unable to engage in the behavior

It is very important that an experienced, trained clinician assist you with an evaluation to help determine if your loved one is genuinely struggling with an addiction. If she or he is a sex addict, the therapist should help the addict develop a sexual health and relationship plan, which outlines healthy versus unhealthy behaviors for recovery. When addicts enter recovery, they typically abstain from sex for a ninety-day abstinence period. This allows the addicts to learn how to tolerate their feelings without medicating sexually. After this abstinence period, addicts usually re-engage in their sexual health and relationship plan. Sex addicts have to learn how to live within their sexual health plan, much like an individual in recovery from an eating disorder learns how to eat in a healthy way.

How did I not know this was happening?

Sex addiction thrives in secrecy. Addicts will often go to any length to protect their double life. Their thinking process becomes impaired and they minimize the severity of their behaviors and take risks that can cause tremendous consequences. Often partners are kept completely in the dark about the sexual acting out. Others might know about some of the sexual activities, but not the extent of the behaviors. When the addict starts to "hit bottom," it usually involves heart-wrenching discoveries for the partner.

There are many ways you may find out about the behavior, such as stumbling across pictures or websites on a computer, learning about your partner's arrests, contracting a sexually transmitted disease, or finding incriminating phone records or receipts. The addict may demonstrate other signs as well, such as unaccounted time and money, late hours, decreased interest in sexual activity, or anger and irritability. You may have had suspicions about the addict's behavior that you dismissed until more evidence came to the surface and it became impossible to ignore.

Early on, most couples focus on getting the addict help. The addict is often the focus of treatment and the partner's pain is often overlooked or seen as secondary. Sometimes the partner is included as part of couples therapy during the course of treatment. But many spouses find themselves in a great deal of pain and confusion and also need support. When the addict's treatment is primary, the partner's issues are frequently neglected. It is important for you to have an opportunity to get the support you need, such as individual or group therapy to help you cope with this painful experience.

Is sex addiction a new term for an old problem?

Awareness of sex addiction has greatly increased in recent years. Even just ten or twenty years ago, some practitioners argued that sex addiction didn't exist. Now, it is a widely recognized illness, although researchers and clinicians still don't agree on what to call it. The most common terms for this illness include sex addiction, sexual compulsivity, sexual impulsivity, and hypersexual behavior disorder. Additionally, there is disagreement over the best types of treatment approaches. Since it has not been accepted as an illness for many years, the field of sex addiction is very far behind in terms of research and evidence-based treatments, although studies have been increasing in recent years. Because many therapists have not been trained on how to work with sex addiction, it is important when seeking treatment that you look for a therapist with specific training in sex addiction. You can search for a certified sex addiction therapist by going to www.sexualaddictiontherapists.com

With the increase in use of Internet pornography, sex addiction has become more common. Friendly faces of celebrities, politicians, and sports figures are now seen engaging in a treatment process for their illness. This has helped reduce the stigma of sex addiction. However, there is still a lot of confusion and misinformation. For example, the media furthers the stigma around sex addiction by confusing it with sex offending and antisocial or sociopathic behavior. For example, the "Craigslist Killer" was labeled by the media as a sex addict, when clearly he had antisocial and sociopathic behaviors.

What's the difference between sex addiction and other sexual behaviors?

There is a difference between sex addiction, sex offending, antisocial behavior or sociopathy, and paraphilias, such as fetish behaviors. For example, someone could have a sexual interest in a paraphilia, such as sadomasochistic sexuality, but not have the compulsive characteristics of addiction. Typical sex addicts have high shame and remorse around their behavior, feelings of despair, and commonly have a history of trauma. They will often seek treatment voluntarily (usually with prodding from their significant other). They can be depressed, anxious, and have difficulties with intimacy and attachment. They can also have a high propensity for being suicidal. Most clinicians would see this typical sex addict as being able to respond to treatment.

People with an antisocial personality, or antisocial features, typically have little to no shame around their behavior. They have more thought distortions and denial, and are less likely to be suicidal. They typically have more physical abuse in their backgrounds and a history of other types of offenses. Clinicians generally regard these people as having a decreased amenability for treatment; they are also reluctant to voluntarily seek treatment.

Are all sex addicts the same?

Dr. Patrick Carnes, in his groundbreaking book *Out of the Shadows,* originally identified three different "levels" of addiction[1]. These levels range according to severity. (See Figure 1.1, Levels of Addiction, on the next page).

Level One is the most common. These addicts struggle with compulsive behaviors, such as Internet pornography, affairs, and anonymous sexual encounters. These behaviors tend to grow progressively more out of control over time. For some, the escalation occurs in terms of how frequently they act out, how much time they spend doing it, and the resulting consequences. Many Level One addicts never progress to Level Two or Three. As a matter of fact, most addicts remain in the same level; however, there are other addicts whose behavior escalates to more risky, intense, and/or dangerous behaviors.

Figure 1.1 Levels of Addiction

Levels of Addiction					
Level of Addiction	Behavior	Cultural Standards	Legal Consequences/ Risks	Victim	Public Opinion of Addiction
Level One	Masturbation, compulsive relationships, pornography, prostitution, and anonymous sex	Depending on behavior, activities are seen as acceptable or tolerable. Some specific behaviors, such as prostitution and homo-sexuality, are sources of controversy.	Sanctions against those behaviors, when illegal, are ineffectively and randomly enforced. Low priority for enforcement officials generates minimal risk for addict.	These behaviors are perceived as victimless crimes. However, victimization and exploitation are often components.	Public attitudes are characterized by ambivalence or dislike. For some behaviors, such as prostitution, there is a competing negative image of glamorous decadence.
Level Two	Exhibitionism, voyeurism, indecent phone calls, and indecent liberties	None of these behaviors is acceptable.	Behaviors are regarded as nuisance offenses. Risk is involved since offenders, when observed, are actively prosecuted.	There is always a victim.	Addict is perceived as pathetic and sick but harmless. Often these behaviors are the objects of jokes that dismiss the pain of the addict.
Level Three	Child molestation, incest, and rape	Each behavior represents a profound violation of cultural boundaries.	Extreme legal consequences create high-risk situations for the addict.	There is always a victim.	Public becomes outraged. Perpetrators are seen by many as subhuman and beyond help.

What you are going through is not unique. There are many others who have gone through similar situations. People have many different responses when discovering their partner is a sex addict. The situations that follow are based on real case scenarios:

- Deborah had always been concerned about her husband Joe's pornography use. Imagine her distress when her adult daughter called and said she had walked in on her father having sex with a nineteen-year-old woman. After this incident, Deborah logged on to Joe's computer and found thousands of downloaded pornography images and videos. Deborah demanded that Joe seek an evaluation.

- Ken was upset when he discovered his partner, Mark, had repeated sexual encounters with different men from his office. He learned that he engaged in sexual acts that he found distasteful and had never done with him. He struggled to deal with the detailed knowledge of these sexual behaviors. Over time, it became clear to Ken that Mark's behavior included many more partners and that he was not ready to change. Ken eventually decided to leave his relationship with Mark in order to move on with his life.

- Lauren was upset when she found women's underwear in her bedroom that didn't belong to her, but she became outraged when she found out they belonged to her niece. Her husband later admitted that he had been molested when he was young and forced to wear girls' underpants. Over time he developed a panty fetish. He reported that he could not stop looking at fetish websites and felt he needed help. Lauren came to understand the nature of her husband's sexual trauma. After going to treatment and seeking marital therapy, the couple reconciled.

- Penny discovered her husband, Andy, was a sex addict when she found thousands of images of downloaded pornography on her computer, many of which were of very young women. She was so hurt, she immediately threatened divorce. Andy decided he was going to commit suicide and called his father to tell him where to find his body. He jumped off a 100-foot cliff but survived. The paramedics found him with a suicide note in his pocket. He was released from the hospital and sent to treatment.

- James found out his wife, Jennifer, was having another affair—her fourth. This time it was with her priest with whom she engaged in hours of ongoing phone sex. Jennifer attempted to commit suicide through carbon monoxide poisoning while sitting in her car with the engine on.

- Rita's nine-year-old son came to her after he walked in on her husband, Scott, having sex with a prostitute in his room. Rita knew that her husband had been seeing prostitutes, but after her son's discovery, she felt she could not go on with the relationship the way it was. She struggled with how to explain it to her son and was infuriated with Scott and decided to seek divorce.

- Pat discovered his wife, Ellen, was meeting up with men at adult bookstores and having sex with them in the parking lot. Although he was very upset about the dangerous situation she was putting herself in and concerned about sexually transmitted diseases, he didn't want to be perceived as a prude. Eventually, he decided to join her. They began acting out sexually with strangers and couples together.

While each family's situation is unique, all of them have something in common: unmanageability, intensity, and crisis. These are core elements of relationships that contain active sex addiction.

Now that I know my partner is a sex addict, what should I do?

The first action steps you should take include establishing your safety, protecting yourself, and getting support. A painful reality is that at this point you may not know the whole story. It is common in the early stages of discovery for partners to know about the "tip of the iceberg." Many hidden behaviors may still be submerged underneath the water. As a matter of fact, there is a common dynamic that occurs among couples at this stage called "staggered disclosure." Here is the typical path of how addicts will disclose information to their partner:

- Deny everything.

- Disclose what they think they can get away with.

- Disclose a bit more.

- Get confronted as more comes out.

- Disclose all.

- (For some couples the addict will repeat this pattern.)

This staggered disclosure pattern is traumatic for partners and destroys the trust in the relationship. The addict basically tells the partner, *I am really telling you everything;* then more surfaces, *No, now I am really telling you everything,* and so on. So the partner doesn't know what to believe and typically doesn't believe a word the addict says after this staggered disclosure process has occurred.

Because of this pattern, when an addict seeks treatment, most clinical therapists will assist the addict with a "formal disclosure process." This is where the addict comes clean with the partner about all of his or her addictive behaviors. This benefits the addict in his or her recovery process to let go of secrets, while at the same time, it empowers the partner with the truth. This can be a very difficult and emotional process for both parties. (See chapter 2 for more details.)

Many therapists will try to delay this disclosure process. The two most common reasons for delaying a disclosure are that the addict is not ready to come clean and is still in some level of denial about the addiction, or the partner is not prepared, does not have enough social support, or is not stable enough to manage the stress of a disclosure. If the therapist you are working with is delaying the disclosure process, take his or her advice on this matter. The disclosure will come eventually. In the interim, while it may be difficult, you can establish initial boundaries for self-protection and garner some critical social support.

What do I need to do to protect myself from further harm?

There are some critical action steps you can take, including the following:

- Get tested for sexually transmitted diseases (STDs), whether you believe the addict has been sexually active with another person or not.

- Use protection or abstain from sex with the addict.

- Seek individual therapy for yourself from a certified or experienced therapist who specializes in sex addiction. If a therapist is available that specializes in working with partners, that is even better. If this person offers a group for partners, attend! This can be invaluable as a source of support for you.

- Insist that the addict receive an evaluation from a trained therapist and follow the recommendations from the therapist/treatment team.

- Work with your therapist to set initial boundaries for self-protection while you evaluate whether or not the addict engages in treatment (remember, actions speak louder than words!). (See chapter 5 for more information on setting these initial boundaries.)

- Work with your therapist to determine who in your support system is a safe person to talk to about this. Confide in a select few trusted individuals who can support you.

Cutting-edge therapy for sex addiction is an intensive process that involves lots of group, Twelve Step work, and individual and family therapy. A typical fifty-minute session with a therapist once a week will not be enough for a new addict in recovery. It's going to take commitment to the process.

If you find the addict is resistant to treatment, is in denial around his or her behaviors, and continues to lie to you, he or she is likely still in the recreational phase of addiction. Just as in substance abuse, addicts have to experience consequences of their behavior and feel some desperation created by losses in their lives in order to change. This is described as "hitting bottom" in recovery circles. Every addict has a different "bottom." In many cases, the healthiest thing to do in this situation is to leave or propose a therapeutic separation. (A therapeutic separation is when the couple splits but agrees to continue to do therapy together to see if they can make progress on the relationship.) Often when the partner leaves, it propels the addict into recovery. If the addict doesn't engage in recovery and remains in active addiction, it is usually a good decision for the partner not to live with the addict. (See chapter 13 for more on leaving the relationship.)

Who can I talk to about this?

Partners often feel tremendous shame about the addict's behavior and feel like they should take this secret to their grave. It is important to remember that the shame about the behavior belongs to the addict and not to you. Many partners will take on that shame and internalize the addict's behavior as being about them. You may think, *If I was more attractive, sexier, a better spouse, etc., he or she wouldn't have done this.* This is entirely not true! Nothing you could have done would have changed the progression of the disease of addiction. You only need to look at all the incredibly beautiful and famous partners of nationally recognized sex addicts to know that this is not about being beautiful and sexy. Their behavior is a disease and it would have happened no matter who they were in a relationship with.

Some partners may be tempted to tell the sex addict to come clean to many people about his or her behavior because they are angry and want others to know what the addict has done. Partners who share this information out of anger with lots of people (including in-laws, people at church, and children), usually live to regret it. Sharing this information should be a thoughtful process, discussed with a therapist if possible. It is typically recommended in the early stages of recovery that the addict and partner be selective on whom they confide in about the addiction. First, it is important that both you and your partner have a few support people selected. You both need people who can listen to your story and be a shoulder to cry on. The people you select should be individuals that you feel will not judge you later if you choose to stay with the addict or choose to divorce.

I feel so emotional about this, is this normal?

In a very important research study on partners of sex addicts, researchers Steffens and Rennie[2] discovered that partners often experience acute stress symptoms and characteristics of PTSD following the discovery of sex addiction in their significant other. This was groundbreaking research for partners. Prior to this, most therapists did not recognize partners as trauma victims. Therapists have since become much more sensitive to the partner's experience and recognize the depth of the pain of the betrayal and how this can impact the partner's emotional stability. It is not uncommon for partners to experience a host of psychological reactions triggered by this traumatic experience, including

- emotional turmoil, such as tearfulness and depression
- fear that may manifest in self-protective behaviors (such as acting like a detective to determine if the addict is acting out again)
- obsessing about the trauma
- avoiding thinking about or discussing the trauma (a common reaction to a traumatic experience)
- intrusive thinking about the addiction or acting-out behaviors, which can make it hard to focus on normal life
- sleeplessness and/or nightmares

According to these researchers, these are natural reactions that occur as a result of experiencing trauma, and are made in an effort to cope. Recognizing that this is an actual traumatic event is important for you as a partner and validates the series of emotions that you may be experiencing.

Where should I start?

There are many things you can do to help yourself cope with this trauma and any symptoms you might be experiencing. First, and most important, sharing your story and pain with others can be very healing. Trauma therapists call this "processing" your trauma. It can be particularly helpful to share your experiences with others who have been in similar situations and can validate your feelings and identify with what you are sharing. This is the healing power of group therapy. Even though feelings of anger, pain, and shame will likely surface, getting those feelings out and getting support are critical to your healing. Sharing the pain and sadness that underlies the anger can help you grieve and prevent the buildup of resentments and unresolved sorrow.

Additionally, there are other types of treatments for trauma that your therapist might recommend. Treatments such as Eye Movement Desensitization & Reprocessing (EMDR), psychodrama, somatic experiencing, art therapy, and experiential therapies are common approaches for people who have experienced a trauma. You may want to ask your therapist if he or she is trained in any particular type of trauma treatment or if you can get a referral to do some specific trauma work.

You may have a whole host of other emotions, too. Some partners find themselves consumed by rage, others blame themselves, and some find themselves detaching emotionally from the relationship. Your emotional response will be unique and will likely be influenced by your childhood and any traumatic events from your past. For example, a partner who has a history of betrayal (an old wound) may feel extreme anger and resentment, as the current betrayal may be bringing up all the painful events from the past. Another partner who has experienced abandonment may internalize the betrayal and make it about themselves (*I'm not lovable enough*, etc.).

Each situation is different. The type of sexual acting out that the addict engaged in can also impact the partner's experience and make it more emotional and traumatic. For example, a partner of an addict who experiences a lot of public embarrassment, or committed serious sex offending behaviors (such as acting out with minors), or had sex with a close friend or family member, will have a level of stress to cope with that can be extreme. This can make an already excruciating process more painful, complicated, and heart wrenching.

Partners who cope the best tend to find an inner reserve of strength and step up and come to their own assistance. They tend to be willing to hit the situation head-on and are motivated to take action steps, such as

- seek critical social support

- go to therapy for themselves

- attend group therapy or Twelve Step meetings for partners and family members

- set healthy boundaries with the addict and stand by those boundaries

- remain introspective about how the past may be impacting current events and are willing to look at these issues therapeutically

- use the trauma to grow personally and to gain clarity on their relationship

- are contemplative and are slow to make big decisions

- are selective about who they confide in for support

- educate themselves

- obtain spiritual support

Remaining open for support and acknowledging this trauma can help you survive the emotional roller coaster you are now on. Most partners pass through six stages on this journey (see chapter 3). The early stages are full of emotional turmoil. As these stages pass, you will become a stronger person.

Picking up this book is a great first step in learning more about sex addiction and what options you have as a partner. This first chapter was designed to introduce you to the topic of sex addiction and to some of the common issues you will face. In this book you will learn about disclosure, the stages you will experience, setting boundaries, the impact of sex addiction on your sexuality, and garnering social support, such as therapy and Twelve Step fellowships. The second half of the book is designed for certain populations (such as families with children and addicts who acted out with people of the same sex). Some of the chapters in part 2 may not apply to your personal situation. Throughout the book, you will have an opportunity to learn about building a foundation for your healing, whether you decide to stay or leave the relationship. Most important, hopefully you will discover that you are not alone and that your situation is not insurmountable.

Chapter Two:
I Need to Know *Everything* That Happened…Or Do I?

Jennifer P. Schneider, MD, PhD

ℰℭ

Lorie, thirty-four, is a nurse and mother of two young children. She believed that her ten-year marriage to Todd, an engineer, was good. True, their sex life had decreased recently, but Todd told her it was because he was involved in an important and demanding project at work and he was usually exhausted by evening. He assured her this was temporary. Lorie's life began to fall apart when she accidentally discovered Todd's secret sexual life on the computer.

A multitude of unwelcome feelings assailed Lorie. She later said, *I felt total distrust in myself, my spouse, and the relationship. I felt betrayed, confused, afraid, and stunned. The person I loved and trusted most in the world had lied about who he was. I felt I had lived through a vast and sinister cover-up.*

Suddenly, Lorie had a hundred unanswered questions *Should I confront Todd? Where can I get more information? Who is a safe person to talk to about this crisis? Is this the end of our marriage?*

Most partners first learn about an addict's sexual behaviors by accident—a friend tells you your spouse is having an affair; you discover a hotel bill; or you overhear a telephone conversation. Perhaps you read an incriminating email, found a large amount of pornography on the computer, or discovered your spouse was having sex with someone online. Maybe your partner was fired because he or she engaged in cybersex at work. Or even worse, he or she was arrested for some type of illegal sexual activity.

Some people first find out about the addict's sexual activities when the addict reveals them out of fear, believing his or her partner has already discovered incriminating evidence. Another reason for disclosing what has been happening is that the addict can no longer tolerate his or her emotions. Perhaps you suspected all along that something was going on, and your suspicions were finally confirmed by looking through your partner's computer, mail, cell phone, or briefcase. No matter how you discovered the sex addiction, this chapter will answer questions you may have about this devastating discovery.

> *I got on my husband's computer and found some steamy*
> *messages to several women. I read all of them. Then I spent*
> *all morning looking through his computer. I found hundreds*
> *of pornographic photos. Some of them looked non-professional,*
> *as if those women had sent them to him. Recently he attached*
> *a camera to his computer, and I'm thinking he probably sends*
> *pictures of himself to those women. I'm appalled, shocked,*
> *dismayed, very angry, and I feel very ashamed—both about his*
> *behavior and about mine, for snooping the way I did. I'm too*
> *ashamed to tell anyone about it. Our sex life in the past has*
> *been pretty good, and I just don't understand this. I feel like*
> *I'm going insane!*

Lorie's reaction is natural and understandable. Today, millions of people are engaging in various forms of sex online, and many of them are now hooked on Internet pornography and other forms of compulsive sexual behavior. Thousands of partners are reeling from this kind of shock. You're not alone.

I've made the discovery, what comes next?

If you're like most partners in this situation, you confront the addict. If your partner agrees he or she has a problem, then a good next step is for the two of you to find a therapist knowledgeable about Internet pornography and sex addiction.

Early on in your counseling session, you will have a planned disclosure so that you can gain a more complete picture of your spouse's or partner's sexual activities. Before the disclosure, you need to clarify your goals with the therapist. For example, a positive intent of counseling could be moving toward greater intimacy or repairing your relationship. On the other hand, trying to obtain ammunition to punish, control, or manipulate your partner is a poor intent. You'll also work with the therapist to determine which details of your partner's sex addiction are important for you to know and how these details may affect you.

The therapist will also likely recommend that both you and your spouse or partner join mutual-support programs based on the Twelve Steps of Alcoholics Anonymous. Such programs now exist for both sex addicts and spouses, partners, and other family members whose lives have been impacted by someone else's sexual behavior. (See chapter 7 for more information on Twelve Step programs and their value in recovery.) In the Resource Guide on page 259, you'll find contact information for S-Anon and COSA, two self-help fellowships for families of sex addicts. Start by contacting them and making a commitment to attend just one meeting. Through these confidential fellowships, you will meet people who can best understand your feelings; these people have had experiences similar to yours, and they have learned how to cope and how to recover.

Feeling like you're losing your mind is common after learning the devastating details of a loved one's sex addiction. The following real-life scenarios show the various levels of frustration and heartbreak involved. As John, whose wife had been sexual with other men, relates:

> I couldn't concentrate. I got into two car accidents and did things like put milk in the cupboard and cereal in the refrigerator. I was afraid I would drive off a bridge or hurt myself using a kitchen knife.

Distraction and depression are common reactions to the crisis of discovery. That is why it's important to get help and support for yourself early on.

> My husband is spending more hours at night on the Internet and less time with me. More than once I walked in on him masturbating in front of the computer. Before he closed the screen, I saw he was looking at a nude woman. He seems much

more interested in the computer than in making love with me. When I confronted him, he said he's just a normal guy. He doesn't think he needs to change. Where do I go from here?

Whether or not your spouse or partner thinks he or she has a problem, your relationship certainly does. Perhaps your partner would be willing to go with you to a couple's therapist, especially one who understands how online sexual activities affect you and your marriage. If your partner is unwilling to go to counseling, go alone to figure out what your options are.

I recently discovered my husband was having an affair. He says it's over now and he's willing to go to counseling with me. I keep asking him for more information about her and their relationship. He's balking, but I feel driven to know everything. I can't stop thinking about it.

Why do I feel compelled to know all the nitty-gritty details?

Partners often initially ask for complete disclosure. This is a way for them to

- make sense of the past
- validate their suspicions about what was happening in the relationship—suspicions the addict often denied
- assess their risk of having been exposed to sexually transmitted diseases, to financial disaster, and to shame
- evaluate their partner's commitment to the future of the relationship
- have some sense of control

No matter how many details you know about your partner's acting out, the ultimate choice to change the behavior lies with him or her, not with you. Having more information won't give you more control. On the contrary, sometimes too much information can cause additional problems. You may end up obsessing even more about your partner's behavior. Intrusive thoughts about the addict can cause additional pain. For example, if you know "they" ate at a particular restaurant, you may decide to never go there again. Judy, who learned her husband had sex in their bedroom, insisted on replacing the bed. If you know your husband and his affair partner did a particular sexual activity together, you may find yourself obsessing about them when you and your husband share that activity. Two women who now wish they had been told less, share their stories.

> *I created a lot of pain for myself by asking questions and gathering information. I have a lot of negative memories to overcome. This ranges from songs on the radio to dates, places, and situations. There are numerous triggers.*

> *I wanted every detail. I thought that would help him with shame, and there was safety in knowing everything. Looking back on it now, I wouldn't have asked for such a detailed disclosure or insisted on complete honesty.*

Twelve Step members caution against giving "free rent in your head" to images that may be difficult to erase later. Consider carefully what information you need rather than asking for "everything."

How much information should I ask for?

Couples who have been through the painful process of disclosure have provided us with some guidelines about what to tell—and what not to tell. In brief, even though it may be painful initially, it's a good idea to ask for the broad outlines of all the significant compulsive activities. Addicts may be tempted to leave out some damaging material, often because they fear their partners will leave them.

This can be a big mistake. If a partner believes she or he has come to terms with the addict's sexual activities only to learn at a later time about other sexual behaviors, this can result in a major setback, destroying whatever progress the couple has made in their relationship. Staggered disclosures can make it very difficult to rebuild trust.

Maria explains:

There were several major disclosures over six months. I was completely devastated. He continued to disclose half-truths, only increasing my pain and making the situation worse. Each new disclosure was like reliving the initial pain all over again. I wish the truth had been disclosed all at once and not in bits and pieces.

Mark adds,

Disclosure came in parts during the first year. I felt immense pain and anger. Part of that was not being told. I felt lied to and didn't trust any part of the relationship.

The lesson here is that although giving and receiving a disclosure is a painful process, it's best for the relationship if the addict doesn't keep any big pieces for later disclosure.

As to what types of details are appropriate to ask for, this depends on the particular circumstances. For example, if the person your partner had the affair with is someone you know, it may be reasonable for you to know who this person is. For example, if the addict was having an affair with a co-worker, you will need to know this. The two of you will have to work out how your partner can limit contact with this person. On the other hand, it is best not to ask for details about sexual activities or locations, because this information often causes more pain.

I can't help feeling that a lot of this is my fault. My guilt and shame make it hard for me to talk about this with other people. What can I do?

Partners often feel excessively responsible for other people. If things don't turn out the way you want, you may feel responsible and that it was your fault. When the problems are of a sexual nature, there's extra shame attached to them. As Joy recalls,

*When my husband first recognized he was a sex addict, I felt a
lot of shame. He went around telling his friends, which just
made me want to sink through the floor. I was sure they would
think I hadn't been a good enough sex partner. I thought, if
only I'd lost more weight or dressed differently, or even cooked
him better meals, he wouldn't have needed those other women.
I kept thinking it was my fault.*

Unfortunately, an attitude like Joy's can keep you isolated at
a time when you need support from others. One of the advantages of
being involved in a self-help group is that you will be around other
people who have similar feelings and experiences. This will help
defuse your shame. Some group members will have been working on
their own recovery for some time. They will truly understand your
situation and won't blame you. They will help you sort out how you
may have contributed to the problem, but they will also help you see
that you had no control over your partner's behavior.

Tell me a little bit more about disclosure; for example, what is a formal disclosure?

The first information you receive about the addict's sexual
activities usually comes to you with no warning. In other words, this
is not a planned disclosure. Your initial reaction is likely to be shock,
dismay, and anger. You may threaten to leave. You may ask a thousand
questions. If you engage in counseling, you likely will have the
opportunity to participate in a formal disclosure in which you will
hear from your spouse and ask questions. This should be done in a safe
setting—in the office of a knowledgeable therapist (or perhaps in an
inpatient setting), after preparations are made to ensure the best
possible outcome.

Several individual therapy sessions come before the formal
disclosure, some with you, some with your spouse or partner. The
addict will be taught to disclose with integrity—to reveal the information while taking responsibility and avoiding blaming others.
Usually the addict receives help writing an "amends" or "I apologize"
letter to you, in which he or she lists the ways his or her behavior has

hurt and affected you. It includes an offer to answer any of your questions about the past. Since rebuilding trust has a great deal to do with how serious the addict is about recovery, the early therapy sessions will emphasize behavioral changes as well as a commitment to work actively on addiction recovery.

You also may have individual sessions with the therapist to prepare you for the disclosure. The therapist will discuss your role in the "dance" of the addiction, which is not the same as being responsible for the addict's actions. You will also discuss what information is useful for you to have. If you want to know all the "gory details," the therapist will work with you on understanding why this may not be in your best interest initially.

Some therapists will agree to plan a session in the future at which time you'll have the opportunity to learn additional information, such as more details about the acting out. The therapist will also encourage you to become involved in Twelve Step recovery. The therapist will likely ask you to think about and write down your thoughts on the following items. These will be the basis for discussion during the disclosure session.

1. Make a commitment to yourself to use the disclosure as a way to start your healing process. You can decide if you want to work on the relationship after you have heard what the addict has to say. Part of working on yourself is acknowledging your fears about the situation.

2. Acknowledge that knowing only part of the truth hurts and that being in limbo contributes to the confusion, fear, and anger.

3. Write a letter of anger about what you do know. Identify all the ways the addict's behavior has had an impact on you.

4. Write a boundary letter about how you want things to be different. Review the letter with your therapist or Twelve Step sponsor, and then read it to your partner.

5. Formulate any questions you have and what type of information you want to know.

6. Identify where you have made threats that represent your fear that you are not good enough and that you seek validation primarily through your spouse.

The formal disclosure may take up to two hours or more. The therapist will monitor both you and your partner's reactions to prevent the session from breaking into acrimony or shutting down completely. Many couples consider this disclosure session to be a turning point in their relationship, an opportunity to begin to establish a healthier marriage. For some, the disclosure will reveal it's time for the couple to begin new lives apart from each other. One partner who has gone through the disclosure process advises, *Do the disclosure soon and in the safety of a supportive environment, such as a therapist's office. Be fearlessly honest, but not detailed. Be willing to share without regard to consequences that might affect your honesty. Try to understand your partner's feelings without judging them or closing down. Realize you are valuable and lovable, regardless of what anyone says or does. Look at being honest as a gift you give yourself. You can say, "That's who I really am." Give others the choice to decide to like you or not, to be with you or not.*[2]

What are the consequences of disclosure?

Disclosure of affairs or other sexual acting out is likely to cause you pain, as well as shame, guilt, anger, or depression. At first you may distrust everyone, fear abandonment, lose sexual desire, or even become physically ill. Other potential consequences include loss of self-esteem and the decreased ability to concentrate or to function at work. The addict may feel guilt, shame, anger, and fear that the partner will leave. The disclosure may, at least initially, damage the couple's relationship even more, or it could result in separation or divorce. The disclosure may also damage the addict's relationship with his or her children or friends.

Facing these negative consequences can make addicts reluctant to admit their behaviors to their partners. However, addicts need to remember that, in the long run, it's the behaviors not the disclosure that led to the negative consequences. Even without disclosure, it's likely that eventually the same outcomes would take place. If disclosure has only negative effects, it's unlikely that couples who have gone through the experience would recommend it to others. Yet, when 164 addicts and partners were surveyed months to years after disclosure, 96 percent of addicts and 93 percent of partners felt it had been the right thing to do.[3] Both groups reported significant positive aspects of disclosure. For addicts, these included

- honesty and an end to putting on a false front
- an end to denial
- hope for the future of the relationship
- a chance for my partner to get to know me better
- a new start, whether in the same relationship or not

The positive aspects of disclosure for partners included

- clarity about the situation
- validation that I'm not crazy
- hope for the future of the relationship
- finally having the information necessary to decide about the future

One of many women whose husband covered up his behavior by casting doubt on their wives' emotional state relates, *One of the most helpful things about the disclosure for me was that it confirmed my reality. My husband had repeatedly told me how crazy and jealous I was. Over time I had started believing him. Finding out I had not misread the situation helped me to begin trusting myself, that I wasn't as crazy as he had said or as I had thought.*

Despite her pain, another woman felt the disclosure could be the start of a better marriage: *It was the best and worst day of my life. I knew for once that he told the truth at the risk of great personal cost. It gave me hope that he could grow up and face life's responsibilities. It was the first time his words of love and his actions were congruent. I felt outraged and sick, yet I also felt respected and relieved. It gave me hope for our relationship.*

In the past, I've threatened to leave should my partner have an affair or even get involved sexually with someone online. How likely are couples to split up after discovery or disclosure?

Threats to leave are a common, easily understood reaction to the shock of learning that your partner has betrayed you by being sexual with another person. Many partners have some suspicions about the addict's behavior long before the addict admits the secrets. Some of these partners confronted the addict and threatened to leave; others said nothing.

But once the partner discovers the acting-out behavior, the majority do threaten to leave or end the marriage or relationship. However, only a few do separate, and in a study of sex addicts and partners, half of those who separated eventually reunited.[4] Of those partners who threatened to leave but didn't, half changed their minds because the addict became involved in recovery work; the partner did so as well, and both went to therapy and worked out their problems. Sometimes the addict sought treatment because of the partner's threat to leave; other times it was because of other consequences the addict experienced.

For the remaining group of partners who didn't leave despite threatening to do so, the reason was primarily out of a fear of abandonment, the study showed. Some partners have childhood wounds that result in a great fear of abandonment. Life without the addict may seem too difficult. They may conclude that living with the pain of the addict's acting out is better than living alone. They may be moved by the addict's promises and decide to give the addict another chance, threatening to leave "if it happens again." Some partners feared confronting the addict. A minister whose wife had online and offline sexual partners stayed with her because he felt he needed to maintain a certain image before his congregation, and he didn't want to subject his children to a divorce.

Couples who stay together and get involved in addiction recovery have to simultaneously work on individual and couple recovery. This is more complicated than focusing on your individual recovery. Sometimes, especially if you don't have young children, one or both partners may feel it's easier to separate. Sometimes the partner feels so much pain, anger, and betrayal that a period of separation is helpful while she or he works through the emotions and issues.

If you're thinking about separation, it's a good idea to discuss it with your counselor or support group. Ask yourself: *What are my motives? Am I threatening to leave to force my partner to attend therapy and Twelve Step meetings? Or do I feel I need the separation for me? How will my children be impacted by this?* In general, it's advisable not to make major decisions right away unless you need to leave for your safety. So think about it, get input from others, and then make a decision based on what's best for you, not what the effect will be on the addict.

Can we do the disclosure right away so we can get on with rebuilding our relationship?

The first thing you need to realize is that disclosure isn't a onetime event—it's a process. In the survey mentioned earlier of 164 recovering sex addicts and partners, 59 percent of addicts and 70 percent of partners reported there had been more than one major disclosure.[5] Sometimes the initial disclosure was incomplete because the addict deliberately concealed the most damaging or shameful behaviors, or he or she minimized the number of partners or episodes of acting out.

You need to recognize that some addicts may not initially remember various behaviors, especially if their addiction included multiple episodes or different types of activities. Or the addict may have been intoxicated or on drugs and does not remember particular events. In other cases, the addict may not have realized that revealing a particular behavior would be important to the partner.

Additionally, addiction is a disease of relapse. Even if your partner is actively working a recovery program, he or she may have a slip or relapse. It's quite possible that there will be additional behaviors to disclose in the future. As part of your therapy after the initial disclosure, you and your partner will need to work out guidelines for how to manage any additional information that should be revealed.

It's a good idea to plan ahead for this. For example, new information about sexual behaviors that happened before the initial disclosure is likely to be less traumatic to the partner than information about relapses. Partners may be able to make a clear distinction between acting out that took place before the addict got into recovery and acting out that occurred afterward, and they may be able to accept additional information about that period of time without major upset.

When recovering partners were asked what information they wanted to know, the most common replies related to the addict's sexual sobriety status. A partner with seven years of recovery says, *If he loses his sobriety, I would want to know when and how and what he plans to do about it, so I can act accordingly.* Another type of information partners want to know about is specific behaviors that might have legal consequences. Yet another recovering partner expresses, *I want to know if he's having sex outside the marriage because that affects my health and our commitments to each other. I don't want to know his addictive thoughts. I appreciate when he can share the inner pain he feels. This helps me understand and forgive.*

If significant additional disclosures are necessary, it's a good idea to do so in a therapy session. When partners were asked what they would like therapists to know, they most commonly requested

- a desire to feel empowered

- to be the one to decide how much to be told

- more support from peers and therapists at the time of disclosure[6]

Contrary to some partners' fears, planning for subsequent disclosures is not an invitation to relapse. It's like a fire drill—it will prepare you for an eventuality that you hope won't happen.

At our first formal disclosure my husband insisted he told me all the big pieces of his acting out, but over the next two years he told me some other things. How can I trust him?

A slip or relapse is the most common reason for additional disclosures. As part of your early therapy, it's a good idea to discuss strategies for dealing with any slips or relapses the addict may have in the future. Some situations that many partners decide they would want to know about include sexual behaviors that put them at risk of STDs, sexual activities involving other people, or sexual behaviors that will impact the relationship.

On the other hand, the couple may agree that minor slips are best processed by the addict with his or her support group rather than with the partner. One partner named Melissa recalls, *One day my husband came home rather grumpy. He explained, "I saw a really gorgeous woman on the street today, and I found myself feeling resentful of you. I was thinking, if only I wasn't still married to you, I could get something going with her." Well, this made me resentful! I told him, "Joe, it really isn't helpful for me or our relationship for you to tell me this. Next time please spare me and instead discuss it with your group."*

Another understandable reason for a late disclosure is that during the initial disclosure, your partner may have forgotten some pieces. Addicts frequently have an extensive history of sexual acting out and may not recall everything right away. Also, the addict may at first not have thought that some behaviors were important enough to mention to you, but further along in recovery, may have realized that you need to know these things. Juanita, a partner, gives an example: *One evening, after my husband and I had been in recovery for over a year, we were having dinner with an old friend of his, and my husband told him what he thought was a funny story about a prostitute he'd been with a couple of years earlier. I was furious! Afterwards when we were alone, I immediately confronted him. "How come this is the first I'm hearing about this? I thought you told me everything important." He said, "I did so many things back then that I'm sure there will be others in the future that will come out. I can't do anything about my past, but I can assure you that since I've gotten into recovery, I haven't done anything untrustworthy." After I calmed down, I found his statement reassuring.*

When you receive new information about events that occurred before the initial disclosure, don't jump to conclusions about your partner's trustworthiness or lack thereof. In addition to the content of the disclosure, think about what it means to be told now. It may be that your partner recently realized that there was another secret that he or she would rather reveal because he or she is committed to your relationship and your future together.

Even though it is painful to go through a disclosure process, the information you receive is critical to your healing. You need to be empowered with the truth about the addict's behaviors, so you can make healthy choices based on the truth. It is important to find support for yourself during this stressful process and have a therapist in your corner who can help you sift through all the information and assist you with setting boundaries and making decisions. You owe it to yourself to get this critical assistance.

Chapter Three:
Is This Going to Get Better?

Stefanie Carnes, PhD, CSAT-S and Cara W. Tripodi, LCSW, CSAT-S

ജ‍രു

*My world has been turned upside down. I can't even remember
the ride home after our "disclosure session." I felt like I was in a haze
for a week, just going through the motions. All of the information
is just starting to come together for me. I fluctuate between wanting to
forgive him and filing for divorce. I have always been the "stable"
one in our relationship and, recently, I feel like I'm going crazy.*

– Joanna, forty-three,
after learning her husband had been exhibiting himself in parks

**My life is falling apart since learning about my partner's
sex addiction. When is the pain going to go away? Am I going
to get better? Is it normal to be so upset?**

    The pain you are experiencing is normal. Learning your
partner is a sex addict is devastating and life-altering. The betrayal
triggers a myriad of emotions. Feelings of anguish, despair, anger,
hopelessness, and shame may threaten to overtake you. This time it
feels surreal, and you may be wondering, *Where do I go from here?* The
shock and crisis brought on by this newfound reality may have you
feeling alone and in unchartered territory. You may not know where
to turn.

    Although your situation feels unique, it's important to know
that there are many people like yourself who have traveled this path
before you. They have come through it stronger, more knowledgeable,
and even grateful for what the addiction has done for their lives. Many
of them followed a similar course of transformation that is outlined in
this chapter. Their decision to enter recovery only came after they were

forced to face the inevitable: that their lives were out of control from living with an addict and that they needed help. True and lasting change can only happen when a personal decision is made to face your own pain and evaluate what brought you to this place.

The Stages of Recovery for the Partner

Partners of sex addicts commonly demonstrate six stages of personal growth and development. These stages were initially developed by Dr. Patrick Carnes in research he did that focused on sex addicts and their partners. He followed ninety-nine partners of sex addicts for more than five years as they progressed from finding out about the addiction to integration of this in their lives.[1]

These six stages of personal growth were compared and contrasted to the progression of sex addicts from crisis to long-term recovery. (See chapter 4 for a discussion of the differences in these two populations.) The Stages of Recovery for Partners of Sex Addicts will serve as a model to help guide you through a rough and necessary journey toward healing and recovery. There are aspects of the stages that will best describe you today. But the stages are also meant to give you perspective on the steps involved in recovering from this crisis in your life. Most important, the stages help you see that you are not alone and that things can improve. Here are the Stages of Recovery for Partners of Sex Addicts:

1. Developing/Pre-Discovery
2. Crisis/Decision/Information Gathering
3. Shock
4. Grief/Ambivalence
5. Repair
6. Growth

How you experience each of the stages will depend on many factors, including your personality, any medical or psychiatric diagnoses you have such as depression and/or addiction(s), and prior losses and traumas. Any of these factors will play a role in how you process your pain, and will influence the timing of when and how you advance through the six stages.

You may find one stage more challenging than another, and you may even stay in one stage for an extended period of time. Conversely, you may move quickly through other stages. You might confront a new crisis or challenge that may pull you back into an earlier stage, such as a triggering event like the anniversary of discovering your partner's addiction or an old cell phone bill that reminds you of when you found out about his or her addiction. These triggers can conjure up old feelings that you believed you had resolved. Similarly, you may see yourself vacillating between two or more stages at once.

Stage 1: Developing/Pre-Discovery

The developing stage is the period of time before knowing there was a problem or before discovery/disclosure. You may find during this stage that you were either completely in the dark about the addiction or had some suspicions but were not fully aware of the extent of your partner's sexual acting out. During this stage, you may have tried to keep the peace in the home and attempted to hold on to an idealized view of the relationship.

For example, one spouse states, *I just wanted us to be the perfect family. I wanted that dream family that I never had, so I unconsciously overlooked problems.* When problems did arise during this time, you may have been quick to blame yourself or define the problem as a relationship issue.

Even if you were completely in the dark about the sexual acting out, you may have had a hunch that something wasn't right with the addict. You likely experienced the unmanageability of the addiction in other areas of life, such as parenting, finances, work, and intimacy. Because life was increasingly unmanageable, you may have found yourself attempting to control these other areas, such as work, the children, and the household.

Conversely, you may have known about certain aspects of the behavior, like pornography use, but had no idea about the extent of the sexual acting out. When you accidentally found suspicious

43

information, you might have overlooked it or believed the addict's convincing explanations. Your gut may have been telling you one thing but your mind told you another. You sensed that something was wrong. However, you didn't have the information to back it up. Instead you questioned yourself and gave your partner the benefit of the doubt. This may have even resulted in you questioning your own self-worth.

During this stage, it's common to tolerate behaviors that others would find intolerable. This may include verbal or physical abuse, lack of emotional and physical availability, and lack of functioning in many areas of life. You may have found yourself caretaking to a fault. Unconsciously, you may have minimized the addict's behaviors and covered up for them by making excuses or concessions despite your better judgment. You may have found yourself defending the addict and believing the addict's words over his or her actions.

Another way you may have tried to address the problem was through couples counseling. If you sought marital therapy after learning about your partner's sexual addiction, it's likely that you found the focus was on stabilizing the relationship and not on the problematic emotional and/or sexual behaviors of your partner. Many partners have been frustrated by couple's treatment because the focus was often on both parties, rather than on holding the addict more accountable and seeking recovery for the addiction, which needs to be treated first.

Core Characteristics of the Developing/Pre-Discovery Stage

- believing the addict's lies
- tolerating and normalizing unacceptable behavior from the addict, such as verbal abuse, dependency, unavailability, and mood swings
- self-doubt, such as second-guessing or not trusting gut feelings
- having a hunch something isn't right
- seeking couples therapy
- unmanageability

- loss of values, morals, or beliefs deemed important to keep peace with your partner

Stage 2: Crisis/Decision/Information Gathering

During this stage, the facade of the secret life of the addict has been exposed, and reality and disillusionment is beginning to settle in. As in any life-altering crisis, how you respond has a lot to do with your personality and whether you suffered from prior trauma or crisis in your life. This means that if you are someone who has experienced frequent losses, then you are apt to be more reactive than someone who has not. The old responses get reactivated and add to your distress. In addition, the duration of the addict's behaviors, the types of behaviors engaged in, and the length of the relationship will also influence how you respond to the fallout of discovery/disclosure.

If you are someone who withdraws from crisis, you will find that you want to avoid knowing about the addict or sex addiction in general. You may act as though nothing has changed and try to keep up with your normal responsibilities. Or if you are someone who is more action-oriented, you may find yourself seeking honesty and accountability from the addict, even though a part of you cannot trust what she or he says.

Due to the broken trust, you may find yourself checking up on your partner or playing detective to determine if he or she is still lying and acting out. In fact, you may find yourself doing these behaviors when typically you are not someone who snoops or even wants to, but you find you are compelled to look for things. You may ruminate or obsess about the addict and his or her whereabouts, and seek to review the details of his or her behavior repeatedly.

Much of this is an attempt to examine what happened and to come to terms with how you were in the dark about your partner's behavior before the discovery. You may be replaying the past in an attempt to capture how you could have prevented it from happening or confronted it sooner. All of these action steps are in response to being lied to and are a strategy to ward off the painful realities you are beginning to experience as a result of the betrayal.

For some partners, the crisis stage is a time when, out of your pain, you seek retaliation. You want the addict to hurt like you do. You do things to catch him or her in lies, like having secret email accounts to track online activity. You may even seek out a sex partner yourself or contact the affair partners in order to confront them. These actions only extend the crisis phase and keep you in a dance of confrontation and avoidance of your own pain.

The crisis stage is a crucial time in learning to care for yourself. The most resilient partners are able to gain perspective and establish a plan of care for themselves. Empowering yourself by seeking information and taking action is a beginning step in developing your voice and directing the course of your life. You may be motivated to seek answers to how you found yourself in this predicament.

This includes learning about sex addiction by reading and attending Twelve Step meetings or educational seminars; considering treatment options in the form of individual, group therapy, and psychiatric consultation; and seeking legal and financial consultation. Establishing concrete resources helps compensate for the feelings of powerlessness that may threaten to overwhelm you.

Core Characteristics of the Crisis Stage

- a catalytic event occurs: you discover or are disclosed to about your partner's duplicitous behavior

- information gathering (evaluating treatment options, reading books, etc.)

- taking action/making decisions, such as sending the sex addict to treatment or joining a Twelve Step group

Stage 3: Shock

Stages 2 and 3 often overlap, and for some may even happen simultaneously. During the crisis you learned about the behaviors, gathered information, and perhaps responded by making decisions. Shock is how you responded emotionally and spiritually to the crisis confronting you.

The upheaval during the shock stage can last for months and, at times, years. Variables that predict how long you are in these two stages depend on your response to the crisis and how your partner does or doesn't progress in recovery. Feelings of betrayal are overwhelming and mistrust of the addict reaches its peak. You seek honesty and accountability from the addict even though he or she has become untrustworthy to you. Despite this, you want disclosure of all previously concealed information or believe there is more when you have been told that there isn't. You don't know what to believe and you suffer from a multitude of reactions.

You may have periods of numbness, contrasted by times of upheaval and conflict. At times, you may find it easier to avoid the feelings. However, you may be simply unable to avoid the many feelings lurking underneath the surface that arise during times of conflict, such as anger, resentment, pain, shame, hostility and hopelessness. You may experience crying spells, depression, and even thoughts of suicide. You might begin to question your worth. One spouse explains, *I began to wonder what he was getting from the other women that he was not getting from me! I tried to dress sexier to win his sexual interest. In hindsight, I wish I had just taken care of myself instead of worrying about his needs.*

Understandably, you will have tremendous self-doubt and will need outside support to help you validate your pain and challenge some of your thinking. Living in an addictive system is about secrets and isolation from others. Recovery becomes about letting others into your world and learning new behaviors and choices that were previously unavailable to you.

Core Characteristics of the Shock Stage

- emotional numbness or avoidance
- feelings of victimization
- suspiciousness
- fear about slips, future relapse
- distrust
- conflict

- feelings of despair

- anger, hostility, self-righteousness, blame, and criticism

Stage 4: Grief/Ambivalence

One of the most important aspects of moving through your pain is recognizing and experiencing your grief. Acknowledging your pain and sadness is essential to moving past feelings of anger and betrayal. At the core of betrayal are feelings of pain, sadness, and rejection. Anger is also often considered a secondary emotion to pain and sadness. So grieving is one of the central processes allowing you to move through your anger and feelings of betrayal. The wounding you have experienced cuts to the very core of your heart and soul, leaving you feeling shattered. Allowing yourself time to grieve the many losses during this time will help propel you into the next stages of repair and growth.

Distinguishing grief from self-pity is important, too. You may believe that feeling sorry for yourself is a waste of time and an indulgence that should not be tolerated. But grief is essential because it is that most private area of yourself that allows you to own your pain on a deeper level. Acknowledging, *Hey, I have been seriously wronged and it hurts* is important. It helps you stop intellectualizing the problem and move into your own core feelings of loss, betrayal, and sadness. It also allows you freedom from focusing on what the addict is or isn't doing, which will assist you in connecting with your authentic self. During this stage you may experience

- loss of the dream of your relationship

- loss of self

- loss of relationship as it once was

- loss of emotional safety

- loss of sexual safety

- loss of financial stability

- spiritual vacancy—*Where was God?*

During this period, you may feel a deep sense of ambivalence about the relationship. When the wound is exposed and healing is occurring, it will be difficult to think of reconnecting with your partner. You may question, *Why should I open myself up to this kind of pain again? How do I know he or she won't act out again? I want a guarantee that my partner won't slip.*

You may contemplate separation, divorce, and have fantasies about how life would be without your partner or wish something would happen to him or her so you wouldn't have to go through this pain anymore. You may also find yourself attracted to someone else or imagine what it would be like with someone new without this addiction. Alternatively, the idea of being attracted to anyone right now may repulse you and conjure up tremendous fear and mistrust.

One of the significant gifts that come from this stage is self-awareness and introspection. Instead of focusing on the addict's needs and wants, you begin to focus on your own needs and wants. Your self-care typically deepens during this time. This is an essential shift in the healing process because without making yourself the priority in your recovery, it will be difficult to move forward into the next stage of repair.

Core Characteristics of the Grief/Ambivalence Stage

- grieving losses
- feelings of despair and hopelessness
- ambivalence about the relationship
- increased introspection and focus on the self
- less focus on the addict's behavior

Stage 5: Repair

For many partners, it can take years of shock and grief before healing really starts to take hold and they move into the repair stage. Repair is marked by increased self-awareness and less focus on the addict's behavior. Although you continue to hold the addict accountable for what he or she did to you, you have moved toward greater responsibility for your own needs and happiness. You know you need to be treated respectfully and honestly by the addict, but you see that how others treat you stems from your own self-worth.

You may also start to make the connections between your past and your present circumstances during this stage. For example, you may consider how your family of origin impacted your choices and influenced your adult actions, especially in your relationship with the addict. This may include focusing on themes from your past, such as abandonment, abuse, and neglect.

Many partners deepen their spirituality at this time. Their Twelve Step program becomes more fruitful, and/or religious ties strengthen or are changed for a new one that best reflects the internal transformations that have occurred.

The Twelve Step fellowships use a phrase from Alcoholics Anonymous: "You will experience a new freedom and a new happiness."[2] This is when some of that new freedom begins to manifest. Coping skills and social support systems become stronger. Secrecy and isolation are replaced with solitude and companionship. Self-defeating behaviors often diminish. Overall, your deep pain and turmoil subsides and a more relaxed, introspective self emerges with a stronger voice.

These changes are reflected in your relationships as well. You will have a better understanding of the addiction and the addict's behavior, which places you in a stronger position to evaluate the relationship. You have a clearer picture of the addict's sexual acting out and the boundaries you need to keep yourself safe. You believe the actions, not the words of the addict, and you don't live in denial of the addiction or the addictive behaviors. You are able to hold the addict accountable with boundaries and are better at following through with them.

If you have doubts about the addict's recovery, you are likely to protect yourself. You are able to see red flags and confront them effectively. If you become re-traumatized by relapses or divorce, you openly seek additional resources to handle it. You are also more emotionally prepared to make the decision to leave the relationship if indicated. If the addict is in recovery and your relationship is progressing in a healthy way, you may explore trust and intimacy that is deeper than before.

Core Characteristics of the Repair Stage

- introspection
- decision-making stage about the relationship
- family-of-origin themes examined and integrated
- prior losses more fully grieved
- increased strength and coping skills
- boundary setting
- emotional stability

Stage 6: Growth

The final stage of recovery is growth. This involves continued self-transformation. One of the hallmarks of this stage for partners is letting go of feelings of victimization and replacing them with resiliency. You may discover a way to make meaning out of your suffering.

Gratitude for the addiction and the opportunities for self-actualization that it has provided occur here. The addiction was a catalyst for change and you responded to it. The many challenges you faced elevated you to a higher level of well-being, and you experience peace and greater appreciation for the work that you had to do in confronting this challenge.

You turn outward, not in a caretaking sense, but in a genuine desire to pass on what was given to you. Your compassion for other people's pain reinforces your commitment to healing. You can now realistically check your motivations and catch yourself when you fall into old self-defeating patterns. You have integrated what you learned about your family of origin and are able to apply these insights into all areas of your life. If you find you are trapped in old patterns of behaviors, feelings, or attitudes, you have choices now that seemed unavailable to you before. Those choices allow you to seek additional help in tackling any problem that presents itself.

You find you have more clarity and vision for your future. You no longer live in denial of what life should be. Rather, you accept what life is and with flexibility address problems that used to scare you. Intimacy is something you can reasonably address, respecting the limits of yourself and your partner. With newfound self-confidence, you likely experience successes in other areas of your life, such as work, parenting, and spirituality.

Core Characteristics of the Growth Stage

- decreased feelings of being victimized by the addiction
- focus on issues not directly related to the addiction
- explore communication skills and conflict resolution styles
- awareness of your role in the dysfunction of the relationship increases
- acknowledgment of gifts the addiction has brought to your life
- ability to be present and fully focused on other areas of life

Frequently Asked Questions

The following are frequently asked questions for spouses or partners who are on this journey into recovery. As you read them, you will see some of the six stages of recovery reflected in the questions.

I had no idea! How could I have been so duped?

You may have been completely in the dark about the sex addiction, or maybe you had a hunch something was not right with the addict. Or you might have been concerned about your partner's sexual behavior, but you minimized or overlooked the seriousness of your concerns, telling yourself, *At least she isn't going outside the relationship* or *All men do this.* This may have quieted your doubts for a time, but the problems never seemed to go away. In fact, maybe they got worse, increasing your sense of concern and catapulting you into this current crisis in your life where you can no longer deny what's really going on.

You were duped because your partner needed you to be in the dark in order to support his or her secret lifestyle. Sex addiction is insidious. It can mask itself in many different ways and can keep a partner deluded into thinking something is not what it appears. It manifests itself in a multitude of ways, such as financial unmanageability, relationship impairment, neglect of parenting responsibilities, reduced occupational functioning, or mood irregularities on the part of the addict. The fact that you didn't know about the addiction is a reality. Your partner wanted to distract you from the real issue of addiction so he or she could continue uninterrupted in the sexual indiscretions.

Addicts deflect, manipulate, criticize, and blame others for their problems to keep them from knowing what they are doing. Even if you suspect something, they will deny your truth and convince you otherwise. Over time, your doubts about your own reality may have gotten the best of you, damaging your self-worth. Addiction precipitates selfish behavior and the addict did whatever he or she needed to at the time to get whatever he or she wanted. Lying to you and coercing you to believe things that were not true were part of his or her attempt to get what he or she wanted, disregarding you in the process.

In the children's story *Little Red Riding Hood*, the young girl thought the wolf looked, smelled, and spoke like her grandmother but, in reality, it was the wolf in his clothing on the prowl to hurt the girl. Just as in this story, you have been deceived and nothing will change that truth. How you prevent that from happening to you in the future requires you to examine those areas of the relationship that were problematic to you. Were you apt to assume responsibility for problems, telling yourself that it was somehow your fault that the addict was behaving in a certain way? Did you find you overcompensated for his or her responsibilities at home, financially, with child care or chores?

For instance, did you support your partner financially and emotionally when he or she was laid off from work only to find out later that your partner had lied to you about why he or she lost the job? Perhaps you then discovered the real reason was poor work performance because your partner was staying up late to view pornography. You may have found yourself bailing your partner out by making excuses for absences, when you didn't know where he or she was. Or maybe you rescued the addict with financial support. Did you feel indebted to your partner because he or she paid the bills and provided you a comfortable lifestyle that afforded you the time to work on your career or raise your children? Did this mean you would take on more of the blame for the problems and, in this way, quiet your suspicions and doubts? Undoubtedly, you experienced the chaos and unmanageability of the addiction in your life, only you didn't know that's what it was at the time.

These examples are common experiences for partners of sex addicts. In a healthy relationship, it's normal to give your loved one the benefit of the doubt and make assumptions and concessions to your partner. Holding a positive image of your partner and the relationship are also helpful ways to thrive and grow together. But in addictive systems, one person, usually the partner, is being taken advantage of by the other, usually the addict. This creates an imbalanced and unhealthy environment.

Addicts take more than is rightfully their share in a relationship. Therefore, applying normal adaptive beliefs and supportive assumptions to your partner in this type of system backfires because the addict is not interested in your well-being when he or she is caught in the throes of the addictive lifestyle. Changing these chaotic patterns starts with you. What you were doing was not working. Begin to own and evaluate how you were treated in the relationship. Start to rely on your own intuition and challenge the beliefs, attitudes, and feelings that you had in the past.

By identifying those areas that were a problem in the relationship prior to discovery/disclosure, and the ways you accommodated or managed those issues, you are piecing together the impact of the addiction on you. Utilizing a support system will help you to learn and practice new attitudes and behaviors.

I feel so despondent about this, and I cannot stop thinking about it. Will I ever get back to normal?

After finding out about your partner's sex addiction, it's typical to question whether life will ever return to the way it was. Because you have suffered such a deep injury that cuts to the core of who you are, your pain will be extensive and repairing these wounds will take a long time. Furthermore, if these wounds in any way replicate painful experiences from your past, your pain will be more complex and confuse the process of your recovery.

Your pain may be expressing itself through preoccupying thoughts about the addiction. Because the betrayal of trust was so severe, the intrusive thoughts often center on the unfaithfulness of your partner. It's common for partners to ruminate about issues directly or indirectly related to this broken trust. Some of the issues you may focus on include

- promises the addict made
- the sexual behaviors he or she engaged in
- his or her whereabouts
- his or her use of time
- his or her attitudes toward you
- the addict's behaviors (such as following through on commitments)
- the trustworthiness of the addict
- the addict's sexuality (is he or she acting out again?)
- whether you should stay or leave the relationship

Ruminating about the addict's behavior is part of the fallout from the crisis and it may be difficult to stop without help. Ruminating serves as a way to protect yourself. It also may reduce your anxiety and help you avoid other feelings related to the addiction. This is a stage and you'll get through it. You may find this experience takes a great deal of emotional energy, and the duration of this stage can commonly last from one to two years.

Don't give up. Having a positive vision of yourself in the future will help you move forward. It will allow you to gain a sense of control over your life. If you find you're feeling stuck in this phase, try to direct your own healing. Become a partner to yourself. How would you want to be treated by others at this time? Begin treating yourself this way.

Seek out mentors who have overcome difficult trials in their life and allow their experiences to strengthen your resolve. The more you recognize that you're deserving of a better life, the stronger an advocate you'll become for your own healing. Own the reality of where you're at today. You will not always feel this way, but you will learn from it if you can open yourself up to the growth that this pain is offering you.

I'm afraid he is going to act out again. What can I expect?

Unfortunately, slips and or relapses do occur, especially in early recovery. It's realistic for you to be concerned about any potential lapses and to prepare for how you will handle them. Setting boundaries, such as *nonnegotiables*, can be helpful for self-protection. Nonnegotiables are those behaviors that you are not able to tolerate in the relationship. You will learn about setting nonnegotiable boundaries in chapter 5. There are differences between slips and relapses. A slip, such as masturbating, can be less offensive to you than a visit to a strip club. In fact, you may not even see masturbation as a problem. Understanding and differentiating between a relapse and a slip will help you to define your nonnegotiables.

What is important is how the addict responds to his or her lapse. Those critical decisions will tell you more than the actual behavior. For example, if he or she is scared and immediately seeks help through his or her sponsor, group, or therapist, that tells you he or she is responding in an appropriate fashion and taking the lapse seriously. If it deepens his or her insight into the causes of the behavior, then it's possible that it can be a learning experience. If, however, he or she minimizes it and doesn't increase his or her program in some way, or if you have to tell him or her to, then that will be a sign to you that your partner may not be ready to stop acting out.

Gathering data over time and comparing it to the list of nonnegotiables you have established will help you in managing any slips and relapses. The differences between slips and relapses, in time, will not matter to you if the addict cannot maintain a continuous period of abstinence, which may force you to make a decision about the relationship.

Rebuilding shattered trust necessitates reliable actions over time. Only over time—months or years of the addict being accountable, working a program, and doing what he or she says he or she is going to do—will it be possible for the trust in your relationship to be restored. In the meantime, it's normal to feel doubtful and suspicious, especially at this early stage of recovery.

I find my feelings are all over the place. One day I am angry and the next I am sad. How come I can't trust what I feel from day to day?

Confronting the painful truth that your partner is a sex addict propels you into experiencing countless emotions. You are embarking on a transformation that brings with it many challenges. One of the most complex challenges you will encounter is tolerating the various feeling states you will go through in your recovery. Below are common emotions associated with the crisis at hand:

- grief
- ambivalence
- anger
- sadness
- loneliness
- abandonment
- fear
- shame

The shock of this discovery sets off a cascade of changes to your body, mind, and spirit. It is crucial that you take the time and seek out supportive avenues that allow you to gain the freedom you need to heal. In this way you are becoming better prepared for the next stage, which is acknowledging your losses and reexamining who you are going forward.

I really don't know that I want to be with a "sex addict," even if he is in recovery. I don't know who he is anymore and this isn't what I signed up for! Why should I stick around? What's in it for me?

Most partners experience a period of ambivalence about the relationship. There is so much shame attached to the disease of sex addiction, you think it would be just easier to leave the relationship behind. Making your ambivalence clear at the early stages of recovery is important for the relationship. *I am unable to tell you if I am going to stay or leave this relationship right now* is an honest expression of your truth and clearly conveys to the addict where you stand. This gives the addict an opportunity to "walk the walk" of recovery and recognize that the relationship is on thin ice and that he or she needs to put recovery first.

Whether you decide to stay or leave the relationship, finding out your partner is a sex addict presents growth opportunities for you. If you stay, the intimacy in your relationship with the addict can deepen through the recovery process. You will learn that the behaviors your partner engaged in, although unacceptable and offensive to you, were a form of escape and coping. Underneath the sexual behaviors lies a person who has used a false sense of self to keep you from knowing who he or she truly is.

If your partner takes on the responsibility of recovery, you have a chance to have a true relationship built on a foundation of honesty. If you choose to leave the relationship, you will also be challenged to grow in many ways, such as living on your own and possibly renegotiating another loving relationship.

Either way, it will be important to assess what led you to being in a relationship with a sex addict and to begin to make connections to how this relates to your own interpersonal and familial issues. Even though this is a painful experience, you're going through this for a reason and there are lessons in it for you.

Why should I forgive? I am so angry about what my spouse did. Shouldn't she ask for my forgiveness? I want true remorse, not "I'm sorry"! When will my spouse get how much she hurt me?

Wanting your partner to "really get" how he or she hurt you is a normal wish, but it may be futile. Don't stop believing this is important for you. However, in early recovery there is very little time available for you because all the energy your partner put into his or her addiction must now be directed toward his or her own recovery. In some ways, you may be like two ships passing in the night. For a period of time you will be wrestling with your own distinct issues that, for now, can't be fully understood by the other. The addict can no more understand your need for remorse than you can understand what it's like for him or her to not act out sexually for thirty days.

It's more important to pay attention to your partner's actions in recovery, because recovery becomes the stepping stone for deeper amends to those the addict has hurt, and that will come with time. The addict may make many promises, but it will be the cumulative actions in support of challenging his or her additive thinking and behavior that will give you small vestiges of hope about his or her growing capacity to experience remorse. Further in recovery, you should expect—in writing and/or with the presence of a trained professional—an acknowledgment of what he or she did to you, and the addict should listen as you explain how he or she hurt you. This will further honor your need to right the wrongs done to you.

Forgiving the addict prematurely is a common problem for many partners. Perhaps your religious beliefs encourage forgiveness and you feel that you "should" forgive. You may have been taught or saw in your family that you shouldn't hold someone accountable for their transgressions. Alternatively, you may feel sympathy or pity for the addict. Realistically, however, forgiveness takes time. It is essential for you to grieve your losses before being able to forgive the addict. There are so many losses you will confront—the loss of the "dream" of your relationship, what you thought you had; the loss of trust; possible financial losses; or losses in social stature and relationships. Most important is the loss of yourself—the trust you had in how you viewed your partner and other relationships.

Not only does your sadness need to be adequately expressed and acknowledged, but also you will need time to heal. Grief takes time. This is an inevitable emotional response, and the last thing you need to do is pressure yourself to forgive before you are truly ready in your heart.

Finally and most important, you will need to forgive yourself. Many partners blame themselves for being unaware of the problems in the relationship, for accepting the unacceptable, or not challenging things sooner. You will find that your self-criticism may be the hardest obstacle to overcome before you can forgive the addict. By making your own recovery a priority, you will find greater self-compassion and move toward self-forgiveness. Eventually, forgiveness of the addict may feel like an option for you.

My husband says he is in recovery, but his behaviors do not consistently reflect a recovery lifestyle. I continue to hold him accountable and set boundaries with him, and he follows through about 50 percent of the time. I am fed up. What should I do?

This behavior is referred to as "riding the fence" or demonstrating behaviors and attitudes that indicate partial recovery. The addict may be trying to convince you that he or she is working a strong program, when in fact is not. You may know on some level that the addict is not fully engaged in recovery. As you get stronger, you may become more willing to set boundaries and follow through with them, hold your partner accountable, and be assertive regarding your needs in the relationship.

If you believe that what you are witnessing is true, verify your data. Common ways to do this are to ask your partner to share your concerns with his or her support network and to follow up with you about it. Next, discuss it with your support system and identify some options for what you could do next. Check the behavior against your partner's words and notice how he or she responds to you emotionally.

Each of these steps keeps you grounded in the truth and protects you from further victimization by the addiction.

One of the most common reasons addicts enter recovery from sex addiction is the potential breakup of a relationship. This means you have more power than you think you do. Your influence in whether the addict stops acting out is important and despite how angry and overwhelmed you might feel, recognizing your own power can help you see the options available to you. For example, although you cannot control whether the addict will seek professional help, you can make it a condition in which to continue the relationship. You may also make separation a condition in which to continue the relationship. Taking the steps toward separation can help the addict recognize that in order for reunification to occur, he or she must get and stay sexually sober. Sometimes the addict needs to experience "rock bottom," which may be the loss of an important relationship, before being willing to embrace recovery. When addicts are faced with the consequences of their behavior, they often experience the desperation they need to be motivated for recovery. In many instances it comes down to timing: *Am I willing to wait until he or she "gets it" or hits bottom? Or will I have already moved on?* This is a very personal choice and one only you will be able to make.

What does my family of origin have to do with this? How did I get here?

You may be questioning how your family background contributed to you being in a relationship with an addict. Addictions travel in families and are passed from generation to generation. Most likely, you were raised in an addictive family or a family organized around a particular family member's needs. You may have learned that chaos and secrecy were part of normal functioning within a family.

When you got older, it's possible that you sought out mates who replicated aspects of your childhood. That familiar feeling was comfortable. You developed a tolerance for this kind of relationship in your family of origin. For example, you may have learned to expect less and then began to seek less from a partner. By accepting little in the way of your needs, you have duplicated how you were treated by your family. You may be able to readily identify the connections to your family of origin, or they may be more subtle and may require closer examination to see parallels to your current situation.

Whatever your situation, it's essential in your recovery that these connections be made. Only when the unconscious is made conscious will you find the capacity and insight to alter the course of your life. Having the courage to look at old hurts and challenge dysfunctional messages from childhood creates a new pathway of choice and freedom for you. Believing you deserve better out of life and personal relationships is a huge step toward self-empowerment.

Again, it's vital to realize that no two partners will experience these stages in the same way or at the same time. By examining these stages, you may recognize yourself on the journey to recovery and be reassured that this will get better over time. You may be currently experiencing one of the more difficult stages of recovery, but this will pass and you will move into a more peaceful stage of introspection and growth.

While considering these stages, don't judge yourself harshly or try to force yourself into a future stage. Every partner goes through the six stages at his or her own pace. Hopefully, reviewing these stages will provide you some peace of mind that the crisis will not last forever, and growth and insight are the inevitable gifts you will receive through this experience.

Chapter Four:
Should I Stay or Should I Go?

Patrick J. Carnes, PhD, CSAT

ℰᏐᏚ

Modern physics shows us that once two molecules touch each other, they have a relationship forever. Mating is similar. Three basic neural networks exist in our brains that involve sexuality. First, there is basic lust in which there may or may not be any attachment. Second, there is romance, which has a cycle of four to seven years. And finally, there is a neural pathway that is about companionship and mating, which when it serves us well, keeps reactivating sex and romance.

So deep is that mating response that one of the great pioneers of family therapy, Carl Whittaker, once quipped that we are "never divorced, we simply add marriages." Many clinicians become wary when they hear the phrase "soul mate," because it is a term romanticized in the media. The implication is that soul mates are exempted somehow from the everyday struggles of real intimacy and commitment. Therapist witness daily how deep, enduring, and perplexing these human-mating attachments can be.

Multiple attachments are sitcom fodder. They build on the difficulties of multiple ex-spouses, stepparents, and reluctant siblings. We see stories in which kids attempt to reunify their divorced parents, or the converse in which the children of remarried parents attempt to destroy the new union. We are moved by the *Sleepless in Seattle* scenario and shudder at *War of the Roses*. Our media simply reflects our new realities as humans.

When our neural networks around sex evolved, life expectancy was less than thirty years, not eighty. In those times, the focus was on survival. Our longevity and abundance creates choices. We have reached the cultural conclusion that one does not have to stay in a relationship that is dysfunctional or worse, destructive. The price we pay is the poignancy of moments such as when three spouses appear at the funeral of someone they were married to, each lost in their private sorrow.

Our abundance and longevity create another set of problems called addictions. To live with an addicted loved one is heart wrenching. To live with a sex addict adds profoundly to the pain and confusion, because the very foundations of the relationship and one's life are attacked. Because so much deceit is involved, partners become distrustful of their own perceptions. They ask how they could not see this problem in the making. They cannot believe anything the addicts say, and this creates unbearable anxiety.

Thus, a partner can go to extraordinary means to find out the truth, turning life into a malaise of obsession that, at times, exceeds the preoccupation of the addict. They hate who they have become and will do anything to stop the pain. The easiest apparent solution is to leave.

To abandon the relationship at this point, however, is akin to having a broken bone and not setting it. Broken relationships require attention as well. Failure to attend to this self-care can be crippling to future relationships. And if there are children involved, problems are inevitable. Whether you go or stay, it makes no difference. Mending will be required. And as painful as it is, there will be less pain and more effective healing when the fracture is dealt with as soon as possible.

The decision to stay or go calls for the deepest personal wisdom. Wise people seem to be able to suspend their feelings and dark thoughts, even in the midst of crisis, to see clearly their best options. This presence of mind is very much in keeping with Twelve Step wisdom. In the Twelve Step program, the key to serenity is having the wisdom of knowing when to act and when not to act. This time-proven approach is articulated so well by members of Al-Anon who recommend, "Nothing major the first year."

The Problem of Mismatched Stages

One of author Melody Beattie's funniest observations is that "seldom does everyone get into recovery on the same day."[1] Therein is one of the greatest challenges to a couple's life in recovery. Not everyone "gets it" at the same time. Chapter 3 outlines specific stages that partners typically experience as they enter recovery.

The addict works through these same stages of recovery. But, the problem is that the addict and partner usually move through these six stages at different times. Working through the stages takes three years or more. This allows time for the brain to grow new, functional neural networks. Plus, there is a host of skills and an array of knowledge to be mastered. To illustrate this, see the following three different scenarios for Jeff and Fran showing how a recovery mismatch can occur.

Scenario One

Fran, the partner, is significantly ahead of Jeff in the recovery process. She has known for some time that he has not been himself. She had discovered the various ways he had been unfaithful, but she now has a good therapist and joined a Twelve Step group. In her recovery, she has gone to workshops and intensive experiences to add to her understanding. She sees how overlooking the obvious has been

---

The Stages of Recovery for Partners of Sex Addicts

1. **Developing/Pre-Discovery:** Partners start to understand that addiction is present in a loved one and that something has to be done.

2. **Crisis/Decision/Information Gathering:** Partners realize they simply can no longer tolerate the problem.

3. **Shock:** Partners absorb the reality of how bad things have gotten and deeply engage in therapy and the recovery process.

4. **Grief/Ambivalence:** Partners profoundly understand their losses and pain throughout life and specifically how the addict's behavior fits the larger patterns.

5. **Repair:** Partners reconstruct how they interact with themselves and those around them.

6. **Growth:** Partners experience a new depth in their relationships and a new level of openness and effectiveness.

---

a pattern in her life. Her father's alcoholism kept her family in chaos, and she married a "high maintenance" man. Plus, her early sexual experiences made sex at times difficult. She was at her best when there was a crisis. Her biggest realization is that if she had not married Jeff, she may have married someone like him. She knows she has as big a problem as Jeff does.

Jeff, however, is still sorting out whether or not he is an addict. He knows he has done a lot of sexual acting out and that he has hurt Fran. Yet, he is not ready to stop all forms of acting out. He fears, in some fundamental way, that he will lose his sense of who he is if he totally surrenders. He goes through the motions of attending meetings and has visited with a therapist, but all he basically wants is to calm down Fran. He vows only to do behaviors that keep him off her radar. Unintentionally, he postpones the inevitable painful feelings that await his acceptance that he is a sex addict.

Fran intuitively knows that Jeff is stuck. He has not grabbed the lifeline of therapy the way she has, so she decides that he will never change. She has tolerated behavior she should never have tolerated. She decides to initiate a divorce, which sets up another problem— eventually she will have to face her own feelings. More than anything, she wants a shortcut through her fear, shame, and anger.

Scenario Two

In this scenario, Jeff has a head start because he got into trouble at work for his sexual behavior. He knows that his problem is profound and there is wreckage everywhere. His Twelve Step meetings are like deep drinks of water for a parched soul. He is excited at what he discovered in recovery. His company sent him to inpatient treatment, which stripped away all the pretenses and lies. He was raw and really needed his wife to be part of all that was happening to him. He also started to understand his wife in a whole new way.

There was so much Fran needed to know, so much hurt she has not been able to make sense of. He knew her family and could see how all the pieces came together. He could see what a difference all this learning could make in her life and in their marriage. She, however, elected not to come to family week. Instead, she informed him she was talking to an attorney.

66

For Fran, you simply could not put the words *addiction* and *sex* in the same sentence. She was stuck with four kids, and the request to take a whole week away from home for behavior that was not her fault seemed to be more of Jeff's self-centered thinking. She resented deeply that all they had worked for was now in jeopardy.

Further, some of her friends knew of Jeff's problems at work and offered to talk. She found the gestures embarrassing since she had nothing to say. No one could really help her now. She had learned a long time ago to do things on her own, and here again she was forced to handle everything. To Fran, it was simpler to go on alone. Only now it would be like having one less child.

Fran actually went to Jeff's therapist and was outraged. There is simply no excuse for what Jeff did. The idea that she needed help was beyond insulting. She walked out of the office vowing never to see a therapist again. It was just a way to make money, like anything else. When she walked out of therapy, Fran walked out on herself. The therapist was kind, but Fran felt attacked. Fran would not let anyone close to her, because to open up to another would reveal to herself wounds that were unbearable. It was easier to be critical and outraged.

As in all grief, anger and denial are closely linked. We push away with a vengeance those who could help us. Fran only trusted her children because she felt safe with them. She failed to notice that having a husband who was like a child replicated the same unhealthy reverse dependency. Further, these children will grow up, and these same issues may be repeated in their lives.

Jeff finally acquiesced to talking to the divorce attorney. There seemed to be no way to help Fran. The more he tried, the more her anger escalated. He realized that he had to let her go.

Part of the wreckage of what he had done was a tipping point. It was a trauma that had activated Fran's deep family wounds. As she lashed out at everyone, he felt sad for what he had done, but he felt even worse that she had decided to banish him from her life. Ironically, he had never been more aware of his deep care for her.

Leaving a relationship is an option for both the addict and the partner. However, leaving the relationship before the couple has a chance to understand each other and the illness of addiction is the tragic loss. Like the Greek heroines and heroes, the problem of hubris—or believing that you are different from other mortals—is a pride we can ill afford. Yet both addicts and partners are vulnerable to it.

Eleanor Payson writes in her book *The Wizard of Oz and Other Narcissists* that both parties in the addictive relationship become "self-absorbed."[2] In that state, neither addict nor partner fully appreciates how they impact others. With recovery, the preoccupation with self falls away and there is this discovery: We are no different than other mortals—including our significant others. Like the Greeks, we reclaim our humanity by giving up our pride.

Scenario Three

Consider a third scenario in which Fran and Jeff both make it to the grief stage of recovery (stage 4). Something amazing happens when you see the pain of your partner. Many partners talk about how they recommitted when they saw the sorrow of the addict. Similarly, addicts report losing the characteristic ambivalence they had toward their partners when they see their spouses' heart-wrenching pain.

Key to this process, however, is that both persons recognize, with remorse, their respective roles in what happened. Both parties discover their unresolved grief over the losses that occurred prior even to meeting one another. All the blame and critical judgment toward the current partner was, in part, a defense against earlier hurts. The irony, of course, is that choosing the current partner has deep roots in the earlier wounds as well. In that emotional environment, deep personal change occurs. The addict and partner also become aware of how much they appreciate each other.

Recovering Couples Anonymous has an exercise that therapists have used for years. Each person is asked to make a list each week of the behaviors that have made life more difficult for their partners. They also make a parallel list of what they appreciate about their partners. Done sincerely, there are few dry eyes in the couple's presence as they share.

In many ways, this shift away from blaming your partner to taking responsibility for your own part changes everything. The most volatile, difficult relationships can be transformed by this level of integrity. And each person discovers the truth of the "wisdom" encapsulated in the Serenity Prayer: *God, grant me the serenity to accept the things I cannot change, courage to change the things I can, and wisdom to know the difference.* We cannot change our partners. The only thing we can change is how we respond in our new truths.

This process is not easy. It is truly a road less traveled. It requires the support of many, therapy, and the Twelve Step process. As the denial wears off, understanding grows and the pain is accepted. Plus, there is so much information about family functioning, child abuse, trauma, addiction, and brain functioning to know. As in any disease, there is much to learn.

We are reminded again of the insight behind that Al-Anon aphorism "Nothing major the first year." The bottom line is there is about eighteen months of learning to make it through the initial stages of recovery. At the beginning, however, you simply do not know what you do not know. So each partner has to risk. There is no guarantee that the relationship can be restored. First of all, there is relapse to be concerned with. Second, some couples, after they become healthier, realize their partnership was never a good match. Sometimes couples reach this point, divorce, and then remarry. There are no guarantees. By going through the process, however, you minimize damage, learn about your part, and are informed about what the stakes are. You give yourself the gift of an informed decision.

Whether you stay or go, the processes will involve pain. You will need help from your therapist and your partner. Your therapist can be expected to bring the knowledge and skills you need. Your partner will bring history, perceptions, and perspectives you will need to hear.

I cannot imagine trusting like that again. How do I risk like that? Can I shorten the time needed for healing? Can I do the work without involving my partner?

When partners become self-absorbed, they want immediate gratification and they want long-term guarantees. The process of healing begins when they abandon the need to control how healing happens. The root cause of this is anxiety. Remember that both addicts and partners likely come from the same type of family structure. They tend to come from "disengaged" families in which bonding had been disrupted. Intimacy in these families is undermined by complex rules systems that create fear of abandonment. Rejection and pain create a chronic state of anxiety and intolerance of intense feelings.

They also tend to come from "rigid" families that have rules about "keeping the peace." Avoiding conflict, keeping appearances, and sacrificing personal needs all serve to keep the lid on the anxiety. Mostly "growing up" has failed to teach them how to take care of themselves, to tolerate life's inevitable challenges, and to be calm when facing difficulty. Basically they have lost their integrity because they will do anything "expediently" to keep the peace. They will do anything to keep the peace externally so everything looks good to others. They will do anything to keep the peace internally so they do not have upsetting feelings.[3]

Divorce looks good to both addict and partner because it is expedient. Blaming everything on the spouse keeps the outside looking good because you can say, "It was my partner's fault." Divorcing provides a short retreat into denial and anger, so that internal grief is held at bay. While divorce is often complex, at first it seems a simple way to disassociate oneself from chaos and pain. What most therapists witness is that divorce intensifies the very worst aspects of both partners. The adversarial nature of legal battle tends to intensify obsession with the activities of the partner and proving that the partner is wrong, deceitful, or even pathological.

The great irony in using divorce as a way to escape the inevitable grief is that it creates more. So much of the addict's life was spent proving something that was not true. Proving, for example, that the partner's fears were not grounded in reality is common to most addicts in relationships—*everything is fine.* Similarly, partners will spend so much emotional energy to prove that the addict is not telling the truth.

Thus, at times, partners will go to such extremes that they lose contact with reality. They make accusations that are not true so others start to dismiss them as overreacting or exaggerating to make a point.

Or they go to great lengths to prove to others that there are no problems in the family. They cover their partner's trail. Again, everything is "fine." Most recovering people, however, learn this fundamental rule: As soon as you are in the "proving mode," you are in trouble.

Here is reality: Divorce is an adversarial process. Litigators are champions at "proving" their sides. It pits former lovers against one another. Issues around children and money dramatically escalate the very worst aspects of this illness. In the midst of the divorce process, it is hard to achieve the perspective, detachment, and process critical to healing in recovery. Further, because passions are so high, things may be said and done on both sides that create more wreckage, deeper wounds, and inevitably more collateral damage to others, including children.

More losses are created when people divorce before they have processed their own part in their addictive dynamics and they have not acquired the basic skills necessary to negotiate good relationship decisions. They have taken a long drink in the river of high drama, intensity, grievance, and obsession. Many years later, those who have divorced without the insights of recovery realize they may have created unnecessary pain for themselves and others. Further, they guaranteed, in their righteousness, that they would repeat certain relationship patterns. The lesson here is this: You can be right, but you may not learn nor will you heal.

Consider Carol who married the same type of abusive addict three times. Each time she told friends that she "had learned her lesson," although she seldom was clear about what the lesson was. Each time she married she was confident that she had made an improvement, that this husband would be a better match. Each marriage, however, was worse than the last.

Finally, she sought therapy, and an astute therapist helped her find a Twelve Step group. The timing was important because all three of her children had different fathers, and all three children were acting out in different ways. Once Carol started to connect with women in recovery, she learned how much she was missing in not having good relationships with other women. She did not date anyone for more than a year. She became much more skilled at handling her emotions and realized how growing up in an anxiety-filled home had affected her. One day her therapist asked her to summarize what she had learned so far. Here is some of what Carol wrote:

> *I learned early to take care of others. It was a way to assure I'd have a place in the family. With men I would be attracted to the flawed and the hurt. I would seduce with my kindness. While I was willing to be Supermom to everyone, I was stubborn about letting anyone help me. I spent decades pushing help away. I overlooked stuff that was obvious to everybody else. I did not want the relationship or my life to be upset any more than it was.*

> *I learned about "negative intimacy" when I kept storytelling about people who had wronged me. All I was doing was keeping them around in my head. I am a drama junkie. My life and the people I picked to be in it were all about my addiction to stress. I misused anger. I used it to bully people and to be controlling. I did not use my anger to empower me or protect me and my children. By being so perfectionistic, I put my shame on everybody else. I cannot tolerate not knowing what is going to happen. My anxiety has made me so controlling, I drive away those I love. I avoid conflict by having conversations in my head—but not with the person I need to have them with. My kids have seen through all the ways I have pitted them against their fathers. That is one of the biggest mistakes I made.*

When asked by her therapist what her greatest source of grief was, she surprised herself by saying,

> *I watch my first husband now when he is with our child. He is a good father and he is in a good marriage. He is happy and successful. And he has a good recovery. For years I lived in resentment thinking of him as a hypocrite. Now I understand that anger really covered my being sad. The woman he is with has my place. I wished I had learned all of this stuff years ago.*

If we return to the three scenarios outlined at the beginning of this chapter, we now can see the advantages of both partners committing to a recovery process and tabling major decisions until recovery has gained traction. Partners who both have committed to the process have new tools to mend what is broken. In many ways, they realize that two abused kids found each other but did not know how to make a relationship work. Now they can make an adult commitment to each other. If it is clear this relationship does not make sense, then they have tools to separate without the volatility and dysfunction they brought into the relationship. They can, for example, create a good, effective parenting relationship.

To discard the opportunity of having your partner in therapy, even if the relationship is untenable, closes off very important information about yourself and the relationship. There is essential debriefing that must happen. It is more than a therapeutic autopsy. Many life issues can be resolved to the extent that the future becomes a much more functional prospect. Nothing is sadder than when one or both partners opt out of this important reality. Recovery groups are filled with people who have a more difficult task of doing therapy because their partners refuse to be part of the recovery process.

What my spouse did is unforgiveable. Since I know I am going to divorce him, why should I go to treatment with him? Is an immediate divorce ever called for?

Situations do exist in which immediate divorce is appropriate. Threats to life, serious crime, further exploitation, financial and legal complications—the list of good reasons seems to be endless. Some situations are simply intolerable. Leading the list is when the addict continues to act out sexually. If there is clearly no effort toward recovery, there should be zero tolerance. In the original AA Big Book, they refer to the person who constitutionally could not commit to the process. All addictions have people who are not able to do what is necessary. For families this is a profound sadness. It is one of the great sources of sadness for addiction professionals as well. And it is the life-or-death part of this disease.

73

In some instances, partners will be tempted to stay in exploitive relationships that are unhealthy because they are addicted to the trauma. We use terms like love addict or relationship addiction or traumatic bonding to describe situations in which a person cannot let go of a partner who is destructive to oneself or others. The bottom line is that partners may also have compulsive behavior that manifests in how they attach to others. This compulsive attachment is a disorder of the self in which the neural pathways of the brain are altered.

The result is the partner has difficulty determining what is normal in a relationship. Noted neuroscientist Louis Cozolino suggests that codependence is rooted in "stress addiction" because of trauma.[4] When noted researchers speak of addiction to the trauma, the world is full of examples. Just think of ones you know:

- spouses who stay in battering situations
- employees who cover for abusive bosses
- sexual abuse victims who work as prostitutes
- battered boys who become mercenaries
- congregations that cover for exploitive pastors

People who stay in threatening circumstances re-create a neurochemistry in their brains in which they will do everything to maintain a destructive relationship. When a therapist says, "That man is your drug," it is more than a figure of speech. There is good science behind it. Fortunately, there are great resources of help in Al-Anon and codependency groups for sex addiction, such as S-Anon or COSA (see chapter 7 for more information on these fellowships).

Part of recovery means no longer tolerating situations that are intolerable. That remains true even if you have to proceed alone in your process. Continuing abuse, physical jeopardy, and sexual acting out would be examples of such a threshold. However, bear in mind the difference between behavior that is intolerable and behavior that is unforgivable.

Oftentimes when situations emerge, they are so beyond comprehension that the partner sees them as unforgivable. When spouses learn about children conceived with others outside of the marriage, that other families exist, or even that sex has occurred with another family member, the issues seem insurmountable. Yet, recovery history is filled with stories about how these situations get resolved. In short, when things are intolerable, it is about boundaries. When it is about forgiveness, discerning what to do truly requires more time and diligence to sort the situation out.

Whether the behavior is intolerable or unforgivable, you should still go to family week or any other learning opportunity that presents itself. Recovery requires that you learn as much as you can. Whenever the partners talk about issues, bond with others, or learn new skills, they actually start to grow new, more functional neural pathways in their brains.

Further, it is heartbreaking to see partners opt out of the therapy process, when clinicians know there is information they do not have that could absolutely change their understanding of everything. Often this comes in the guise of the addict not having told the partner everything. And much of it has not to do with sexual behavior. The addict did not know the significance of the information. Or they felt the partner already knew. Therapists cannot help because they cannot break confidentiality, and addicts will not reveal them if the partner does not show up to a safe environment so these issues can be aired. Almost every therapist has been in the bind of knowing that people are making decisions with insufficient data and there is nothing that can be done until those involved are willing to talk.

Given the scarcity of resources, it's important for couples to utilize all the inpatient and outpatient resources that are available. Building a recovery requires diligence. Not to do so usually means poor decisions about staying or leaving. Read everything you can find. Go to Twelve Step meetings. Find a good therapist who has been trained to help people coping with sex addiction issues. Find intensive workshops and group experiences. You may even choose to seek inpatient treatment.

You simply must build a support network with people who understand this problem. They become the consultants who help you keep perspective, provide critical tools you need, and give you the care you need and deserve. Ultimately, they will also be the reality checks you need for good decision making. Most partners will admit that, on their own, their decisions have not been good. That is because they attempted to do it without help, without all the information, and without the tools they need.

So how do I make the decision to stay or leave? How do I know I have done enough to take this step?

Let us assume you have excellent support by people who are experienced in the problem of sex addiction. You have taken sufficient time to let the dust settle and the brain to start to shift to a higher level of functioning. You have done enough therapy and recovery work and have been proactive about learning about the disease. You have incorporated Twelve Step principles and practices into your life. To make a decision, there are some things you must remember.

Partners often experience the erosion of a sense of self. This fact is why therapists may suggest a therapeutic separation. By living some months separately, and doing therapy, couples can do what clinicians call *individuation*. This means the partners get a new take on what it means to be responsible for only themselves. Part of the goal is to develop enough ego strength to negotiate a new relationship.

This strategy is scary for couples, but it reveals so much and can be really useful. It illustrates a critical task necessary for making a decision about staying or leaving. Recovery means being able to discern what is right for you. You do not have to go through a therapeutic separation to learn that, but many still have the learning to do. The habits of being with someone are so ingrained, a dramatic change may be necessary to see how easily the self is lost.

One of the tests for an intimate relationship is answering one simple question: *Can I be most myself in your presence?* Then, ask your-self, *Can I be creative, funny, vulnerable, productive, strong, weak, flamboyant, shy, or even smart? Can I couple any of those words with sex and romance? Can I be tough, forgiving, generous, spiritual, intuitive, graceful, clumsy, lazy, self-indulgent, and disciplined? Do I feel equal, successful, attractive, encouraged, trusted, and believed? Can I be fully as competent as I can be and not have my partner disappear? Do I feel challenged? Can I be accountable and hold my partner accountable? Is it okay to make a mistake? Does our time together really seem to matter?*

There are many ways to discern if you can be yourself in your relationship. The more fundamental issue implicit in the question is *Are you willing to risk yourself with this person?* Intimacy really comes down to what you bring to the equation. And happiness stems from what we bring to that table called intimacy.

There are two decisions on the table. The first is the choice to be in a relationship. A committed relationship is a way of life that requires much of the partners. And it is has little to do with who you are with. This commitment has more to do with how much you have grown up, learned skills, developed integrity, understood your own limits, and healed your wounds.

From a therapist's perspective, people's unhappiness is often of their own making. To be an adult, especially with children, work responsibilities, and the nightmare of addiction, it is a difficult context to discover you still have growing up to do. For some, the best choice is to take the time until you know you are really ready to be in a relationship.

The second choice is to whom you are willing to commit. When intimacy boils down to its essence, physical characteristics, such as breast size or an athletic build, become tangential. The size of the bank account becomes irrelevant. The level of learning, while important, pales by comparison. Ultimately, two things determine whom you successfully choose to commit to—after the initial rush of sex and romance wears off. First, ask yourself:

- *Does my partner freely admit his or her mistakes?*
- *Do I feel safe enough to readily admit my mistakes?*

The answers to these questions make or break successful intimacy. Nothing lasts without those basic qualities of integrity. Everything else—sex, romance, success—goes through that filter. No long-term intimacy can survive without this essential sense of our own limits.

Psychiatrist Carl Jung long ago pointed out that the most important part of any relationship is the willingness to share the darkest parts of ourselves. It is critical to good parenting. Children need to understand that their parents struggle in life. Otherwise, unrealistic expectations create shame in children. Similarly, no primary relationship survives without the full disclosure of self. Again there is this great irony that shame is reduced by telling the most shameful things about ourselves. When partners keep secrets from one another, they invariably introduce shame into the intimacy of the relationship. So the second key determining factor when deciding whom you can successfully choose to commit to is revealed by asking yourself:

- *Can I share the darkest part of myself?*
- *Can I hear about the dark side of my partner?*

Being vulnerable doesn't require that the partner fix anything, but rather witness the strength and courage it takes to be an adult human being. In the movie *Shall We Dance*, Susan Sarandon stars as a suburban wife who hires a private detective to find out about her husband's secret life. She learns that her husband has secretly been taking dance lessons. While he hasn't been unfaithful, he did have a secret life. The private detective clearly wants to use this discovery to become involved with her, so he asks her why she stays with this man. She responds with one of the best statements of what it means to be in a relationship with another, "Because we need a witness to our lives."[5]

There are more than six billion people on the planet. What does any one life really mean? But in a marriage, you are promising to care about everything. The good, bad, terrible, and mundane things. All of it—all the time, every day, you're saying, *"Your life will not go unnoticed because I will notice it. Your life will not go unwitnessed—because I will be your witness."*

All relationships are challenges. The ultimate test of human life is making a successful long-term relationship. It is part of life's refining process that calls us into being better people. Family therapist Carl Whittaker once observed that all relationships are a struggle. It is simply a matter of finding the best "struggle" you can. Many times we find it is the one we are already in.

Chapter Five:
How Do I Set Boundaries and Keep Myself Safe?

Cara W. Tripodi, LCSW, CSAT-S

ℰℭ

Boundaries can be one of the most confusing—yet freeing aspects—of healing from sexual addiction. Sometimes people don't even really know what boundaries are, where they come from, why they are important, or how to establish them. Learning about this now is crucial for people like you who are navigating the unchartered territory of life after discovery of sex addiction.

What are boundaries?

Boundaries are defined as something that bounds or limits. Think of it as a fence around the perimeter of your property—the place where you live. It shows others where your property clearly begins and ends. Personal boundaries aren't as easy to see as that. Everyone sets their own boundaries around their physical, emotional, spiritual, and sexual self. These are not visible to others and are unique to each person.

Where did I learn how to set boundaries?

Boundary development starts in childhood and continues throughout your life. They reflect the cultural, social, familial, and religious affiliations in which you were raised. Children raised in environments where the rules were flexible yet predictable learn that what they say matters and that the appropriate limits will be adhered to. If children are taught to be respectful of others, for example not to interrupt when someone is speaking, they learn to expect the same from others. If they are not treated in the same way, they recognize that their feelings of anger are okay, and they expect their caregivers will support their feelings and explore possible actions regarding the offense to them.

Why are boundaries important?

Boundaries provide structure in your relationship. When boundaries are unhealthy and unpredictable, problems around self-identity arise. For example, if there was a no-talk rule in your family and you learned feelings were not welcome, you may have developed a fear of dealing openly with emotions. If your brother physically abused you and no one intervened to protect you, you learned that your physical safety and emotional needs were not important. These types of experiences can leave you vulnerable in intimate relationships, resulting in a poor sense of what your rights are as a person, and results in unhealthy boundaries.

Boundaries are critical to your recovery from your partner's sexual addiction. You will find that they will become a cornerstone for lifelong change and help to redefine the direction of your life and your relationship to the sex addict. They can also be the most difficult part of the healing process. You will make a lot of mistakes as you attempt to challenge old patterns of behavior with yet untested but more adaptive ways of relating to the sex addict. Realizing that you are living with an addict shakes the deepest parts of your identity, and setting and enforcing boundaries will become an essential part of how you manage your recovery going forward.

Where do I begin setting boundaries with the sex addict?

A good place to start is the beginning. Know your rights.

I have the right to . . .

- not tolerate any unwanted sexual advances
- expect a commitment to recovery defined by actions, such as Twelve Step Meetings and individual and/or group psychotherapy
- set boundaries and expect they be respected

- not accept sexual acting out (includes viewing pornography or having contact with sex partners)
- not be victimized again by the sexual behaviors
- not be lied to or deceived

You may have mixed reactions about voicing these rights. Your critical voice may say you are wrong, controlling, or rigid for setting limits with your partner. Maybe the addict has also criticized you, furthering your self-doubt. Setting limits with your partner can make you feel controlling.

Am I establishing boundaries or trying to control behavior?

In early recovery, they often do not feel all that different. A basic distinction has to do with intentions. Boundaries are about self-care and serve as a means of self-protection. Setting a boundary begins with you. Controlling is "other focused" and is centered on managing the outcome of someone else's behavior or attitudes. Asking a few questions can help in discerning your intentions when questioning your boundaries:

- For whom is the boundary intended?
- What is the desired outcome I seek?
- Am I protecting myself or trying to change the addict's behavior?
- What am I trying to achieve?
- Do my actions and words match?

Often in early recovery the boundaries you set will involve external controls. For example, choosing to live apart after learning about the addiction, having separate bedrooms, or having a no-sex contract. In distinguishing the difference between controlling behaviors versus establishing boundaries, examine your motivations pertaining to the circumstances. For example, you may decide an appropriate boundary is sleeping apart from your partner if you find out that he or she has lied about attending Twelve Step meetings. If you are establishing the limit to retaliate and make your partner change, this would be control. In the early stages of recovery, establishing safety should be your number one goal. You can't attain a higher level of emotional growth until there's stability in your home. Your physical, emotional, and spiritual safety was jeopardized as a result of your partner's sex addiction. You may not know what you need initially, but as time goes on the parameters will become clearer to you.

If your partner spent hours isolated in the basement office "working," and you later learned it's where he or she viewed online pornography, then having the computer moved to a neutral space, even if it is not you who moves it, can be seen as controlling. In reality, it's not. The goal and the intended outcome you are seeking is primarily for yourself. You are saying through your action that pornography is not acceptable in the home. Moving the computer to a more open space in the home acknowledges the impact of the addiction on you and the need for safety in your home as you define it. A desired secondary or simultaneous gain is that the addict will stop the behavior and change. However, what motivates you to set the boundary is to regain control over your life and to limit the toxic effects of sex addiction in your home.

Emotionally believing in yourself despite what your partner tells you will be a hurdle in your boundary development. Typically addicts respond to demands for accountability with accusations that deflect responsibility onto others, most likely you. Labeling you "controlling" or saying you are "managing his or her recovery"—these are common ways addicts may try to manipulate you to avoid your requests for change. These types of comments can make you doubt yourself. It's imperative that you listen to yourself and seek guidance from supportive people in these matters. Trusting yourself by learning to explore and implement new behaviors will help foster healthier boundaries.

What should I consider as I begin setting boundaries?

Before implementing your boundaries, it's useful to thoughtfully consider your needs and discuss your ideas and plans with trusted people who understand your situation. If the addict's duplicitous behavior extended over years, the severity of the violation will be greater, especially if you confronted the addict but your suspicions were repeatedly denied or explained away. If the sexual behaviors you've learned about are a recurrence of other previous indiscretions, then your level of mistrust will be further magnified. If the behavior is illegal, you may face greater social, legal, and financial consequences. It is important to recognize that your partner deceived you and violated your trust and no excuses need minimize this reality.

You may think, *She didn't mean to hurt me,* or *He did this because of how he was raised,"* but these rationalizations, although they may be true, may sidestep you in setting the necessary boundaries for yourself and your partner. Making a commitment to developing healthier boundaries will help protect you from being victimized by the addiction in the future.

Boundary work is a fundamental step in your recovery. You will need a lot of practice in identifying and respecting your boundaries. Your partner's addiction brought you here, but it's up to you how you handle this going forward. The choice to heal and transform your pain into meaning is one worth making. A step in protecting yourself is to not minimize the damage from the addiction. The pain will lessen in time but much depends upon how you care for yourself and face the difficult task of learning better ways to communicate your worth to yourself and others.

What are some examples of boundaries that people set?

In the first few years of recovery from sexual addiction, you'll need to create very specific, definable boundaries, also referred to as *nonnegotiables.* These should be specific behaviors or situations relevant to your circumstances. Nonnegotiables can range from determining the need for additional boundaries with the addict to grounds for ending the relationship. Here are some examples of nonnegotiables:

- No sex outside the relationship.
- Internet access at home is to be regulated by a monitoring program.
- Money spent over _____ must be discussed beforehand.

- Recovery must remain consistent.

- No viewing pornography.

- No masturbation.

- No contact or alone time with prior acting-out partners. This can include emails, phone calls, text messaging, or use of secret bank accounts.

- No verbal abuse.

How do I determine what to do if these boundaries are violated?

In addition to defining your nonnegotiables, you need to create consequences that will help you become more consistent and allow you to be clearer in what you can and cannot accept in your relationship with the sex addict. Be as specific as possible when creating this list. For example, if having sex outside of the relationship is a nonnegotiable and the consequence is separation, how will you respond if you learn your partner went to a strip club? Does that equate to sex outside of the relationship? If so, are you prepared to act upon your stated nonnegotiable?

Be prepared to have a list that best defines the parameters of your boundaries and consequences if a boundary violation occurs. Be careful and think through the excuses you might tell yourself that may communicate a mixed message. If you say one thing but do another, think through how that will affect you and the sex addict. Most addicts avoid and displace responsibility for their actions. Many rebel against rules meant to limit their behaviors and avoid accountability. This can be especially prevalent in intimate relationships where accountability is most likely to be expected. Limits you set can activate defensiveness and reactivity, which in the past may have caused you to compromise and acquiesce to the demands of the addict.

If you learn that the addict has violated one of your nonnegotiables, cultivating a practice of "gathering data" will help. When a problem arises, like a slip with masturbation or an unexplained phone bill, first allow yourself to experience your reactions and seek safe people to talk to about what happened. Next, if you decide to confront your partner with the information and if you are not satisfied with the response, stay focused on what your feelings and perceptions are telling you. Enlist a detached stance just as if you were an observer to the situation. Notice if any other issues arise over a period of time that gives you pause and triggers suspicions. Review and compare the information pertaining to the infraction to other evidence gathered. Does the behavior match other aspects of the addict's actions and attitudes with you or others? Some questions you might ask include, *How is he or she treating me emotionally? How invested in recovery is he or she?* or *Do his or her words and actions add up consistently?*

Taking these steps doesn't mean avoiding or denying your concerns. Rather, they help you act from a place of preparedness rather than reactivity. Confronting your doubts and your concerns makes you an active participant in the facts, empowering you toward the right action.

Practicing an observer stance can conjure up feelings of impatience or fear of being duped again. It may feel as though you are avoiding the suspicious behaviors, when in fact you are actively addressing issues in a new way. Threats or ultimatums haven't worked in the past and learning newer ways to handle situations that used to confuse you is difficult in the beginning. By pacing your responses, you allow yourself time to gain perspective in an objective way, which distances you from personalizing the behaviors and empowers you to act in more effective ways. The addict acts out because of difficulty in relating to life in a responsible and adult fashion—not because of who you are. By delaying your response, you build confidence in enforcing boundaries and in asserting your worth as a person. You find you are better able to make choices. "I'm not going to take it anymore!" is no longer a meaningless threat but an action you are prepared to take to create greater safety and predictability in your life.

Creating this boundary and consequence list is going to take some time. What should I do in the meantime?

If you're not prepared to act and want to take a wait-and-see approach, that's understandable. It's even advisable because many of the addict's behaviors may fall into gray areas and you may be uncertain what is or is not acceptable for you. It's better to wait before establishing boundaries than to set them and not be prepared to act on them. Understanding your nonnegotiables will advance your own healing process because you will gain knowledge and clarity for yourself that will help you when confronted with addictive behaviors and attitudes.

What happens if I can't uphold my boundaries or change my mind?

"I say one thing and then do another!" "I told him no sex for a month and then the next week I wanted to have sex with him and he said no!" or "I found emails from escorts and told him I wanted a divorce and then never did anything about it." "What's wrong with me?" "I have said the same things time and again and nothing changed; she still did what she wanted. Why should I believe I can affect change now?"

Give yourself permission to be in a *process* of change rather than an event. The event was learning that your partner is a sex addict. The process of change is what you do with the consequence of the event and will be lifelong. There will be a lot of mistakes in the early stages of establishing healthy boundaries, because trusting yourself over the addict may be uncomfortable and downright scary. *If I feel and think this way, then I have to act accordingly,* or *She is going to tell me I am wrong and what if she's right?* Sometimes the old ways are more familiar but also keep you stuck. Other times boundary failure occurs because you might confuse new behaviors with old ones. *Because I felt this way in the past, does that mean that's how it has to be now?* Seeking the understanding from others who share and support your change process will help you gain perspective on those roadblocks.

Many partners commonly have made the mistake of focusing on what addicts say rather than what they do. You've been accustomed to listening to the addict's explanations, rationalizations, or promises. Pay attention to the inconsistencies between the addict's words and actions, and challenge these inconsistencies. Remember the concept of the observer—notice what you think or feel about the situation. Reevaluate and slow down how you communicate with the addict.

Pointing out inconsistencies may trigger defensiveness. Be prepared for how you will respond in this instance. Remember that it will take practice to communicate differently and effectively and you will not be perfect.

You have listened to the addict at the expense of yourself. Commit to yourself that your needs come first. In the beginning, this is difficult because you may not yet understand the addictive part of the partner you knew. Recognizing how you were manipulated, cajoled, and persuaded to think other than what you did, is the first step in separating your truth from the addict's truth. Until you become a better judge of the addictive aspects of your partner's personality, you need to remember that you're vulnerable to the addict's opinions and perceptions of you. Go easy on yourself. Remember that healthy boundary development is a learning process. Commit to the hard work involved. Apply a "trial and error" approach. It's essential to long-term growth. Take the time to learn where your boundaries were porous within the relationship prior to the discovery of sex addiction. Begin to apply new ways to prepare and follow up on changes for yourself. Be curious and observe what worked and what didn't. Talk to others. Don't do this alone.

Is it okay to tell my close friends or family about my situation and some of the boundaries I am setting? I feel so alone and want those close to me to know.

The discovery of being involved with a sex addict is like stumbling upon a rude and unwelcomed guest in your home. It's there, you want to get rid of it, and yet the memory of this intrusion is always with you. Upon first learning of sex addiction, the shock and devastation you experience is overwhelming. As with any other life crisis, it's normal to want to talk about what's happened. You're tempted to turn to those who know you best, yet afraid to tell them because you're embarrassed and ashamed about your partner's sexual behaviors. Sex is a taboo topic for much of society. Sexual indiscretions can be an intolerable topic. Little is still known or talked about regarding the compulsive use of sex, much less the disorienting impact it has on families.

What are your motivations for wanting to share with others? Is it to retaliate against the addict for having done this to you, or is it for your own emotional support? It may be hard to distinguish your motivation, particularly in the beginning. For example, if you've been with a partner whose mother has always been critical of you, your first instinct may be to tell her. In this case, you would be trying to validate your pain at the cost of the addict's relationship with his or her mother. Perhaps the addict hadn't planned on disclosing the information to family members. This may become a nonnegotiable to consider if acting out continues. One option in addressing this nonnegotiable is to have the addict tell his or her mother or another mutually agreed upon family member. You're angry and hurt, yet you may not feel comfortable talking about your partner's sex addiction with those closest to you. Who is appropriate to tell? And how will they respond? Keep in mind the following issues as you ponder disclosing to others.

Safe versus unsafe people

Imagining the future is a good way to decipher if someone will be supportive or judge you down the road, especially if you reconcile with the addict. Consider how this person will react. Will he or she hold it against you? How will their reactions impact you? Will they tell you to leave the relationship, making it harder to know what to do for yourself?

Long-term ramifications

You want to be sure the person you tell is someone who will keep your confidences. What you say now isn't something you can take back in two months or two years, so weighing your decisions against the long-term ramifications are factors to consider.

Prepare what you will say

Depending on the person, you may want to modify the details. With one person, you may be more open yet with another person less so. Write out what you will say. This prepares you for any unwanted questions you may feel compelled to answer. Give the scope of the problem but not necessarily the graphic details. For example, *John and I are in therapy because John discovered he has an addiction that has become*

out of control. Or, I learned some devastating news about Sally and I am in
a lot of pain. I'm not comfortable talking about the details at this time, but
would greatly appreciate spending some time with you for support.

Inform the addict of your intentions

During this time you will find your needs are very different
from the addict's. The need to tell others can be a boundary for you.
Talk to your partner and let him or her know who and what you plan
to share. If your partner asks you not to share, compromise in terms
of when, how much, and who to tell. For the addict, telling others
about the behavior may be shaming. If confiding in someone close to
you is part of your healing and not as retaliation for the pain your
partner's behavior has caused you, then your partner's reaction can be
considered a consequence of his or her behavior. For example, telling
the addict, *Because of your behaviors I plan to let _____ know.*

You may be embarrassed and don't want anyone close to
you to know what you're going through. That's okay and is your
choice. But keep in mind that talking to at least two people, including
a therapist, will help you move through the various stages of healing.
Sometimes partners find they absolutely don't want others close to
them to know. If that describes you, consider what contributes to this
feeling. Do you feel you will be judged or told disparaging comments
and later regret confiding in them? Do you worry that your partner's
behavior somehow reflects poorly on you? If so, you may be internal-
izing some of the shame of his or her behaviors and feeling responsible
for what he or she did, as though you could have prevented the
addictive behavior. Exploring some of these themes with a therapist
will help you sort through your internal boundaries and define where
your issues end and the sex addiction begins.

How will setting boundaries help me cope during this difficult time?

In the beginning you may feel compelled to act on your
feelings or thoughts about leaving. In fact, you may have tried leaving
or asked your partner to leave. You'll likely feel pressure from others to
end your relationship, as though that would end the emotional turmoil

you're in. Or you may be determined to make it work. Whatever your situation, boundaries will help you get through it. Most therapists suggest you make no significant life changes during the first year of recovery. This initial time period will feel long and often very open-ended, but it affords you the necessary time to sit with the myriad of feelings without having to act on them. Making a decision to not act *is* an action. Just because you're not making any significant life changes doesn't mean you're doing nothing. You are actively engaged in a process of discovery necessary for your well-being. Attending to your own pain, recovering from the trauma in a safe place, setting bound-aries, and allowing yourself to witness whether your partner is able to commit to recovery will move you forward if you allow yourself the time to heal.

Delaying major decisions can be valuable, even for those where the damage may be too great to reconcile. If the acting out was too pervasive, extreme, or involved significant consequences, you may feel almost certain you cannot re-enter the relationship. However, investing in this initial time period does not deny your certainty. Rather, it allows you to process all the losses associated with the relationship while not getting distracted or caught up in the decision making involved in ending the relationship. By acquiring skills like boundary setting, you will be better prepared to enter a relationship with another partner. All of these steps take time and attention.

You have had an attachment to someone important to you, and giving yourself the time to disengage is acknowledging the depth of this bond. Allow yourself time to grieve and heal. Setting boundaries is an essential tool in this process and will better equip you in all future relationships. Defining, acknowledging, and implementing are all separate yet intertwined steps in boundary development. How you were raised and the messages you received about your self-worth and value in relationships have played a large part in how you entered into a partnership with someone with distorted sexual and intimate boundaries. Recognizing how your needs were not met prior to discovery or disclosure will assist you in evaluating where your boundaries were impaired. Establishing nonnegotiables sets into motion a new and solid foundation of self-protection and self-assertion. You are worth it. Taking the time to heal from the pain by setting and keeping boundaries will give you a freedom you've never really known.

Chapter Six:
What about Me and My Sexuality?

Omar Minwalla, PhD

ℰℭ

When it comes to sex addiction and sexual compulsivity, there is tremendous focus on the addict's sexuality, not the partner's. Therapists, sponsors, support groups, couples, and the addict all pay close attention to the addict's sexuality. All this attention makes sense because, after all, it is the sexual acting out of the addict that in many ways characterizes "the problem."

Seldom does the spotlight spin around and shed light on the sexuality of the partner or spouse of the sex addict. In all the effort to help address the addict's problem, the sexuality of the partner or spouse is most often conspicuously minimized, neglected, and ignored. Rarely does the partner's sexuality become a focus of clinical attention or discussion and, when it does, it's most often in the context of couple's treatment—an attempt to help the couple become sexual in the later stages of the recovery process. Since the majority of partners are female, one of the reasons for this is the still-prominent patriarchal dynamic of neglecting female sexuality and rendering it unimportant and illegitimate. It also reflects the clinical field's squeamishness and avoidance of female sexuality, including sexual and gender-based victimization.

What happens to the sexuality of the partner or spouse of a sex addict? What's the impact of sex addiction on the partner's sexuality, and what can he or she do about it?

This chapter speaks to you directly as a partner of a sex addict and aims to address some of the ways that your sexuality, your sexual sense of self, sexual psychology, and sexual functioning may be impacted and wounded by the sexual addiction and its consequences.

In addition, a treatment model is proposed to help you embark on a sexual healing journey and reclaim aspects of your sexuality.

The Sexual Trauma Model

When you begin to understand the sexual symptoms experienced by partners of sex addicts, it becomes apparent that the symptoms are strikingly similar to those known to occur from sexual trauma, such as rape, sexual assault, sexual abuse, and molestation. When we look at well-established symptoms of sexual trauma and abuse, partners of sex addicts can identify with many or all of them. Many experts hold a new, emerging perspective that partners of sex addicts experience a form of sexual trauma.

Using this model, the partner's symptoms, reactions, and what is otherwise perceived as "erratic behavior" may be understood as symptoms of trauma, including sexual trauma. Ignoring these symptoms only serves to exacerbate them. They may be similar to those that people with post-traumatic stress disorder (PTSD) and rape trauma syndrome (RTS) experience. Working from a trauma model, the partner's symptoms are understood and framed as natural and expected responses to trauma—a way of coping and trying to adapt and survive. This perspective respects and validates the partner's sexual wounding and victimization and emphasizes the importance of looking at his or her sexual symptoms and healing them.

When we shift our thinking to include and acknowledge the sexual trauma that you may be experiencing, your reactions and symptoms make much more sense. This perspective also helps the professional address the issues at hand in a way that will more likely lead to healing and change—helping you move through your wounding rather than remaining stuck in your pain.

Professionals also know that one of the most challenging aspects of recovery for addicts and their partners is regaining a sense of sexual health. Even when some of the emotional and relational aspects seem to have been worked through, confronting and addressing the sexual aspects of healing often go unaddressed. The sexual trauma model may help explain why sexual healing and developing healthy sexuality can be so challenging for partners and couples in recovery. If symptoms of sexual trauma have been ignored, finding healthy sexuality as a couple can be a near-impossible task. Underneath the attempts to regain intimacy and sexual pleasure lie trauma wounds that are open and still bleeding. Again, the trauma perspective helps the journey of sexual healing in that it specifically acknowledges any sexual trauma and makes imperative the need to address and attend to the specific sexual symptoms as part of treatment toward sexual health.

Sexual Wounding

The process of discovery can clearly have many consequences: psychological, emotional, relational, and spiritual. One of the dimensions of your experience that's often affected, yet frequently unacknowledged, is your sexuality. Of course, simply avoiding your sexuality doesn't lessen the impact. Many partners impacted by the addiction are left to either address these issues in isolation with little support or ignore them altogether. Silence, however, only perpetuates the symptoms.

Sexuality fundamentally affects the core of our psychology and sense of self. This is why the impact on your sexuality cannot be compartmentalized and ignored without it affecting other aspects of your life, in addition to your healing process as a couple. It is vital for you to acknowledge, validate, and address how the addict's sexual acting out affected you. It's also important for the addict to recognize the impact of his or her behavior on your sexuality as well.

Every partner is affected differently by the addict's sexual acting out. Some may experience few sexual symptoms. However, others experience a greater effect on their sexuality. It's imperative that every partner or spouse struggling with these issues go through the process of assessing his or her sexuality and recognize any wounding in this area.

This chapter discusses some of the ways your sexuality may be affected. Much of this discussion is based on qualitative research, where partners describe their experiences in their own words. Not every type of sexual wound will be described here and many may not apply to every partner. However, this chapter will give you awareness that, indeed, many partners of addicts do experience sexual wounds that are significant, painful, and clearly indicate the need for attention and healing. The types of wounding described here are based on the sexual trauma perspective.[1]

As you read these wounds, take time to reflect on the ways you identify with the experiences of other partners, and try to become more aware of your sexual wounds. Remember, you are not alone and many partners out there share in your pain.

Why do I avoid, fear, or lack interest in sex?

One of the most common sexual wounds that you may experience, particularly early in the process and often immediately after discovery or disclosure, is a type of sexual shutting down and sexual aversion. The idea of sex is painful and overwhelming. You may no longer feel pleasure or have any interest in it. Some people in your same situation have described the experience this way:

> *I couldn't masturbate for at least a month or two after disclosure.*

> *I can't imagine ever being sexual again. I have no interest.*

> *I feel dead sexually. I couldn't care less whether I have sex again.*

> *I fear sex in the future. I don't think it's just because I've been with the same man for sixteen years and am no longer youthful. I think it has a lot to do with how my sexuality has been impacted by the sex addiction.*

Specific behaviors that you once enjoyed you may now feel an aversion toward and they may produce anxiety or fear.

> *I never again performed oral sex. Possibly it was the submissive nature to it. Or it was just me pleasuring him. I never wanted to do that for him again. Possibly because I could so easily imagine all the other mouths, bought and paid for, that had performed that little service before. It took on the feeling of service, rather than intimacy. I just refused to go there again.*

*I still feel sexual. I still want to have sex. But I know I will
never feel as sexually free as I did before I became involved with
my sex addict husband. I'll always be leery about what lies
beneath, possibly feeling that there is always darkness, shame,
hidden secrets associated with a man's sexuality.*

Why does sex feel like an obligation?

Many partners describe sex as an obligation. In these cases,
you're not engaging in sex because there's an internal desire or
motivation, but rather because you feel that you "have to." Often
what's behind this is the idea that if you are not sexual with your
partner, he or she will act out. If you don't attempt to satisfy his or
her sexual needs, then your partner will get them met elsewhere. This
may translate into having sex when you don't feel like it. Given that
you may not have been educated on the nature of sex addiction and
the underlying causes, it's understandable that you may assume,
erroneously, that you can control the addiction through your sexual
behavior or that the addiction has to do with your sexuality. You are
not alone. Read on to discover others in your same situation.

*All along, I had thoughts that if I just went along with
everything he wanted sexually, then he would get better. . . .
I ended up doing things that disgusted me.*

*I thought that if I gave him enough sexually, he would stop
acting out. When he entered recovery, I would feel obligated to
be sexual with him when he wanted to even if I didn't want to,
because I felt if he was abstaining from all sexual stimulus
outside of our relationship, then I owed him sexually. But this
made me feel resentful because it was not what I wanted and
I still feel unsafe.*

Why do I participate in compulsive or inappropriate
sexual behaviors?

Sometimes you may find yourself engaging in sexual
behaviors or activities that you would otherwise not want to or don't

match your comfort level or value system. Again, this may have to do with obligatory demands you may feel. You may believe that your partner's sexual acting out is dependent on your sexuality. You may also be using sexuality in a compulsive manner—using sex as a way to medicate your pain caused by the addiction. This may then leave you feeling your own sense of shame as a consequence of using sex as a way of coping—creating your own cycle of compulsive sexual behavior.

While it's understandable to think that a partner's sexual acting out could be curtailed and controlled by providing more sex or the type of sex that he or she seems to seek in his or her acting out, it's critical that you recognize that your sexuality is independent of your partner's sexual acting out. Dependence on problematic sexual behavior and arousal is not about you or your sexuality—it's about the addict's underlying psychological and emotional dynamics. Others have discovered that using sex to try to control or "help" another person doesn't constitute healthy sexuality.

> *I found myself becoming more sexual and willing to engage in behaviors I didn't like.*

> *I felt pressure to comply with his sexual desires…that if I acted like a porn star, he would like me and not act out.*

> *I felt obligated to wear lacy or sexy underwear even though I hated the way it looked under my clothes. I hated wearing the underwear, especially when I would wait up for him to see it and he wouldn't come home until 2 a.m. I felt unwanted by the one person I wanted and powerless to please him. Now I am resentful of the years of dressing the part and regret that because of how hurt I still feel about it.*

Why do I experience negative feelings such as anger, disgust, or guilt when touched?

You may find it challenging to experience touch, particularly sexual touch, in a way that's pleasurable, comforting, or loving. Instead, you may fear touch, find it aversive, and feel uncomfortable with being touched. This is particularly significant when we consider how important touch is to human functioning. Touch is a basic need; thus your desire to avoid touch demonstrates the depth of your wound. For some partners, the idea of "sexual touch" may become overwhelming.

> *I feel disgusted by the idea of sex and a man's body. I am scared of physical contact.*

> *I recoil from touch now. I just don't want anyone touching me anymore. I am damaged.*

> *I can't imagine what a passionate kiss feels like anymore. I cringe when he attempts to embrace me—even platonically.*

Why do I have difficulty becoming aroused or feeling sensation?

One possible symptom experienced by partners is a lack of physical and sexual responsiveness. Sensation may be experienced as diminished. Arousal, orgasmic response and the ability to lubricate may all be impacted on some level. It makes sense that when there are so many psychological and emotional disturbances occurring that the physical body will also be affected. Many people can relate to this.

> *I definitely had difficulty becoming aroused and feeling sensation. I wasn't sure if that was a factor of the sexual trauma or what was lacking between my husband and myself.*

> *I have been unable to experience any type of sexual pleasure or intimacy for a very long time.*

> *I didn't feel anything anymore…it was like I was numb.*

Why do I feel dirty and contaminated?

Some partners describe feeling dirty and contaminated. The disgust that partners feel toward the addict's behavior is often projected onto themselves. The addict's behaviors are seen as dirty.

As a result, partners perceive themselves as dirty. When people associate with that which they feel is disgusting, they become contaminated as well.

> *I feel dirty and disgusting and objectified. I feel crazy for thinking and feeling that way.*

> *I feel dirty, marked, and scarred.*

Obviously, this includes more than just a perception of being contaminated; it includes anxious fears of actually contracting a sexually transmitted infection.

> *I not only feel dirty and contaminated, but I worry about becoming infected with a disease.*

> *My health is hugely at risk. I am terrified of HPV, AIDS, and other STDs.*

> *I feel angry and anxious because I have to use a condom with my husband. I can't trust that he's clean and doesn't have a disease, and this is supposed to be the man I trust the most. I feel like he's dirty and I am too for being with him.*

Why do I feel emotionally distant or not present during sex?

Feeling detached and not in the moment is common among partners of sex addicts. There's often a part of you that feels unsafe, suspicious, untrusting, and uncertain about the presence of your partner. You may wonder if she or he is fantasizing about other partners or pornographic images, or if your partner is enjoying sex with you. There's often a part of you that's still wounded, hurting, and in considerable pain. It makes sense that you may be unable to be fully present under these conditions. You may be preoccupied with anxiety about an STD or if your partner has been acting out again. You, like many others, may be focusing on your own sense of inadequacy, feeling preoccupied with your body image and whether you are arousing your partner.

I felt detached from my body. I dissociated.

I feel emotionally separate from him and have a really hard time being present when trying to be intimate. I panic when he won't look at me and wonder where his mind is.

Why do I experience intrusive or disturbing thoughts, images, and flashbacks?

This is common and highly disturbing for some partners. You may discover images on the computer or in videos that become firmly etched in your visual mind. These can often be of a highly graphic nature because contemporary pornography has become highly intensified and diversified. Particularly as an addict's pornography addiction escalates, he or she often will look at increasingly more intense sexual imagery and content—often moving into domains such as rape scenes, extreme torture, bestiality, and child pornography. Many partners, on the other hand, often have little exposure to pornography. If exposed to the extreme content found in an escalating porn addiction, such images can have a shattering and horrifying impact on your psyche.

This is particularly so when you have little knowledge of how porn addiction works and the reasons for increased intensity among addicts. Because men tend to be more visually sexual, a female partner with little exposure to porn will be even more affected by it. It's difficult to let go of such disturbing images, because the psyche has a way of noting material that is highly emotionally and psychologically charged. Just as a rape victim may experience flashbacks of the traumatic event, graphic images can be experienced in the same way and can significantly impact sexual functioning.

The intrusive and disturbing thoughts and images were some of the most difficult experiences post-disclosure. For more than a year, I was haunted by all kinds of pornographic images involving my husband...during sex, in dreams, or just in the course of my day.

Intrusive thoughts are the most apparent way that I have been scarred by this, the most compelling symptom of trauma. I had my own sexual fantasies and thoughts, but what goes through my mind now doesn't really feel like my own. It feels like something forced into my psyche against my will. It's very disturbing. It's something I still contend with two and a half years later.

I also experience a type of flashback and I wonder if I don't have something akin to PTSD. Certain behaviors of his, arguments we had, moments of doubts I had about his veracity, these would trigger thoughts and images accompanied by a rush of adrenaline and all that goes along with that.

I can't make the flashbacks stop. I see him with prostitutes all the time in my mind. I see reminders every minute, every day. I'm exhausted from all the symbolism.

Why do I have trouble establishing or maintaining intimate relationships?

One of the most painful and wounding aspects of the addiction dynamic is the breakdown of trust in a relationship. Without trust, it's almost impossible to create a healthy and stable intimate relationship.

While distrust works on all levels of a relationship, it certainly impacts sexuality in a relationship. Since healthy sexuality most often requires vulnerability, the lack of trust will often impact your ability to fully relax during sex and will significantly impede your ability to enjoy the experience.

Furthermore, many partners come to view the addict's sexuality as fundamentally compulsive and unhealthy. The lack of trust in the addict may leave you feeling that it is simply unrealistic to expect your partner to stop acting out. This can often leave you feeling hopeless about intimacy and relationships in general. You may experience a feeling of resignation. You may reason that it is better to stay with the addict whom you already know, rather than investing in a new relationship that may ultimately lead to similar pain.

I feel a general distrust of men and what they really think and feel about women.

I began to fear that all men act out using pornography and obsessively fantasize about other women. As a woman, if I wanted a romantic relationship with a man, I have to tolerate it. The idea of that being true is so unbearable, it makes me want to never have a relationship with a man again.

It's hard not to think of all men as being unable to control themselves if tempted. I question whether all men think of women as being only sexual objects. Are all men this sick inside their heads?

I am unwilling to have sex with my husband or any man. My trust was destroyed and I cannot put myself in harm's way mostly physically and somewhat emotionally.

Why do I have vaginal pain or difficulty achieving orgasm?

The impact of discovering a partner is sexually addicted can go beyond "sexual shutting down" and diminishing sexual response and sensation. It can actually create psychosomatic sexual symptoms such as vaginal pain for some women.

I have been unable to achieve orgasm for a long time, and for the past few months when I am kissing him and would normally become aroused, I instead have aching (and sometimes sharp) vaginal pain, which also used to happen whenever I would catch him acting out or think about sexual things he had done.

When my husband expressed sexual dissatisfaction (during his acting out), I experienced painful cramping with intercourse. The cramping lasted for hours after the intercourse. I no longer had this symptom after initial disclosure and then formal disclosure.

Why do I have body image issues?

A common outcome experienced by partners is body image concerns and an increased sense of insecurity about physical attractiveness. In a culture where most people, particularly women, carry insecurities and concerns about physical appearance and body image, you may have a heightened sense of inadequacy about your body.

Whatever issues you may have had prior to the addiction, they are often exacerbated and intensified. You may become preoccupied with evaluating and criticizing your body, your sexuality, and your sense of attractiveness. If you once felt confidence and enjoyed your body, you may suddenly find yourself doubting your appearance and feeling inadequate. These are common feelings.

I felt like damaged goods. I didn't want to look at my own body. I felt detached from my own body. I had trouble even looking at myself naked.

Feelings of self-consciousness about my body would overcome me during times I was trying to be free and sexy.

I have felt detached from my body, disgusted by it. I have felt unattractive, fat, ugly, insecure, and like I must be inferior to other women for them to have captured his interest.

I asked him about my vagina size. I never used to give this stuff a second thought, but now I wonder.

Among the body image concerns that you may experience, specific sexual and genital image issues may arise, resulting in significant negative consequences on your overall sexual functioning, sexual self-esteem, and sexual health.

I had never worried about whether or not my vagina was tight enough before, but now I do.

Knowing that every pornographic image or prostitute he looked at undoubtedly had large, and most likely, enhanced breasts, my small breasts, which I had always thought had appealed to him, seemed flaccid and spent to me. They were unappealing and limp after two children, and I never really enjoyed him touching them again, something that had always been a part of my pleasure in lovemaking.

After learning of his desire that I have bigger breasts, I went through a period of wondering whether I owed it to him to try to enhance them. Mostly I felt angry that my breasts were deemed less than desirable. I used to spend a lot of time comparing myself to the sexual ideal he described.

Why do I feel secrecy and shame?

A common problem experienced by partners is the shame they feel and the embarrassment that the addict's problem is sexual in nature. Such feelings may leave you isolated and silent about your pain. Because sexual addiction is still a relatively new diagnosis and lacks the legitimacy of alcoholism as a disorder or problem, telling others that your partner is a sex addict leaves you vulnerable to the misconceptions and myths of sex addiction.

Many spouses fear, for example, that their partners will be automatically perceived as pedophiles and that they themselves will be judged for staying in the relationship. This affects your sexuality as well, leaving you hiding secretly with your sexual wounds, afraid of reaching out to others for help or support.

I have difficulty sharing information about his addiction with friends because I am embarrassed and afraid of what they'll think of him and me for being with him.

I felt like damaged goods. I thought about how others would view me: "Oh, she couldn't satisfy him sexually." I felt marked.

Why do I feel responsible for this victimization?

As mentioned, shame and secrecy often accompany your symptoms. Like many victims of sexual trauma, you may feel somehow responsible or in some way that you contributed to the addict's behavior. You may struggle with notions that you caused the addiction and see it as a reflection on you. You may have been encouraged to take responsibility for your part in the addictive processes in the relationship. This might lead to self-blame and confusion about your role in the addictive process.

> *We are told that we are codependent and contributed to the problem. I find myself asking if I had been less emotional, if I had been less volatile, if I had been more emotionally in control, this would have enabled him to work his program better. He's done a number on me in terms of putting so much blame on me. It's hard to sort through it all.*

> *Therapy, books, and support groups—they all ask us not to blame ourselves, but we are also told that we contributed to the problem. This is something I am trying to work on.*

> *I have a hard time getting away from the idea that this addiction has something to do with me.*

How do you know if it's sexual abuse?

To further explore how you, as a partner of a sex addict, may have been abused sexually, it may be useful to review author Wendy Maltz's four indicators of sexual abuse.[2]

Consider your own experience and in what ways you can identify with the following indicators:

1. Were you unable to give your full consent to the sexual activity?

   > *He has never touched me without consent or forced anything on me. But, in lying, he has robbed me of my ability to consent with full awareness of the truth. If I had known about the sexual addiction, I never would have consented to a sexual relationship.*

2. Did the betrayal involve the betrayal of a trusted relationship?

   It's very traumatic to find out that the decisions I've made in our relationship (including entering it and becoming attached in the first place) and the way I've felt about my partner hasn't, in large part, been based in reality but in deception.

3. Was the sexual activity characterized by violence or control over you as a person?

   I feel like I've had my sexuality stolen from me and that even as an adult, I've had very little say about what happens with and to my body and what kind of sexual relationship I will have and what my partner is allowed to do and bring into our bed.

   I feel as if my sexuality has been ripped from me and I wonder if I'll ever be able to have sex again.

4. Did you feel abused?

   I have been raped and molested in the past...and I have done some healing around that. This too feels like a rape, but even worse—because I know and love this person. He is my husband.

   I feel that I was sexually abused and that I suffer from post-traumatic stress syndrome. I have flashbacks regarding the prostitutes.

Targeting Sexual Trauma among Partners of Sex Addicts

Working within the sexual trauma model, it's important for partners to acknowledge any symptoms of sexual trauma or wounding and to address these symptoms. Of course this can be a painful process requiring patience, insight, and a tremendous amount of effort and courage.

Current clinical interventions often don't include the partner in the initial stages of the addict's treatment. As a partner, you may feel that the problem is the addict's and therefore, understandably, resent the idea that you may need professional help. Most current models of treatment focus primarily on the addict. If the partner is included, it may only be in the context of couples work during later stages of treatment.

In cases where the partner does engage in his or her own work during the initial stages of treatment, the focus is typically on issues related to codependency. This emphasizes learning to draw boundaries, self-care, getting out of the victim role, and gaining support through Twelve Step groups such as COSA or S-Anon. When trauma or victimization is addressed, it's typically limited to the emotional and relational betrayal and trauma, which is obviously critical and important.

Integrating the sexual trauma perspective expands treatment to include a focus on the sexual wounding. Your need for healing becomes emphasized and your own need for professional help should be explained in a way that helps you appreciate your wounding and need for self-care.

As a partner, you may want to consider integrating some of what's offered into your own recovery journey. One of the first steps toward healing as a partner impacted by sex addiction is to recognize that you might need some individual therapeutic work that is done independent from your partner. Due to the potentially traumatic nature of the wounding that occurs sexually, it's imperative that you first address some of the sexual wounding on your own, on your own terms, before trying to be sexual with your partner or another person.

How should I approach my sexuality in early recovery?

Take a vacation from sex. One thing to consider early in your healing journey is taking some time to heal. This means permitting yourself to take a break from being sexual and allowing yourself some time to adjust and process the consequences of the addiction in your experience—the emotional betrayal, the change in how you view the relationship, and the hurt of having been lied to. You may feel pressure to be sexual—that if you don't, your partner will act out. You may find yourself wanting to help take care of your partner's needs at the expense of your own. Both reactions are unhealthy.

You may also feel compelled to be sexual in order to comfort and reassure yourself that the relationship is still viable and your partner still loves you. You may use sex as a way to medicate and comfort your pain related to the addiction. This, too, is unhealthy. Many partners are relieved when they are given "permission" to abstain from sex. You can let go of the pressure and feelings of obligation and attend to your wounds without sex becoming a distraction and confusing your healing process.

Don't let your partner or anyone else, including a professional, pressure you into the idea that you need to be sexual before you're ready. Whether you're going to remain in your partnership with the addict or move on, taking some time out to heal your sexual wounds is important to healthy sexuality. If you remain in the partnership, it still makes sense to first concentrate on repairing the emotional betrayal and focus on creating a basic level of relational and emotional intimacy before being sexual. It doesn't make sense to work on sexual intimacy with your partner until there's an adequate level of trust and intimacy in the other areas of the relationship—whether it's emotional intimacy, work intimacy, spiritual intimacy, communication intimacy, or aesthetic intimacy.

Reclaiming Sexuality

One important part of healing is to make a conscious, internally driven decision to reclaim your sexuality. While those around you may encourage and want you to heal on the sexual level in light of your partner's addiction, it's ultimately critical that you find a place inside yourself that wants to heal and make a commitment to a healing journey. One way is to articulate the specific ways you want to heal your sexuality. Some examples include

- *I want to develop a more positive view of sexuality.*
- *I want to stop thinking about my partner's acting out during sex.*
- *I want to be able to say no to sex when I don't want it.*
- *I want to be able to appreciate my body.*

- *I want to be able to share my sexual desires and needs with my partner.*
- *I want to be able to believe that my partner's acting out was not about my inadequacy as a lover.*

Make sure that you approach healing your sexuality in a specific and realistic way. Always recognize that healing is an ongoing process—progress not perfection.

Sexual Assertiveness—Finding Your Sexual Voice

Another critical aspect of healthy sexuality is the ability to negotiate and be assertive, to communicate and make sexual negotiations, to protect yourself, and to draw sexual boundaries. You should educate yourself on why this may be a challenge and why many of us find it difficult to own and assert our voices, particularly in terms of gender dynamics and damaged boundaries from trauma. Being able to communicate, particularly about sexuality, becomes vital in the healing process and may take practice.

When will I be ready to be sexual again?

One of the most important steps of the healing process is asking yourself if and when you are ready to be sexual with someone else. As a partner of a sex addict, you have hopefully educated yourself, come to recognize some of your sexual wounds and have done some work on them, and have found support. Part of healing is reaching a place of willingness to be vulnerable again sexually. It's only at this point in your process that you should engage in sex therapy.

Couples Trauma-Targeted Sex Therapy

Couples sex therapy, for couples recovering from sexual addiction, should acknowledge and process the sexual wounding and any trauma experienced by the partner. This requires the addict to take full responsibility for his or her actions and the consequences of the behavior on the partner. If this doesn't occur, the addict will have trouble finding appropriate empathy and understanding the partner's symptoms and reactions.

It will also be difficult for the couple to be able to negotiate sexual boundaries and communicate honestly if the addict doesn't fully appreciate the sexual wounds of the partner and how it may be impacting the sexual experience. For example, if the partner needs to stop during lovemaking because he or she is feeling averse to the lover's touch, the addict needs a framework and prior discussion about this issue in order to deal with this reaction in an optimally healthy manner.

Another important aspect of sexual recovery for a couple is learning and practicing how to communicate sexually. After learning how to draw boundaries and reclaim your assertiveness, it's important to communicate vulnerability with your partner. One helpful exercise is for each partner to share a list of likes and dislikes. They may also share a sexual fantasy. Couples are often amazed at how little they really ever communicated or knew about their partner when it comes to sex.

Recovery Is a Journey

Recovery from the sexual trauma of discovering your partner is a sex addict is a journey. It requires willingness for self-exploration, honesty, and openness. It can be painful as the wounds are acknowledged, but it's important to grieve about your experience with other supportive people. Reclaiming your sexuality will be an essential element of your healing.

Chapter Seven:
What Can the Twelve Steps Do for Me?

Mavis Humes Baird, BFA, CSAT-S

ℰℭ

Sex addiction is a devastating disease, and all members of a family are impacted. It's crucial that you, as a partner, spouse, or family member of a sex addict, take the time to recognize the many ways in which the addict's behaviors have affected your life. Simply leaving the relationship without seeking the healing you need could affect your future relationships. Many partners have discovered tremendous insight and growth by surrendering to their own recovery process. This chapter will provide you with guidance on how to work your own recovery program.

Alcoholism was first recognized as a disease by the American Medical Association in 1956. Among its other traits, alcoholism was described as a "primary, chronic, progressive, *family* disease." Since that time, we have discovered all addictive disorders have a family component and create similar symptoms among family members. "Addiction as a family disease" means it runs in families and affects the whole family. Addiction is often passed down from generation to generation. Researchers have established a genetic component as well as an environmental one.[1]

Many partners of sex addicts are dealing with the traumatic shock of discovering sexual secrets, lies, and betrayal. On top of that, anyone who is close to an active addict becomes affected to some degree in certain ways. To top it all off, just as in families of alcoholics, many partners of sex addicts have come into the relationship with particular traits and vulnerabilities that make them more likely to get into and remain involved in relationships with sex addicts. Thus, you are more easily drawn to *and less aware of* the addictive cycle than someone from the general population. In other words, even while you might be horrified if you truly knew what was going on and might never go along with it, you may tend to have more denial, more tolerance, and/or more attraction to addicts. It's not uncommon for partners to report getting out of one relationship with a sex addict, determined never again to let the disease into their lives, only to find the same problems reappear in future relationships.

Twelve Step programs are a major part of comprehensive relief from the effects of all kinds of addiction. Most people have heard of Twelve Step programs like Alcoholics Anonymous (AA) and Al-Anon Family Group (Al-Anon). AA is for the addict seeking recovery from alcohol and other drugs while Al-Anon is there to provide strength and hope for friends and family members of the addict. Just like Twelve Steps groups such as AA and Al-Anon, there are Twelve Step groups for sex addicts and friends and family of the addict too.

If you have never been to a Twelve Step meeting, you may have certain assumptions about what Twelve Step programs are and what they can or cannot do for you. This chapter will help clear up any misconceptions you might have and will serve as an excellent resource for you as you prepare to join a meeting.

General Information about Twelve Step Groups

Which meeting should I attend?

Twelve Step programs designed specifically for spouses and partners and other family members of sex addicts are

- COSA (this is not an acronym, but the name of the organization)
- Co-SLAA (CoSex and Love Addicts Anonymous)
- SRA-Anon (family group that is a mirror fellowship for Sexual Recovery Anonymous)
- S-Anon (family group that is a mirror fellowship for Sexaholics Anonymous)

All four of these fellowships adhere to the Twelve Step philosophy created by AA and focus on recovery from sex addiction. In accordance with what are known as the Twelve Traditions of these fellowships, each operate autonomously, and although they may cooperate with each other, they are not affiliated with their counterpart fellowships or with each other.

At the time of this writing, S-Anon has developed and has more active meetings than COSA. Some cities have only COSA meetings; others have only S-Anon. Some cities have both. (See the Resource Guide on page 259 for further information.)

Are all fellowships basically the same except for the name?

There are some minor conceptual differences between these fellowships. Some of the programs define sexual sobriety differently. SAA (Sex Addicts Anonymous), SCA (Sexual Compulsives Anonymous), and SLAA (Sex and Love Addicts Anonymous) all instruct their members to come to terms with their own individual patterns of compulsivity. They recognize that members have different patterns of compulsivity, so each member identifies his or her own personal sobriety plan. As they learn to face their particular patterns, addicts will recognize which sexual behaviors are compulsive and problematic for them, allowing them to choose the ones they need to abstain and recover from.

In contrast, both SA (Sexaholics Anonymous) and SRA (Sexual Recovery Anonymous) give across-the-board definitions of sexual sobriety. According to SA, "...for the sexaholic, any form of sex with one's self or with partners other than the spouse is progressively addictive and destructive." SRA differs from SA and others in defining sexual sobriety as "the release from all compulsive and destructive sexual behaviors...sobriety includes freedom from masturbation and sex outside a mutually committed relationship."[2] SA has received attention for its stand against sex outside of marriage and, therefore, against sober homosexual actions for sex addicts. Its publications classify any form of nonmarital sex, even within a committed monogamous relationship, as acting out addictively. Therefore, within the SA program, the only sexual sobriety for most homosexual members is sexual abstinence.

In ruling out all forms of masturbation and all noncommitted sexual activity, some therapists believe SA and SRA may be giving its members the messages that one's experience of healthy sexuality is dependent on having a partner and that sex can only be non-addictive as part of a committed partnership. Sex educators and sex therapists express concern that these definitions could limit the development of responsible sexual awareness. They point out that monogamy and commitment to a relationship do not necessarily equal sexual health. On the other hand, many addicts and their families find the sobriety definitions in those fellowships to be reassuring and clear-cut, and they are fearful of an open-ended process for finding one's own definitions as is practiced in SAA, SCA, and SLAA.

Each program also uses some terms particular to just its own program. For example, in SA and S-Anon, the terms *sexaholic* and *sexaholism* were coined, and the word *lust* is used to conceptualize sex addiction. Many of their members report that the word *lust* helped them begin to find a way to separate from their compulsive drives. Members of other fellowships don't generally use *lust* as a synonym for sex addiction out of concern that it may contribute to our societal confusion about whether addiction is a disease or an issue of amorality. Outside of SA and S-Anon, common usage defines *lust* (small "l") as sexual appetite, and *Lust* (big 'L') as a religious concept found in the "Seven Deadly Sins." Members of SA report that they can make the mental distinction and find the terms *lust* and *lusting* to be helpful labels. While the fellowships for sex addiction all have their differences, they all adhere strongly to the Twelve Steps, Twelve Traditions, and the spirit of recovery.

Can I attend the same meeting as the addict?

By attending open meetings of the addict's fellowship, you may learn to see the nature of the disease *in others* as well as coming to understand the nature of addiction and recovery *for others*. Being introduced to recovery in this way sometimes helps you to recognize your own need to recover. However, there is also a danger. Many partners struggle with obsessing about the addict's recovery. Attending the addict's meetings can reinforce your focus on the addict's progress or lack of progress, which would impede your own recovery process.

Additionally, most addicts find it unbearably distracting to have their family members with them in meetings. One reason for this is that it focuses their attention more on worrying about what you are thinking, rather than on relating to the message being shared. Therefore, the general guideline is that family members should only attend open meetings of the addiction fellowships where their family members will not be present. In some cases, the addict will feel relaxed enough to invite you to one of his or her regular meetings, but this is not the norm and family members shouldn't expect such an invitation.

Special recovery events such as conventions, learning days, couples retreats, or pre-planned dinners are more acceptable times to share directly in fellowship with the addict and his or her support systems. Once you have your own program of recovery firmly in place for a while, you may find that occasionally attending open Twelve Step meetings for sex addicts enlarges your perspective in a healthy way, especially in balancing your sense of compassion for the addict with your own need for self-care and safety.

By attending your own meetings you will see addiction is a *family* disease, and you will receive much-needed support. You will also come to understand the nature of addiction and recovery for the addict and for *yourself*.

What is anonymity?

Anonymity is a spiritual principle of all Twelve Step fellowships. It is practiced in a variety of ways. First, members usually identify themselves by first names and last initials only. This removes the potential focus from what members' roles, responsibilities, and status may be in the world and puts the focus on your equal footing as fellow humans. No matter what the differences, all members are suffering and are in need of peace and healing.

By challenging all its members to put their societal identities and roles on a shelf before they come in the door, Twelve Step fellowships establish a new basis for belonging and status. If you have qualified to belong to the group, you have earned your seat and no one can remove you. In that sense, you are all equals. Anonymity also protects your identity. Because of the stigma surrounding addiction, many addicts and their family members choose to keep the addiction a private matter.

How do I identify myself during meetings?

Twelve Step fellowship members have developed a practice of self-identifying their conditions every time they share. Learn to recognize the disease for what it is, and put the blame where it belongs—on the disease itself. By seeing the disease for what it is and reminding yourself regularly, you break through the negative and shaming messages and labels you may have received. One of the many positive effects of attending Twelve Step family groups is being around others who are letting go of the shame and finding the best solutions together.

One of the fellowships, COSA, recognized that their members had a variety of preferences for how they identify themselves. As a result, they encourage members to adopt whichever term works best for them or to create their own.[3] Commonly used terms include

- partner of a sex addict
- co-addict
- co-sex addict
- codependent to a sex addict
- sexual codependent
- codependent sex addict
- sexual co-addict
- addicted to a sex addict
- adult child of a sex addict
- family member of a sex addict

After reading through this list, you may have problems with some of the terminology used, especially terms such as *addict* or *co-addict*. You might see these terms as more negative judgments. It is natural to be wary of these terms, especially if they are unfamiliar. In recovery, however, these terms are used not to mock you or your partner, but rather to help you recognize the symptoms of your problems for what they are and to separate from the active disease process.

Codependency is the most common term used to describe the suffering of anyone affected by someone else's addiction. It has often been misunderstood by the public and the media. The term *co-addiction* is a variation on the same concept. These terms do not imply that family members are also addicted. Rather, they originate from the idea that the addict is dependent on a drug or process, and the family member or concerned other is "co-" or "also" affected by that dependency.

Do Twelve Step programs address the issue of blame versus responsibility?

One common misconception is that by prescribing recovery for family members, we are assigning blame to the family. In fact, one of the common Twelve Step sayings offered to family members to aid in their recovery is, "We didn't cause it, we can't control it, and we can't cure it."[4]

The Twelve Step fellowships for the family members of addicts directly addresses "the blame game." There is no blame assigned to addiction or codependency, and when we use terms and labels it is not as a way to blame you or the addict. For now, members hope at least that they can be used by addicts as tools for clarity and direction in the face of this "cunning, baffling and powerful"[5] disease.

The Twelve Step process enables and encourages you to let go of feelings of shame, anger, blame, and guilt and to move instead toward an empowering sense of taking responsibility for your recovery. Part of taking responsibility is actively finding the help, guidance, and support that you need.

Do I have to speak during the meeting or can I just listen?

Some meetings have a custom of screening newcomers to make sure you're in the right place. If the meeting does screen new members, one or two members will most likely speak with you privately. The only requirement for membership is that you have been affected by someone else's sexual addiction/compulsive sexual behavior. Some meetings have a custom of going around the room and introducing everyone by first name only, or going around in turn to allow members time to share if they so choose. It's always okay to say, "I pass" when it's your turn.

What if I'm a male partner and the Twelve Step meetings for partners in my town do not allow men?

Unfortunately, there are not yet as many men as women who are active in recovery. Fortunately, due in great part to the growth of the Internet and COSA's recent commitment to recognize men as partners of sex addicts, there has been a greater influx of male members. Men now have the opportunity to create support networks and establish quality recovery.

If your local COSA, S-Anon, Co-SLAA, or SRA-Anon meetings are women-only meetings, try writing them. Explain why you'd like to join the meeting and ask them to consider changing their membership policy. You may also consider starting your own meeting and invite members from the women's group. Some will likely want to support your efforts. You may also need to look for long-distance support groups and attend annual conventions or retreats.

I'll be embarrassed if I see someone I know. Is this something I should worry about?

Sex addiction is a disease and not a moral issue, despite the fact that it sometimes leads to moral decay. People in recovery as well as addiction professionals have campaigned to correct the cultural stigma of addiction in general. This stigma especially applies to sex addicts and their families. The risk of being shunned by members of your community is real. Those who you see inside the meeting are also there to seek help. Family members who have been scared to attend meetings report experiencing relief to finally find a place that welcomes them and enables them to become a part of a group that understands them and has experienced similar situations.

Learning and Understanding Addiction Terms

There are many new words and phrases you will learn in Twelve Step communities. Some may be familiar to you, while others may seem confusing. Understanding these concepts is crucial to your recovery and requires some contemplation.

What is powerlessness?

This Twelve Step concept, along with several others, has often been misunderstood and misrepresented. The Twelve Step fellowships teach that by surrendering to the disease and accepting its existence fully, you can begin to find the strength to recover from it. Accepting that you are powerless doesn't mean you're hopeless and hold no accountability. Rather, it's the serene acceptance that you have no control over addiction. When you embrace that notion, it provides clarity and empowerment for your own recovery to work on the things that you can change.

Phrases like "being my own worst enemy" and "needing to learn to get out of my own way" refer to the tendency to revert to the old, self-destructive thought patterns and behaviors. Addicts and families alike, when fully suffering from their diseases, can become similarly invested in willpower and control as the answer for every problem.

Your attempts to maintain control—whether it's controlling your own acting out, your partner's acting out, or other challenging aspects of your life—rarely work in the long run. In reality, the tighter you cling to your attempts to control, the more people rebel against you and take advantage of your "good will." AA refers to the disease of alcoholism as "cunning, baffling and powerful"—and sex addiction certainly shares these qualities. The addicts and partners who eventually surrender and experience a sense of peace have come to accept the incurable yet treatable nature of this disease.

What is detachment?

Detachment means learning how to step back and see the big picture. With practice, detachment allows you to separate yourself from your own reactions in order to make better choices. Newcomers often misunderstand the recovery concept of detachment to mean "the ability to no longer care" or "the ability to cut yourself off." Detachment is actually a spiritual response to the problems of addiction. After all, you didn't cause the addiction and you can't cure it. What you can choose, however, is your response. Detachment is the art of learning to stop yourself from reacting automatically in order to choose a recovery-oriented response that takes healthy boundaries and self-care into account. Your detachment can sometimes have a positive impact upon the addict as well.

Working a Program

Why are these recovery concepts so difficult?

Some recovery principles are not easy to internalize or use on an ongoing basis. Fortunately, ample evidence exists that these principles work beautifully in confronting the family disease of addiction. At first, many of the principles of recovery may seem contradictory. It has often been said that the Twelve Steps are simple but not easy. Perhaps we could say that they are *deceptively* simple. On closer examination, however, you will see that these principles are actually *paradoxical*. For example, when an addict admits his or her powerlessness over sex addiction, he or she may for the first times in years feel a sense of relief and hope.

The principles of recovery often seem counterintuitive, especially when you are first looking for black-and-white answers. Primary examples of this are "powerlessness," "detachment," and "putting the focus on yourself." It is a natural instinct as a family member to try to help your loved ones. When the problem is addiction, these attempts will not often succeed but instead will allow the illness to consume both your lives. Thus, it is important to deliberately pull your focus away from the addiction and put it onto addressing your own needs.

Alcoholics Anonymous, known as the Big Book, and *The Twelve Steps and Twelve Traditions* describe the disease of addiction as feeding on one or more of your human drives,[6] or on your natural human instincts. The Big Book describes the addict's belief that the problem lies with the outside world and other people. In general, addicts believe that it is other people who need to change, not them. Addicts handle their relationship problems much like a director would manage a play, the actors, and various elements. If all these externals could be corrected or adjusted, the addict's illusion is that he or she would be satisfied. Partners report the same outward-focused beliefs and efforts to manage their feelings. Both suffer from a disease that uses defenses to block the afflicted from their own internal integrity and equilibrium. As the disease takes hold and begins to progress, it actually seems to satisfy something missing within us. As it progresses further, however, it actually rewires our brain's neural pathways, driving us into increasingly compulsive behavior. When you try to break free of the addictive pattern, your very instincts will convincingly urge you against it and your defenses will rally.

How can I ever hope to break free from this depressing nightmare?

Twelve Step fellowships believe that the natural spiritual state of the individual can be restored to a condition of core integrity. With maintenance of the supports and practices needed, spiritual awakening can be maintained over the long term. To do so, that restoration process needs to be repeated and adjusted frequently. It's a lot to learn and to allow, and it takes time, desire, and commitment.

In this spiritual awakening, you'll be able to

- achieve and maintain a balanced sense of awareness and a connection greater than yourself

- mentally come to know open-mindedness, calm and clear thinking, and even excitement about your future

- consistently practice positive communication, with a balance of restraint and expression

- learn to channel the rich and unique experience of your own inner knowing to contribute creatively to the world around you

- operate from a place of compassion, gratitude, and humility without setting yourself up for ego crashes

- come to know your life purpose as you develop the ability to choose and to act instead of react

- value your various emotional states

- know how to take care of yourself emotionally

- learn more about yourself from the lessons and messages your emotions bring you

Ultimately, you will develop a unique sense of your place on the earth and a practical, grounded outlook.

How do Twelve Step fellowships work?

The three primary elements of Twelve Step healing identified by AA are unity, service, and recovery.[7] The concept of unity is captured in the spirit of fellowship between members. Members often gather at a local diner for conversation and plan other recovery-centered family activities and outings. The concept of unity is also captured in the Twelve Traditions and in the principles of inclusion, anonymity, equality, and interdependence. The common problems and solutions you all share is what is relevant, not who you are and what you do out in the world. You need each other in order to recover. The strength of the group bond and being included is crucial. The "Higher Power" of recovery lies in the act of surrender. All are welcome.

The concept of service is captured in every aspect of the structure of the fellowships. All members, even newcomers, are expected to do service. Newcomers are often grateful for the opportunity to complete a useful and unselfish task. It helps them to break their obsessive focus on the addiction and makes them feel like part of the solution. Members' service positions are volunteer tasks. Some are simple, such as setting out chairs before a meeting. Others are more complex, such as chairing a meeting or helping to create a public service announcement.

Twelve Step fellowships have vast decentralized service networks. It's a challenge to learn the inner workings, customs, and policies and how much they vary from one meeting or one area of the country to another. The skills learned over time for participating in business meetings and the spirit of cooperative service are some of the same skills required in healthy, sober relationships. These include skills such as safe communication, mutual respect, finding win-win solutions, healthy decision making, "progress not perfection," "minding your own business," and singleness of purpose.

The concept of recovery is captured in the ongoing actions of listening to each other, sharing your progress, working the Twelve Steps, and applying recovery principles to your daily living, one day at a time. The power of learning to see past your own subconscious defenses, and the ability to change inside, lies in part by listening to other members' stories of recovery. Change occurs as you work the Steps, do service work, and support others. Members support each other through speaking at meetings, sharing their stories of recovery, giving out phone numbers or email addresses for times of distress, and sponsoring other members. This is a part of Step work and "carrying the message."

Anthropologists, psychologists, physicians, treatment specialists, and people in recovery have studied the experience of Twelve Step recovery and analyzed its success formula.[8] They have found several major healing components, including

- viewing addiction as a chronic, progressive biopsycho-spiritual illness
- the primacy of sobriety
- the single purpose of the sharing of mutual help to address the disease
- the single focus on the disease and its recovery
- the power of the group and the magical and ancient power of storytelling[9]
- the power of repetition and a concrete structure
- rigorous honesty and "reality checks" with yourself and with others who have been in similar places
- resolution of the contradictions in one's personal beliefs and commitment to place your trust in and live according to those beliefs
- the spiritual tools, slogans, and processes

How much work does recovery involve?

The Twelve Step goals cannot be achieved by our intellect. They are better absorbed by making the effort to try them through a series of repetitive actions and experiences. In this way, learning the Steps can feel rather like learning to ride a bicycle. Actually, recovery is more like riding a variety of bicycles as a remedial treatment for a degenerative muscle condition. When we accept the chronic nature of the underlying condition, we begin to understand the metaphor of bicycle riding differently. Members believe that recovering addicts—as well as recovering family members—don't do as well when they live life without these tools.

While a bicycle is usually built for one person, the nature of working the Steps is relational. With the Twelve Steps, people often need the witnessing, acceptance, love, and direction from others in order to truly see how to apply the principles to each new situation. Therefore, the wisdom and safety of the Steps continues to unfold and is revealed as one applies them to life's challenges—one day at a time. People do get the hang of working the Steps, and they experience that same sense of freedom and balance that one feels when riding a bicycle. Recovery is a new way of life that can take a while to understand and apply to all your issues that have piled up, but it does become easier with time, practice, and consistent commitment.

How do I "work" a program?

The most typical way to get started is to join one of the Twelve Step fellowships, attend meetings at least weekly, and get to know other members. As you acclimate to the lingo and customs of the group, you'll observe how others are "working the program." While the meetings include people from different cultures, educational levels, socioeconomic backgrounds, and political, sexual, and religious orientations, all attendees have something in common—they all been affected by sex addicts. They have gone through situations similar to yours and can relate to what is happening in your life.

The basics of working a program include attending meetings, calling members for regular check-ins, learning how to apply the slogans, and reading the literature. Establishing a daily routine will help ground you in recovery principles so that you can start responding to your daily challenges with new tools and from a balanced and serene frame of mind. As soon as you can, start collecting phone numbers and calling other members to build up your "recovery support system." Once you're acclimated to your surroundings, establish a regular habit of attending meetings and practicing other recovery tools. The next challenge is to find a sponsor (someone to guide and mentor you) as you begin working the Steps. Both COSA and S-Anon have published literature containing Step study questions. They also encourage local groups to hold regular structured Step meetings. Both hold retreats and conferences on working the Steps, while COSA provides Step study supports online and via email.

Working the Steps in any Twelve Step fellowship begins with learning the general meaning of the Step through a series of readings, discussions, and listening to others. Second, you complete a series of contemplations and written exercises, which will help you begin to integrate the Step into your awareness. As you progress, you share your work with a sponsor or support group. Gradually you'll be able to apply the Step to various situations or circumstances in your life.

Because someone else's addictive disease is intrinsically a part of your situation, you may sometimes feel as if you are doing double the Step work. First, come to terms with your powerlessness to control somebody else's addictive disease. Second, work the Steps to help yourself with your own issues. This can help you examine areas where you may have lost control over your own life.

Will the Twelve Steps teach me about boundaries and accountability?

The Twelve Steps help us develop our awareness and give us an appreciation for developing new, healthier boundaries. The Steps also provide us with a system of accountability. Consistent accountability over time will help you keep your bearings—with your thoughts, feelings, actions, and decision making. As you work the Steps, you will develop your boundaries naturally.

For example, as you absorb the full significance of Step One, you'll begin to find your center, sometimes for the first time in your life. As the gifts of healing continue along with your Step work, you'll likely develop a sense of gratitude for your recovery. That gratitude will become a part of the foundation for restoring health to your spirit.

What is a sponsor?

A sponsor is like a big brother or big sister in the program—someone who is further along in recovery and can pass on what she or he has learned. A sponsor is also someone you can turn to for special guidance in working your Steps and someone who will be a listener. As you start to build your support system, you'll usually find someone you connect with.

Will finding a sponsor be difficult?

Due to the recent epidemic of Internet sex addiction and because Twelve Step fellowships for family members of sex addicts are still small, the influx of newcomers is often greater than the availability of members with the time and experience to be a sponsor. In these isolated or newly forming areas, members either seek long-distance sponsorship or practice co-sponsorship, which is supporting each other to do Step work and taking turns. In these cases, it's best to also plan day-long Step workshops or attend fellowship Step retreats to experience more seasoned messages of joy and healing.

Do the Twelve Steps help with couples' issues?

The Twelve Steps can help couples in a variety of ways. Working the Steps allows addicts and partners to find freedom from acting-out behaviors, clears up distorted thinking, balances emotions, and allows development of vulnerability and communication skills over time. Both members of the couple may occasionally want to speed up the couples' healing in order to relieve their sense of losing control or to get past deep feelings of guilt, remorse, or fears of loss or abandonment. Other times, couples—or one member of the partnership—will try to avoid the couples' work out of fear, anger, shame, or a combination of mixed feelings and insecurity. As a partner of a sex addict, you may want to work on your partner's recovery or at least on the coupleship more than your own recovery. It's important, however, that partner focus on his or her individual recovery first. Once individual recovery is stable, you may want to consider attending special meetings for couples offered in SAA and COSA, or Recovering Couples Anonymous (RCA). In this fellowship, couples gather to apply the Twelve Steps to strengthen and nurture their relationships.

How will my religious beliefs be affected by working the program?

Contained within the Steps are many commonly practiced spiritual principles. Twelve Step programs are unique in that they focus on the particular conditions their members face. Twelve Step programs do not adhere to any particular religion, but welcome you no matter what your beliefs are. They are open to all people who suffer from these conditions. Everyone has a right to recovery.

The Twelve Step fellowships focus on establishing and maintaining recovery from a progressive illness. They also teach that your condition has probably disrupted your spiritual footing and that your recovery will need to include sorting out all your various beliefs, not just your religious ones. You will not be expected to change your religious beliefs unless you feel the need to do so. You'll be shown respect for your beliefs and learn to respect the beliefs of other members who may have beliefs different from your own. Some members do not believe in God. They learn how to practice the recovery principles from that perspective. The Twelve Step fellowships view each member's religious beliefs as a private matter. All members identify whatever it is they believe will restore them to sanity as part of working their second Step. They continue to work the Steps by learning to put their faith in those beliefs.

Because Twelve Step fellowships encourage members to develop a relationship with a God of their own understanding, all members can find a way to interpret the use of prayer and meditation in a way that works for them. Some members think of prayer and meditation as the practice of sacred attitudes, such as wonder, gratitude, humility, and contemplation. Others believe in a fully traditional religious prayer life. Still others gradually change their beliefs as they maintain their recovery by seeing what works for them.

What if I don't feel a connection with my group?

You may not like everyone you meet at a Twelve Step meeting. You will most likely see people in varying states of health and functioning. It's important to remember that everyone is there for the same reason and may be in a great deal of pain. When we can't offer a shoulder to cry on or a kind word, we can practice not adding to others' troubles and steer clear. You can ask others to do the same for you. You can practice learning about boundaries among your peers as part of implementing the same boundary practices you will develop with loved ones.

While you will find no one member to be perfect, as you develop your interdependence with the group as a whole you'll discover it frees you and allows you to find your true self. Asking for help will no longer have to wait until it becomes a desperate act, but can become a simple and well-deserved tool to use on a daily basis. This does not mean that you would ask group members to lend you money, get in the middle of your conflicts, or provide for you. They will, however, provide plenty of support in the form of encouragement and guidance. Over time, you'll be able to recognize a true sense of balance. When you're working your program consistently over time, you'll learn how to sense when the balance is off and often will know what to do to restore yourself, including reaching out for support.

Conclusion

For many partners, the thought of reaching out to a Twelve Step community can be daunting. Understanding more about the Twelve Step fellowships—how they work and what to expect as a member—may make the process of reaching out easier. One of the promises of the Twelve Steps is that you will experience a "new freedom." Embracing recovery and allowing yourself to reach out for support may be the first step to experiencing a new freedom in your life.

Chapter Eight:
How Can I Begin to Take Care of Myself?

Sonja Rudie, MA, LMHC, CSAT, C-EMDR

ℰᏅℭℛ

"Love is a condition that exists where the other's well-being
is AS important AS one's own."

— Harry Stack Sullivan (psychiatrist)

Discovering your partner is a sex addict can be a traumatic and stressful event. It can compound the grief of previous unhealed emotional wounds. During times of great difficulty, it's common for people to neglect their own self-care, especially if they are not in the habit of getting their wants and needs met. This chapter underscores some of the fundamental ways partners of sex addicts can take care of themselves after their world is turned upside down.

Many partners report they knew something strange was happening in their relationships, but they had no idea that their spouses or partners were sex addicts. Common thoughts for partners attempting to absorb information that feels too overwhelming for them might be: *What's wrong with me? Why am I so mistrustful? Am I crazy? Why am I feeling this way today when some days are just fine?*

As you move from disbelief into reality, you're likely to have many questions. How did I miss this?

Feelings of shame or embarrassment often prevent a partner from turning to resources that could normally be a source of comfort. Partners will also blame themselves for the sexual acting out of their sex addict partners because they don't understand that the sex addiction has nothing to do with them. Deception may have gone on for a long time, so when the truth comes out, a partner's denial may return with full force. Many times partners will know about a few "infractions" against the fidelity of the relationship as a couple, but they will dismiss their instincts to keep the peace. Sometimes there's only an intuitive sense that something's wrong. Often this sense is quickly minimized, then dismissed as paranoid, especially if the addict has provided convincing evidence of how "insecure" the partner is behaving. This use of an emotional or psychological "smokescreen" can fool partners. Feelings of confusion and even revulsion are normal when faced with deliberate lies and covert behavior.[1]

My gut told me something was wrong. Why didn't I listen?

In recovery, partners start to listen to their inner voice. Dr. Emeran A. Mayer, a professor of medicine, physiology, and psychiatry at UCLA, notes:

> *The enteric nervous system can be seen as an extension of the emotional center of the brain. Evolution has placed part of our emotion-generating circuits in the gut, an area where you have major mechanical influences such as contractions and a direct interface with the environment.*[2]

Professor Mayer hopes to find scientific explanations for "gut-thinking" and that our visceral information is what we have come to understand as our "felt-sense." While this does not give all the facts to a partner who is questioning his or her reality, it certainly gives more understanding of how important it is for a partner not to dismiss the body's ability to discern important unconscious recognitions that something is amiss in a relationship.

In his book *Blink: The Power of Thinking without Thinking*, Malcolm Gladwell describes the work of Dr. John Gottman, a marital therapist and researcher from the University of Washington.[3] He reports how Gottman was able to determine successful or unsuccessful marital outcomes with remarkable accuracy by the use of mathematics and video observations of couples interacting with one another. Gladwell uses the term *thin-slicing*, defining it as "the ability of our unconscious to find patterns and behaviors based on very narrow slices of experience." He believes when our unconscious engages in thin-slicing, what we are doing is an automated, accelerated, unconscious version of what Gottman does with his videotapes: instinctive processes of rapid cognition.

Often partners of sex addicts may experience truth in their unconscious through this thin-slicing process. On some level, they recognize the addict's deceptive behavior. It's a gut feeling. Part of taking care of yourself is letting yourself know the truth. Even a private investigator cannot tell you whether your gut is giving you information that's accurate. However, if you're hiring a private investigator, there's normally a good reason for your mistrust. Acknowledging that you're uncomfortable, fearful, uncertain, angry, hurt, or feeling betrayed are healthy steps to caring for yourself.

You deserve to honor your body wisdom—that gut feeling. The concept of thin-slicing may not mean you have all the details, but it does mean you're absorbing the shock and can begin to take the next steps toward safely making good decisions for yourself. You have the right to your own reality.

What are some ways I can take care of myself?

First, you must recognize your unmet needs. To help you with this, we'll use psychologist Abraham Maslow's hierarchy of needs. Using a pyramid shape with five different layers, Maslow helps us understand the basics of human need and self-care and why it's important.[4] Needs at the bottom of the pyramid fall under the basic needs category and include food, water, and shelter. People can progress to the next level of needs, which are for safety and security once the first level needs are taken care of. As people move up the pyramid, needs become increasingly psychological and social. Further up the pyramid, the need for personal esteem takes priority. The tip of the pyramid is self-actualization, which is a process of growing and developing as a person to achieve individual potential.

Maslow's Hierarchy of Needs

Using Maslow's hierarchy of needs, we must first get the basic needs on the bottom met before we can proceed toward the top. It is not uncommon for partners who have made the shocking discovery of sex addiction in their relationship to neglect their most basic needs. Safety needs may take on a whole new meaning. Partners may need to access a new or different social support system. When presented with a crisis such as this, it is important to take stock of your basic needs and evaluate what you need to do to take care of yourself.

Are you meeting the basic needs from the bottom layer of the pyramid? Are you safe physically, emotionally, and spiritually? If not, how fast can you get yourself there? Does this mean you need professional assistance or therapy? Once your basic needs are taken care of and your safety is established, you can begin to move further up the hierarchy. The next rung is building up your social support network, which is critical after discovery of sex addiction. Once you have this network built, working on your self-esteem and psychological growth is possible.

My world is falling apart. I don't have time to take care of myself. What should I do and who can I turn to for help?

The crisis of discovery can cause tremendous emotional turmoil and may sometimes bring about symptoms of common psychiatric ailments, such as eating disorders , PTSD, depression, and anxiety. Maybe you're just now considering the possibility that your partner may be a sex addict, or perhaps you have already made the discovery and are in a significant amount of pain and suffering. If you're attempting to recover from the shock of infidelity, seek a community of people in recovery and a competent professional who can assist you in finding your equilibrium again.

Undiagnosed illnesses, such as depression, can wreak havoc on a person's life. Depression is a treatable illness, and it's important to understand that unnecessary suffering can be eliminated. If you believe you may have an illness and are not taking care of getting it treated, you are operating from either a place of poverty or denial. If you are in a place of denial, take this opportunity to invest in yourself. You're wiser than you think; you deserve to give and receive love and self-care. Make a decision to act on your own behalf!

Discover Your Worth

Being positive about yourself and challenging perfectionism are ways to promote self-care. Glenn Schiraldi writes about "Howard's Laws of Human Worth."[5] Schiraldi's book addresses the need for understanding one's core worth. He believes that worth is never determined by externals, such as what kind of car you drive, clothes you wear, your occupation, or how many meetings or therapy sessions you attend. Worth is never in jeopardy. It is infinite, unchanging, and intrinsic for all human beings, as we are created equal from birth. He describes these concepts as vital frameworks for health and healing.

Do you have unconditional positive regard for yourself? Have you been giving yourself the message that you are worth the effort of living a healthy and sane life? Are you continuing to challenge any chaos in your life and take responsibility for creating a healthier way of being? Not having self-esteem is considered by many to be an invisible handicap.[6] Creating healthier self-esteem is possible by practicing new ways of thinking and behaving toward yourself.

On airplanes, as a safety measure, passengers are always instructed on how to use an oxygen mask. Passengers are told, "First, put your *own* oxygen mask on before assisting others." Saving yourself first is an act of courage and self-preservation. If you can save yourself with the help of your Higher Power, you're better prepared to consider the needs of others. Children need their parents to be "fully oxygenated." With proper and swift action, children and loved ones can be positively influenced by the resiliency and determination of a stabilized parent. What ways are you "oxygenating" your body and self today?

Cultivate Healthy Behavior Patterns

Behaviors have specific patterns. Find ways to create healthy activities and behaviors in your life. By doing so, you will help bring structure to chaos, sanity to a crazy situation. See the Recommended Reading list on page 261 for more information on how to understand your behavior patterns. Educating yourself will empower you to make a difference in your own life circumstances. Taking positive steps toward making changes in the way you live your life is vital for your mental health and, if you have children, for theirs too.

Working on your own patterns of behavior doesn't diminish the appropriateness of feeling angry or devastated about betrayals you may have experienced. If you've been harmed by your partner going outside the covenant of your relationship as a couple, it's possible that your behaviors and emotions have impacted the people around you. You are responsible for your feelings and actions—even when you find out about betrayal. How can you behave in ways that are consistent with your value system and also stay firm within your need for emotional and physical safety?

Self-Care versus Selfishness

What does *self-care* mean? Self-care refers to a commitment to one's own good health. Pauline Boss, PhD, describes health as "relational...the ability to enjoy a positive connection with another person and with a community of others; preventive health is the presence of resilience in the face of stress and trauma."[7] Former President Jimmy Carter describes health as "relational, able-bodied, involves self-regard, and includes control over our own affairs, strong ties with other people, and a purpose in life."[8] Carter says some of the best advice he ever received was that it was "better to use recreation to preserve health than to use medicine and treatment to regain health" once it was gone. He goes on to say a few dollars or days spent pursuing a hobby or pastime is a sound investment, paying off both in enjoyment and in avoiding medical expenses.

In the recovery community, people use the acronym HALT, which helps serve as a reminder of self-care concepts. If you're **H**ungry, you need to eat; if you're **A**ngry, find a way to express anger safely; if you're **L**onely, reach out and connect with trusted friends, family, or family of choice; if you're **T**ired, then rest. Many times people are taught that taking care of our own needs is being selfish. Sometimes your needs may conflict with the needs of others and that's okay. Selfishness usually is accompanied by a lack of mindfulness, humility, or compassion, which isn't the same as self-care. Unless someone is a dependent child, adults can take the responsibility necessary to take care of their own needs and be mindful of their loved ones. Being mindful of self-care doesn't mean behaving in a controlling way; rather, it reflects a care deeply felt and observed for the self while considering others.

There are ways to keep track of your self-care. Consider Sarina's approach. She was married to a man who was the deacon at their local church. She discovered he had been regularly viewing online pornography of teen girls. She was devastated. She and her husband sought counseling after he was caught by his church and reported to the authorities. When Sarina started working on her own recovery, she began focusing on herself and her unmet needs. She began to make a list of different categories: health, spirituality, friends, creativity, family, and relationships. She then broke these categories down into two or three things that represented her own personal self-care plan. For example, under "family" she wrote: "Take time to do fun things with the kids, write my siblings, and go to a family reunion." In the category of "health" she wrote: "Take time to find my core self, make time to play, and get at least seven hours of sleep each night." Sarina was amazed at how little self-care she had actually done in recent years because she had been so focused on her husband and children. As she began making her own health a priority and her husband continued his own therapy, the couple began making strides toward greater intimacy and healing their marriage.

> *When will we become loveable? When will we feel safe? When will we get all the protection, nurturing, and love we so richly deserve? We will get it when we begin giving to ourselves.*
>
> — Melody Beattie, The Language of Letting Go[9]

You may know what you need to do to take care of yourself, but actually taking action is more difficult. People who are deliberate and create an opportunity for rest, relaxation, and self-care will reap the many benefits. Stress that builds up cumulatively will wear down our bodies. Our ability to cope with situations becomes quickly compromised when we become exhausted. We are more vulnerable to illness, injuries, accidents, and disease when this condition becomes chronic. Consider how one stressor will be compounded when another stressor is added before the first one is resolved. Illness such as heart disease, high blood pressure, obesity, ulcers, anxiety, insomnia, depression, arthritis, asthma, colitis, diarrhea, sexual dysfunction, and headaches have been linked with prolonged excessive stress.[10]

I want to get better. What are my treatment options?

Psychiatric Care

Making a decision to enter treatment is one of the most important decisions you'll make in your lifetime. First, you must be willing to truthfully explain to a mental healthcare professional what you believe is the primary cause of your distress. Treatment professionals will usually do a thorough assessment of your life events and medical background. Providing this information is essential so they can begin creating a treatment plan. Sometimes this will also include an action plan that recommends a medical evaluation from a physician. This is nothing to be afraid of. It simply means you're receiving careful attention and support.

Full medical evaluations from psychiatrists are often used as a baseline in assessing medical history before a full treatment plan can be effectively completed. The purpose of the evaluation is not intended to corroborate or justify someone "is crazy." Don't buy into any societal stigmas associated with medical evaluations. Not everyone will need to see a psychiatrist, nor will everyone who sees a psychiatrist necessarily need medication.

Individual Therapy

There are many treatment options available to you when seeking therapy. The treatment option you receive may depend on which professional you choose to do your therapy with. If you're seeing a psychiatrist, he or she will have a specific way of doing therapy that's based on a medical model. Some psychiatrists will manage medications after the initial medical evaluation, and others will prefer to do both the therapy and the medication management during the initial visit. You may choose to see a psychologist, who will use a specific therapy model. Licensed Clinical Social Workers, Licensed Mental Health Care Professionals, Licensed Professional Counselors, and Licensed Marriage and Family Therapists also provide individual therapy using different therapy models. There seems to be as many choices of therapy and counseling options as there are choices in automobiles to drive!

Obtaining a referral from a trusted family physician, local hospital, crisis line, the Society for the Advancement of Sexual Health (SASH), International Institute of Trauma and Addiction Professionals (IITAP), or member of the Twelve Step community is often an excellent way to discover names of clinicians who have experience working with sex addiction issues.

There are a host of treatment model options and tools available to treat partners, spouses, companions, children, and family. Some of these include art therapy, psychotherapy, psychopharmacology (medication), EMDR (Eye Movement Desensitization Reprocessing), cognitive behavioral therapy (CBT), trauma-focused cognitive behavioral therapy (TFCBT), equine-assisted therapy (EAT), gestalt, somatic experiencing, mindfulness-based cognitive therapy for depression, cognitive therapy, interpersonal therapy, psycho-dynamic psychotherapy, dialectical behavioral therapy (DBT), existential therapy, humanistic therapy, and dance therapy.

Many therapists are trained in more than one kind of therapeutic model and may possess skills in several of these areas. They also may have specialized training in the use of psychological tools such as hypnosis, Neurolinguistic Programming (NLP), or Thought Field Therapy (TFT). A comprehensive review of the different types of therapeutic approaches is beyond the scope of this book. However, some of the aforementioned are possible treatments with good results.

If you decide to attend therapy, be sure to pay special attention to the therapeutic relationship. *Is this someone you believe you can work with? Does it feel generally like a good fit for you?* It's important that you experience a feeling of safety with your therapist to help you gain some sense of control in your life again, especially if you're being treated for PTSD or PTSD-like symptoms.[11] Effects of traumatic experiences spread throughout the family, so do not let it go untreated.[12] If you have experienced trauma, your ability to function with your children, spouse, or partner may be affected. Other areas of your life, such as work, school, church, social life, and finances. can also be impacted negatively without appropriate intervention and treatment.

Groups

Counseling and support groups are advisable to help reduce the pain and anguish experienced by infidelity, divorce, or other kinds of traumatic events.[13] The combination of individual therapy with group therapy gives the added benefit of stabilization and comfort for people who are suffering. Many partners have found a tremendous amount of support by meeting with other partners and spouses struggling with the same issue. This helps to normalize the situation and reduce shame. Practitioners all over the country have begun to offer groups for partners of sexual addicts.

Marital and Family Therapy

Your primary individual therapist will be your best resource to determine when couples or family therapy is called for. It is common for couples who decide to stay together and work on recovery from sex addiction to need the assistance of a marital therapist. If both of you are also in individual therapy, it is advised that your marital therapist is not the same therapist who treats either of you on an individual basis, if possible. However, your marital therapist should work with both of your individual therapists. Ask your therapist about the recommended treatment plan for your situation.

Inpatient Treatment

Sometimes the pain of a situation goes beyond what feels bearable. If you are suicidal or are unable to function, inpatient or residential treatment may be an option. Centers that focus on stabilization will have a shorter length of stay and often focus on medication management. There are also residential programs that focus on trauma or codependency. Talk with your primary therapist about what level of care is right for you.

How much will treatment cost?

Financial stress is often a key issue in marriages where sex addiction exists. Affording proper treatment for self-care can be difficult for many families. This becomes a particular challenge when a specialist is needed. If you have medical insurance, many plans will not cover marital therapy, but sometimes they will cover individual sessions when there is a clinical diagnosis of depression or other kind of mental health diagnoses. Insurance coverage is more likely if you see a psychiatrist, psychologist, or a professional who is licensed or certified in the field of mental health. Seeking out qualified profession-als either "in network" or "out of network," as provided for in your insurance contract, may save you a lot of money.

Therapists who are CSATs (Certified Sex Addiction Therapists) as well as licensed professionals or doctors may help you avoid possible increased financial stressors simply because their experience working with sex addicts and their partners can save you time in therapy. You may also find there are associates within a company, community mental health facility, or hospital under supervision for certification offering a lesser fee for service. You may be able to avoid out-of-pocket payments for therapy completely if you do some research ahead of time.

What are my needs?

According to Maslow, our progression up the hierarchy of human needs is essential to foster a secure sense of love and belonging. Wants and needs are separated here into different categories because people usually aren't aware that they are so fundamentally different from one another. For example, a person may want to be sexual, but what he or she may need is the intimacy afforded by a real emotional connection to express feelings of hurt, worry, or frustrations. Maybe they are simply lonely and their unmet need for companionship has been replaced with food. Overeating or poor nutrition can become a substitute for knuckling down and making a real effort to reach out into a healthy community or truly working a recovery plan.

Doing what is best for you may feel strange, wrong, or upsetting at first. For example, spending money to get your teeth fixed when family members are clamoring for the latest video game may feel counterintuitive, but it is a terrific exercise in self-care. Picking up the phone and calling a trusted friend or family member instead of eating a quart of ice cream perhaps doesn't seem as easy as overindulging.

Communicating your need to safely express your pent-up hurt or anger is one way to be congruent with yourself by fostering true intimacy and continuing in healthy self-preservation. Your need for a safe intimate connection is valuable and honorable. Being harmonious with yourself is a healthy response and avoids the act of abandoning your core self for the sake of the other.

Professionals have long understood the correlation between repeated abandonment of the self and the shame-bind that perpetuates further cycles of harm and despair. Those who were neglected or abused in childhood will often experience high levels of toxic shame and feelings of unworthiness as adults. Because they may feel "worthless," they may treat themselves as worthless and even reenact unsafe situations in their adulthood.

When faced with repeated exposures to emotional or physical harm, we may further our own destruction through the substance use or aggressive acts of physical self-harm, such as obesity or self-mutilation. We may develop illnesses like eating disorders, chronic pain disorders, or dissociative disorders that impair our ability to properly function in the world. All of these issues are generally treatable, so if you or a loved one has symptoms similar to those described above, seeking a qualified therapist to sort them out is a step toward relief.

Meeting Your Wants Can Bring You Joy

As mentioned previously, wants are different from needs. Wants are "the essence of a heart decision that evokes pure joy."[14] For example, if you have dreamed of learning to fly, obtaining a degree in higher education, owning a dog, visiting Alaska, parachuting, or traveling to a foreign country, these are all examples of wants that can delight the soul. Focusing on some areas that can bring you joy during a time of distress can help lessen the load and help you focus on something positive.

Some people find it useful to create a *bucket list* of fifty things they want to experience before they die. Writing down your bucket list can help you define what activities will enhance your health and well-being or help you move forward in a life that you uniquely aspire to achieve.

Learning to decipher your wants and needs can take you a long way in creating a better life for yourself. Martin Seligman, PhD, author of the book *Authentic Happiness*, discusses the million dollar question that most of us would like the answer to:

> What is it that makes people happy? Is it money? Fame? Marriage? Status? Does happiness depend on what country you live in or your ethnic background? Does happiness depend on what church you belong to, how many children you have, or don't have?[15]

According to Seligman, the secret to happiness is to find your own "flow" or "calling" by utilizing what he calls your "Signature Strengths." He describes these strengths as qualities that each of us possess naturally: the intrinsic strengths that make us unique from others. The feelings of joy, zest, and enthusiasm that people experience when operating from their signature strengths are a reflection of what Seligman is talking about when they say such statements as, "This is the real me."

What makes your life worth living? What is it that lights fire in your soul, gives you a chuckle, or brings passion into your existence? Are you using your signature strengths in your day-to-day experiences? How can you begin shifting your focus to create a life filled with abundance, gratitude, and authentic happiness even if you're faced with uncertainty? Start at the beginning. Begin by being determined to change the way you think.

How can I rise above this situation and feel stronger?

The answer is simple—resiliency. Resiliency is the ability to rise above difficult circumstances. It can be mastered by diligently focusing on self-care one day at a time. A recognized expert in resiliency, Dr. Albert Sebiert, identifies the following steps to building resiliency:[16]

- Optimize your emotional stability, health, and well-being.
- Focus outward and develop good problem-solving skills.
- Focus inward and develop a strong inner gatekeeper that includes self-confidence, self-esteem, and self-concept.
- Develop resiliency skills.
- Discover your talent for serendipity.

In his book, Sebiert goes on to say, "*…resilient people don't wait for others to rescue them, they work through their feelings, set goals, work to reach their goals, and often emerge from it with a better life than before.*"[17]

It's not enough to "talk the talk" without "walking the walk." This may be one of the most difficult times of your life. You would likely encourage anyone else in your situation to follow through on taking care of themselves. Why not take this advice for yourself? Start creating that bucket list. You can begin today by making the choice to discover yourself and find your heart's sincere desire.

Experiencing this crisis may actually give you the opportunity to see your circumstances from a new perspective. New perspectives have the potential for propelling you forward into positive change. You can choose to create new dreams or revisit old ones you have not yet fulfilled. You can learn to trust again with the experience of trustworthy loved ones around you. There is a whole world of other people out there who are willing to walk beside you. Take the time to take care of yourself, reach out for support, and pursue your dreams. Are you ready to begin?

Part Two: Specific Situations

Editor's note: Part Two contains specific information about sex addiction based on your particular situation. Not every chapter in Part Two will apply to you. Skip the chapters that aren't relevant to you. For example, it's not necessary to read about addicts with an interest in minors, or the same sex, if your partner does not have these interests. In fact, it could cause you unnecessary worry. Concentrate on what you need to know and leave the rest.

Chapter Nine:
What Should I Tell the Kids?

Stefanie Carnes, PhD, CSAT-S

ℰℭ

Cindy was mortified when she learned about her husband's sexual improprieties at work. She had long suspected Gary might be having an affair with his secretary, but she always believed his explanations: their relationship was platonic and his long work hours would result in a promotion from dean to provost at the state university. Cindy was shocked when Gary told her he was being investigated for sexual misconduct and harassment—and the allegations had been made by five different women. Moreover, he would probably lose his job. Nothing, however, prepared her for what she learned next: the investigation would be publicized by the news media because of Gary's position at the university.

Cindy and Gary had always been respected members of the community, and she took pride in that. She imagined the way people would gossip about them at church and the country club. She was wrestling with all of these concerns when it dawned on her that they would have to share this information with their twin daughters, Emma and Rachel, age eleven.

Emma was a sensitive girl who was very close to her father. Rachel, while always closer to Cindy, was having a difficult time at school. Cindy was overwhelmed thinking about sharing this information with her daughters. She couldn't imagine the impact her husband's conduct was going to have on them.

Should the children be told, or should we try to "protect" them?

For many parents, determining how much information to reveal to children presents a huge dilemma. In the best circumstances, the decision is made after careful discussion and planning with a therapist who has specialized training in treating sexual addiction, and possible additional experience in child development and child counseling.

Determining whether to disclose—and deciding how much to reveal—can be an agonizing decision. Parents must consider many variables, including the age and developmental maturity of the child, content of information to be shared, the child's current level of stability, and the dynamics in the family. And while it's common for therapists to make recommendations, it's equally important for parents to remember that, as expert of their children's personalities, they are ultimately best suited to decide how much information to share with them.

Disclosure to children is a touchy issue, and even the most seasoned therapists may struggle when making recommendations to families. Following are different types of disclosure scenarios.

> **Forced disclosure:** This occurs because the children will soon learn the information through a non-nurturing disclosure process.

> **Delayed disclosure:** This occurs when the parents jointly choose to wait to share information until the child is old enough to process the information.

> **Softened disclosure:** This usually involves developmentally appropriate sharing that doesn't include detailed information about the sexual behavior. Sometimes a softened disclosure is followed by a delayed disclosure. When the child is older, he or she receives more information.

> **Unbalanced disclosure:** This disclosure comes from the partner instead of the addict, and often it doesn't include the addict. It can be done in anger or with poor boundaries, and it usually results in the child becoming caught in a triangle, choosing sides, then reacting on behalf of the person who is perceived to be the victim parent.

Discovery: This happens when the child discovers the sexual acting out on his or her own. For example, the child learns of an affair or finds the pornography stash. In some cases, the child may learn this information before the partner does, and in others, the parents may believe the child doesn't know when in fact she or he does.

Some paths of disclosure are healthier than others. It's essential when planning a disclosure process that the best interests of the child always remain the focus. Good reasons for disclosing to children include the following:

- We want to teach direct, open, and honest communication in our family.

- We don't want to perpetuate family secrets.

- We want our children to know us and understand our path to recovery and health. We want to share this part of ourselves with them.

- We want to stop the transmission of addiction from generation to generation in our family by educating our children.

As with most situations that involve children, the child's needs supersede the parent's needs. During trying times, it can be difficult for parents to have strong boundaries and protect their children, but this is usually what is in the children's best interest.

I think my child knows something is going on. What should I do?

My best friend saw my dad in a park with a man. My parents are now separated and I have to pretend that I have no idea what the problem was. I feel so uncomfortable around him now! I put on a happy face when I see my dad, but privately I'm grossed out!

— Jeremy, eleven

If your gut is telling you that your child knows what's going on, you are probably correct. In a survey conducted by Black, Dillon, and S. Carnes, researchers found that in 67 percent of cases, the children already knew about the sexual acting out prior to the disclosure.[1] If the parents continue to deny or hide the problem, it sends some powerful messages to the children, such as

- This is such a shameful secret I could never talk about it.
- We do not openly discuss difficult issues in this family.
- Sexual acting out is okay as long as it is kept secret in the family.

If you find yourself in this predicament, it's often helpful to uncover more information about what the child does or doesn't know. It may be useful at this point to involve the child in therapy. The child's therapist can be instrumental in finding out what the child already knows and can then work with the parent's therapist in facilitating a family session that involves a disclosure and open communication about the addiction.

If the parents only suspect the child knows information about the sexual acting out, they may find themselves in a difficult quandary. On the one hand, they don't want to perpetuate shame and dishonesty through secrecy and cover-ups; on the other hand, they don't want to disclose information to the child that he or she may not be ready for. Parents in this situation should work with a qualified therapist in determining the best choice for them given their circumstances.

What is an appropriate age to disclose this type of information?

It's important to keep in mind that no matter the child's age, some open and honest communication may be appropriate. The key to remember is that sharing should be developmentally appropriate.

Alice's Story

When Alice was just out of her teens, she discovered online pornography. She soon found herself addicted to the readily available images. She was attracted to websites that included some romantic and sexualized chat. Her participation would often lead to hookups with men for casual sexual encounters. She also dated, looking for Mr. Right. When she met Dan, a corporate attorney, she instantly fell in love with his romantic and witty personality. But even after she married Dan, she continued to secretly surf for pornography online. After the couple had two children, Alice attempted to quit looking at porn and tried to put that lifestyle behind her.

As a stay-at-home mom, Alice's life was full, until her children began attending school. Then she suddenly found herself with a lot of unstructured time during the day. She soon returned to those old websites that once offered her so much excitement. Alice began feeling increasingly isolated from Dan and was stressed about her continued unemployment. Her time online escalated, and it wasn't long before she was hooking up with men she met online for casual sex.

As Alice spent more time online, she began to neglect her role as a mother and wife. She continued to grow distant from her family and began feeling close to her online buddies. Dan became suspicious when he came across some suggestive pictures on their home computer. When confronted, Alice was initially defensive. There were fights and arguments. Ben, seven, and Tiffany, five, were puzzled by their parents' sudden moods. Why was Daddy so angry? Why was Mommy so tense? Dan continued to pressure Alice for answers. She reluctantly admitted what she had been doing online. Alice decided to seek treatment for her sexual addiction. Once there, Alice told Dan about her sexual encounters.

Once the couple engaged in the recovery process, they made a renewed commitment to the marriage. They were both concerned about Ben and Tiffany, and they knew the children had felt the tension between them. They wanted to openly address this tension with the children and be able to speak about their recovery and renewed commitment.

With the help of a therapist, they planned a family session with the children. Alice told the children she had lied to Daddy and caused tension in the relationship. Dan and Alice assured the children that the conflict had nothing to do with them. They also emphasized that they were committed to the marriage and the family, and were working on honesty and recovery with one another. Ben and Tiffany were relieved and could see that their parents were starting to get back to normal.

As you can see in the above example, the disclosure was "softened" because the children were so young. According to child development expert Jean Piaget, who developed stages of cognitive development for children, children have a limited capacity to understand abstract thinking around concepts such as "addiction" prior to age twelve.[2] Additionally, most children have a limited understanding of sexuality prior to mid-adolescence. So the concept of "sexual addiction" is confusing to most children. Not to mention that children are typically uncomfortable discussing sexuality, especially when it refers to their parents.

Parents of older children may consider a full disclosure. A "full disclosure" would include that the parent is in recovery from sex addiction and general information about the acting out. For example, *Dad is in recovery from pornography addiction or prostitution use.* Ideally, children should be a minimum age of mid-adolescence before considering a full disclosure.

It's also imperative to consider many other variables when making this decision: maturity of the child, stress level of the child, family relationships, and other factors specific to one's family. Talking over all the extenuating variables with a good therapist can be helpful. Of course, if the child is likely to learn the information through a non-nurturing disclosure process or already knows, then full disclosure at a younger age should be considered.

Examples of Language Used in Disclosures

Softened disclosure and acknowledgment of reality:

Daddy hurt Mommy, so he's going to sleep in another room for a while.

Mommy and Daddy have been fighting because Daddy lied to Mommy. This is between Daddy and me. We love you and it has nothing to do with you.

Full disclosure if the situation warrants:

I am a sex addict. I was dishonest and broke my marriage vows by hiring prostitutes. This has affected my relationship with you in the following ways…I am in recovery and this is how I'm planning on taking care of myself…

I am a sex addict. My cybersex use has gotten out of control and has impacted my ability to work and stay involved with you and the family. I have received treatment and have a plan around this. I would like to be open with you if you have any questions about this.

My child is struggling in many areas of his life. I'm worried that learning about his father's sex addiction will put him over the edge. Should I go through with this disclosure?

Children also go through difficult times in life. It's wise for parents to assess the proper timing of the disclosure whenever possible. At-risk children should be considered vulnerable. Your child may be considered at-risk if he or she struggles with any of the following

- drug abuse and addiction
- an eating disorder
- major mental illness
- thoughts of hurting themselves or others
- running away
- school truancy or other school difficulties
- behavioral or conduct problems, such as stealing or vandalism
- problems with social or peer-group functioning (although some is normal)

If your child is experiencing any of these problems, you may want to delay or soften the disclosure process. Remember that many children already know about the acting out. Sometimes when children are struggling, they may be struggling with information about the sexual acting out and the parents may be unaware that their children already have the information. In these circumstances, discussion with a therapist to determine your course of action is warranted.

My children are young adults. I don't think they would ever find out unless I told them. Should I bother sharing this information with them?

While it may be a bit unsettling for adult children to learn their parent is a sex addict, typically the benefits far outweigh the consequences. Famous psychologist Carl Jung once said, *"The most important gift a parent can give their child is to tell them about their dark side. Telling children about your struggles helps them developmentally to have a realistic picture of what it means to be human."* [3]

When parents share their darkest struggles, sorrows, and pain with their children, it normalizes the children's darkness. The children realizes that they, too, will have dark times that they can share with others and overcome them. It also deeply enriches the intimacy between parents and their children, and the children will be more likely to share their pain and struggles with their parents.

Of course, when sharing the information with adult children, reassure them that you are working on your recovery, so the children don't worry about having to care for the parent. Many addicts in recovery want to avoid talking to their adult children, due to their shame, but the exercise in disclosure can be shame reducing for the parent, as most adult children can handle the information and still demonstrate love for the addict.

Can I share with my oldest child, but not his younger sibling?

It's important to be realistic that when siblings are close, they will share information with one another. Most siblings, especially those that are close in age, have a high degree of openness and sharing, especially when it comes to information about their parents. In these circumstances, it's important to use the age of your youngest child when considering disclosure, keeping in mind that your children will likely share the information. In the ideal situation, parents will determine what's appropriate to share and keep information consistent for all children. It can be distressing to children when they receive different information from different parents. For example, if the older child is closer to the addict and the younger one is closer to the spouse and they are given different information, when the children talk it will be confusing for them. They will be hurt that they weren't told everything or be distrustful of some of the information.

On the other hand, if there's a large age gap between your children, you might consider disclosing only to the older child. For example, if your older child is sixteen and your younger one is eight, it's likely the sixteen-year-old is mature enough to not tell the younger sibling. However, keep in mind that even young children pick up on the subtleties of communication and can be confused by nonverbal communication between an older sibling and parents in a situation such as this.

My partner and I have decided to share this information with the children. How should we do it? How can I make this process easier for them?

Keep in mind that, ultimately, it's the addict's responsibility to disclose to the children. It's a key part of the addict's recovery to take responsibility for his or her behavior and be accountable. This is the foundation of an addict's Twelve Step work. Family members also need to see the addict as remorseful and accountable. This can promote the necessary healing so the family can move past the shame and pain caused by the addiction.

In an ideal world, the addict and partner will plan exactly what will be shared with the children. Corley and Schneider recommend the disclosure focuses on the values that were violated and the direct impact on the child.[4] For example, *I was dishonest, and as a result Mommy was upset,* or *I was unavailable because of my addiction, and as a result I wasn't able to attend your baseball games.* It's often helpful to spend some time and anticipate questions the children may have and how you'll respond. Below is a chart developed by Corley and Schneider that can assist you in anticipating questions children might ask.[5]

What Kids Want to Know by Age

The following questions are what children might ask depending on their ages:

Preschool (ages 3 to 5):

(They have often been witness to fighting or have heard that you're an addict and don't know what is happening.)

- Are you going to die or leave me?
- Am I in trouble?
- Do you love me?

Early Elementary (ages 5 to 6):

- Is this my fault?
- Will something bad happen?
- Who are you now?

Upper Elementary (ages 9 to 13):

- Am I normal?
- Will I get this addiction because I have sexual feelings?
- Am I going to end up an addict because you are?
- What will happen to me if you get divorced?

Teen/Adult Years:

- How could you do this to Mom? To the family?
- How does this specifically relate to me?
- How could you ruin my life?

You may also plan disclosure with a family therapist you trust. In this situation, the addict shares general information about his or her addiction and the consequences. It's important not to share any detailed information about the sexual acting out with the children, if possible. Also, it's beneficial for the addict to share his or her current plan for recovery with the children on an age-appropriate basis. This will provide hope for the children and reduce their anxieties and fears.

If possible, the partner should take a supportive role and be genuine in terms of his or her feelings. Children will pick up on it if the partner or spouse is not genuine. If there are feelings of anger or sadness, the spouse can share with the kids that he or she is hurt, angry, or sad. However, it is important that the partner not take a victim role in front of the child.

During the disclosure, it's crucial that the partner doesn't berate or shame the addict in front of the children, because they will have so many feelings of their own. This will be a difficult moment for children, whether they show it or not. You need to make their feelings and ability to process the information a top priority.

Disclosure is a process, not a onetime event, and this applies even with children. Children may have additional questions over time, or as they mature you may feel it's appropriate to share more information. Keep in mind that the strength of your relationship with your child will influence his or her ability to handle this information. Consequently, continue to do fun things together and keep working on the positive aspects of your relationship.

My child is now upset. What can I do to help?

There are times when upsetting information has to be shared with a child. A good example is the "forced" disclosure situation or circumstances when the child "discovers" the acting-out behavior. The vast majority of children are going to react negatively to the disclosure experience. In the study by Black, Dillon, and S. Carnes, twenty-nine children were asked if they were glad they were told.[6] Of these, twenty said yes. However, the majority of respondents didn't like the process of disclosure and didn't want the information to be true.

Naturally, the more deviant the behavior, the more detailed the information shared with the child; and the more public exposure in the incident, the more distressed the child will be. For example, if the father is the principal at the child's school, was caught with child pornography, and it was in the media, this would be a complex and difficult situation for the child to handle.

Sometimes it can be helpful for children to receive some education about sexual addiction to assist them in normalizing the problem. Data demonstrates sex addiction is a common problem that is typically not discussed, and education can be helpful in reducing shame. If the partner or spouse is involved with the Twelve Step community, she or he may be aware of any events associated with COSA or S-Anon the children may be able to attend. Attending a recovery-oriented lecture or meeting, or hearing someone share his or her story, depending on the content of the lecture or meeting, may be beneficial for older children. You should also consider therapy for the child. Children do an amazing job of covering up their concerns and pain. If they have a good therapist whom they see as an ally and who can also do some occasional family work with the parents, it can facilitate healing.

One of the most important things parents can do is maintain a sense of stability in the family. Having the addict move in and out of the home or having the child switch schools will only cause more pain and disruption for the child. Giving your daughter or son permission to still spend time with and love both parents is essential. Some of the most painful situations involve the addict moving out of the home and rarely spending time with the child. For example, if Ben learns his father is a sex addict, his father moves out of the house, and his mother will not let Ben see his dad, this will only further alienate Ben from both parents. Ben will be hurt and confused by this type of behavior. Of course, if the child is at risk for sexual abuse that may be an exception.

Giving the child reassurance and hope can make this distressing situation easier. If you feel able to genuinely and confidently reassure the child that nothing is going to change, doing so can be helpful. Sharing elements of recovery, such as special things that you and your partner have learned in the recovery process, may also reassure the child. Other positive steps may include introducing the child to safe, strong recovering people.

My child was exposed directly to my partner's acting out, what can I do to help her?

I don't think I would have ever become a sex addict had it not been for the discovery of my father's pornography stash when I was eight. I was so intrigued with what I saw. Whenever I was in pain, I would reach for that stash. This was the beginning of my addiction.

— Scott, twenty-nine, a recovering addict

There are many ways children can be exposed to a parent's sexual acting-out behaviors. For example, they might accidentally discover a parent's pornography collection or find out about an affair. Keep in mind that children are absorbing information about sexuality at all the times during their youth. They learn from their parents, other family members, friends' families, and even the media.

When they see a parent's sexual acting out, it has the potential to influence the child's developing sexuality. For example, it's not uncommon for affairs to be a repeated pattern of behavior from generation to generation. The child learns affairs are acceptable in relationships after that behavior was modeled for him or her. Similarly, pornography use can be passed down from generation to generation. Many pornography addicts report being exposed to it at a young age.

If your child has been exposed to sexual acting out, some damage control is in order. It's best to keep from shaming the child or giving negative or very strict moral messages. Rather, simply validate that it's normal to be sexually curious at their age and that sexuality is a healthy part of life. An open discussion about intimacy and healthy sexuality is helpful in these circumstances. If the sexual acting out had overtones of objectifying or degrading one partner, then a discussion of healthy sexuality as mutual and respectful should take place.

Occasionally, children will worry that they, too, are going to become a sex addict. This is especially true for teenage boys, who are experiencing a normal increase in hormones. An open dialogue normalizing these feelings can reduce anxiety.

In the worst situations, the child may have been molested or experienced incest as part of the sexual acting out. Clearly, treatment

161

would be critical for these children. Keep in mind that some children who have been sexually abused do not develop long-term problems, so it's important not to pathologize the child under these circumstances, while still trying to listen, validate, and understand the child's experience.

My partner and I cannot agree on whether to disclose. What should I do?

Consider the case of Mary and Roger. Nothing could describe the pain Mary experienced when she discovered Roger's sex addiction. Not only had he been involved with prostitutes, but he had engaged in several affairs, the last one was with one of Mary's closest friends. She was devastated. She could not bear to talk with him, sit across the table from him, or even look at him. Plus, they had two children together, Jonathon, nine, and Rebecca, eleven.

Mary believed the kids needed to know the truth about their father's sexual acting out. Roger, on the other hand, thought it was none of their business. Jonathon and Rebecca had always been close to their dad, so when Mary shared everything with them about Roger's sexual acing out, it was quite a shock.

When Roger denied Mary's accusations, Jonathon and Rebecca were hurt and confused. They felt sorry for their mom, and they felt like they had to choose sides. Extended family was also dragged into the conflict. Everyone in the family suffered, especially Jonathon and Rebecca.

As seen in this case example, when parents can't agree on a course of action, it's usually the children who suffer the most. Unfortunately, couples struggling with sex addiction are often in so much intense pain, it's hard for the needs of the child to be placed above the parents' needs. If the couple is heading for a divorce, sometimes separation counseling can be helpful. This type of therapy is not geared toward reconciliation or emotional processing of feelings. Rather, it focuses on issues relating to ongoing contact, such as negotiating co-parenting issues and boundaries. This may be a helpful venue for discussing how to share information with the children.

Again, remember that the child's needs supersede your needs in these situations, and it's usually in the child's best interest to work toward an agreement on this issue.

In summary, there are many factors to consider that can make this an easier process for your children. The list below highlights some of the key characteristics of healthy disclosure that can make this process healthier.[7]

- Disclosure is facilitated by a therapist and is not a onetime process.

- Both parents are present and participate.

- Both parents are in agreement to disclose to the children.

- Both parents articulate why this is important and of value to the child.

- Both parents have strategized and agreed upon what is and is not disclosed.

- Parents speak for themselves. The addict and partner each speak about their own behavior.

- The addict speaks in generalities about addictive behavior, not specific details.

- Parents display signs of recovery.

- Neither parent takes the role of victim.

- The child is not used as a confidant.

- Parents are clear that it is not the child's responsibility to fix or take care of them. It's easy for the child to become caught in a triangle, choosing sides, then reacting on behalf of the person who is perceived to be the victim parent.

- Open dialogue and discussion with a therapist is shown.

- Set the tone for children to know they can discuss it with you as they need to or as you believe it is appropriate. To say or imply, "We'll talk about this today and never again" reinforces the shame of disclosure and the behavior.

Educating your children about sex addiction can be one of the most important lessons you can teach. Empowering them with information so they don't repeat the mistakes you've made can save them a lot of pain. Conversely, if they do wander down the same path in the future, your recovery can serve as a source of hope for them and give them the power to stop the cycle of sex addiction in their family.

Chapter Ten:
What Does It Mean if My Partner Has Shown an Interest in Minors?

Barbara Levinson, PhD, CSAT-S

ℰℭ

Nearly every day you hear or read something about pedophiles, predators, child molesters, or the abduction of children. We are so aware of the issue that we have become a society that sees the boogeyman around every corner. It is important to be knowledgeable about these issues and be sensitive to the needs of our children and keep them safe. However, for people with partners who are sex addicts with behaviors that have included an interest in children, the trauma can be almost too much to bear. Finding out your partner has secret sexual behaviors is enough of a shock and trauma. Add to that the realization that his or her conduct also includes thoughts, behaviors, or fantasies about minors is frightening, abhorrent, mind-boggling, confusing, and disgusting. Knowing others have dealt with some of the same situations as you and have survived it can be comforting.

Susie's Story

Susie was angry and frantic. A recent Pap test came back positive for human papillomavirus (HPV), an increasingly common STD. She was confused and had no idea how this could have happened. Although her gynecologist explained she may have contracted the STD long ago and it didn't manifest until recently, Susie was mortified. Her doctor also told her she would need to tell her husband, Stan, who had likely also contracted the disease.

Susie had had sexual partners before marrying, but had always used protection. Stan had told her he had not been very sexually active while single, and she believed him because he had inhibited attitudes and behaviors about sex.

The couple had been married seven years and had no children together. Susie, however, had a ten-year-old daughter from a previous marriage. Although her and Stan's sexual relationship was good in the beginning, over the years the couple struggled to keep up an active sex life due to Stan's work obligations. When Susie did suggest sex, Stan would often be uninterested. Susie began to wonder if her desire was abnormal.

Five years into their marriage, Susie's daughter went to live with her father, who resided in another state. Once she and Stan were living alone, Susie believed their sex life would become more spontaneous. Instead, the couple had even less sex. Prior to her visit to the gynecologist, the couple had only had sex once in two months. Susie was petrified that Stan would think she had contracted the STD through an affair. But she also secretly wondered about Stan's lack of interest in sex. And she had a "gut feeling" that something was odd about the way Stan stared at younger women and made sexual comments such as, "They shouldn't dress like that. They're just asking for it."

Stan spent hours on the computer, and there were times she couldn't reach him at work, which she also thought was suspicious. She had mentioned these behaviors over the years, but when Stan got angry, she dropped the subject. Her suspicions only increased after she discovered an open web page that contained pictures of partially dressed teenage models. When she confronted Stan about it, he became angry. She called him a pervert and told him she no longer trusted him.

Despite his denials, Susie couldn't let it go. She became a detective, looking for evidence that Stan was cheating on her. She soon discovered not only that Stan had sex with prostitutes, but that he was also interested in viewing images of underage girls. She wondered, *Is my husband a pedophile?*

What is pedophilia?

Pedophilia is defined as a persistent sexual interest in prepubescent children.[1] Clinicians rely on several different sources when considering the diagnosis of pedophilia, including self-report, a history of sexual behavior involving children, and psycho-physiological assessments. All of these sources have limitations, and people will tend to deny pedophilic interests for fear of being reported and getting caught up in the legal system.

Having interests, thoughts, or fantasies is different from acting them out. A person's history of past sexual offenses in terms of the number, age, gender, and relatedness of child victims is informative but is only approximate because it is limited to known victims.[2]

For a clinical diagnosis of pedophilia, a person will have had the following:

- recurrent, intense, sexually arousing fantasies, sexual urges, or behaviors involving sexual activity with a prepubescent child or children for a period of at least six months. Moreover, the person has acted out on these sexual urges; or

- the sexual urges or fantasies cause marked distress or interpersonal difficulty. The person is at least sixteen years old and at least five years older than the child or children.[3]

This diagnosis of pedophilia suggests that the person must suffer internal conflict or social consequences. Only a small percentage of sex offenders meet these criteria for pedophilia.

A pedophile often starts offending at an early age and can have a large number of victims that are not family related. The pedophile is usually driven to offend and has actual sexual contact with victims. All too often, the term pedophile is used incorrectly and is misunderstood. Most of the time, sex addicts are interested in much older children who are past puberty and have sexual characteristics that are more developed.

Pedophiles are usually obsessed with children and they can behave in addictive ways. They usually have a belief system that could support a predatory lifestyle. There are also subtypes of the pedophilia diagnosis to further complicate the issue. These are

- *fixated pedophiles* who identify with children and seek sexual relationships with them

- *regressed pedophiles* who are passively aroused by children

Pedophiles can have a rigid set of double standards and also can be very religious.[4] Some studies report that a high number of pedophiles have been victims of childhood sexual abuse themselves. However, this is not always the case. True pedophiles are simply fascinated with children. They can describe children in very idealistic terms. They're often interested in childlike activities, rather than adult activities, and frequently continue to have the hobbies they had in childhood. However, that doesn't mean anyone who collects toys or comic books is a pedophile; collecting behavior can be perfectly normal and appropriate.

Pedophiles will frequently make friends with single parents or work or volunteer in youth-related activities or professional positions that have contact with children. Again, that doesn't mean every teacher, youth minister, or pediatrician is a pedophile. A pedophile usually prefers children who are close to puberty, but others may target younger children. If the pedophile was abused as a child, he or she will often target children who are the same age the pedophile was at the time of the abuse.

For the most part, sex addicts are distinguishable from sex offenders, who are also distinguishable from the true pedophile, although there may be some overlap in these groups. *Sex offender* is a legal term and should only be used for persons who have been adjudicated and involved in the legal system.

If your partner looks at or objectifies teenagers or comments on how "hot" they are, or you find some inappropriate images on a computer, don't panic. It doesn't mean he or she is a pedophile. Sex addicts often explore sexual avenues they may never have thought of before the Internet existed. Because all kinds of information, images, and videos are readily available online, the addict can get easily aroused or interested in behaviors that he or she may never consider doing.

There is, however, a difference between curiosity and preferential interest. Finding information about particular websites your partner has visited or downloaded images from, although concerning and possibly illegal, again doesn't mean your partner is a pedophile. A careful assessment must be done to understand the behaviors. Pedophiles will typically have a large collection of pornography, if they use the computer to gather information and view pictures, and will categorize the images in separate folders. Often the collection will contain particular images or a series of images of particular children.

There are other red flags that can distinguish a true pedophile. For example, the type of movies or videos they buy or rent, souvenirs they keep, or how the home is decorated may indicate that their interest in children is problematic. Binoculars by a window facing a school, playground, or park can also be indicators. Fixated pedophiles can generate their own "erotic" materials from relatively innocuous sources, such as TV advertisements, clothing catalogs featuring children modeling underwear, and other available sources.[5]

Can pedophiles be cured?

There's much talk in the media about how all pedophiles are dangerous predators with a poor prognosis. In reality, most pedophiles can be treated and managed. Treatment of pedophilia is difficult, but not impossible. Often adults who have an interest or fantasies about teenagers or "adult-looking children" or "childlike adults" are not pedophiles.

If you believe your partner is a pedophile, it's essential to start with a comprehensive evaluation or assessment. There are many variables that would direct the course of treatment. For example, are they regressed or fixated? Are they a pedophile, an incest perpetrator, a child molester, or someone who has had fantasies but never acted on them? The diagnosis may be further complicated if he or she has a personality disorder, developmental problems, or a significant mental illness. Many partners in your situation find tremendous relief when they seek the counsel of a qualified professional who can assist them in understanding the details of their situation.

Sex Offender or Sex Addict?

As noted earlier, *sex offender* is a legal term that refers to someone who has already committed a crime and has been adjudicated in the legal system. Sex offenders are usually referred to clinicians through the legal system or by attorneys or probation or parole officers. Providers of treatment for sex offenders must have specialized training. In some states, practitioners must be licensed to treat sex offenders in addition to holding other licenses. Other states have only certification or registration requirements for treatment providers. Some states have no special training requirements, although this is becoming rare.

The treatment of sex offenders requires a very structured program geared toward group therapy. It's usually a cognitive behavioral and psycho-educational approach, and most often the offender uses a workbook designed specifically for the treatment of sex offenders. In most states there are strict requirements about treatment guidelines and strategies. Homework assignments are almost always given, and offenders must adhere to a strict "treatment contract" that outlines what they can and cannot do. The guidelines are usually prohibitive, and the treatment provider almost always works in conjunction with probation or parole.

The laws governing sex offenders outline where they can live and work. There are restrictions regarding contact with children, both theirs and others, and the activities in which they can be involved. The main goals of a sex offender treatment program are

- no more victims
- community safety
- for the offender to have a successful and happy life

Not all sex offenders are sex addicts and not all sex addicts are sex offenders. Just because your partner is an addict, it doesn't mean he or she has overtly committed a sexual offense. The following figure outlines the similarities and differences between sex offenders and sex addicts.

Figure 10.1 Similarities and Differences between Sex Offenders and Sex Addicts

Similarities and Differences between Sex Offenders and Sex Addicts		
Situation	Sex Offender	Sex Addict
A loss of control and life consequences	X	X
Come from rigid and disengaged families	X	X
A history of addiction in the family and trauma in childhood, with a high percentage of emotional abuse	X	X
Multiple addictions	X	X
High stress levels	X	X
Use of pornography	X	X
A high use of thinking errors (cognitive distortions), such as rationalization, excuses, blaming, "poor me," victim stance, denial, justification, lying, anger, keeping score, and sense of entitlement	X	X
A history of sexual difficulties	X	X
Criminal lifestyle history	X	
Criminogenic thinking	X	
Distrust of authority	X	
History of violence	X	
Past sexual aggression	X	
Escalation of violence	X	
Overall pattern of assaults	X	

Sex offenders have victims, not only the people they offend against but also their victims' families, friends, and loved ones. The offender also abuses people who care for them, since they are affected by the crimes they commit. Often, sex addicts don't believe they have victimized anyone, which perpetuates their behaviors. The person who looks at child pornography may believe it doesn't hurt anyone; however, the children in those images are living humans who have been victimized.

A person who finds out that his or her partner is attracted to or participating in sexual behaviors with others is deeply hurt. Both sex addicts and sex offenders have victims. A major difference is the sex offender has been accused of or did something that was illegal or criminal.

Will my partner go to jail?

If a crime has been committed, your partner may become involved with the legal system. In fact, this may be how you became aware of your partner's secret life. Here are some examples:

- A man caught with 20,000 images of child pornography on his computer was sentenced to five years in prison.

- A man who engaged in an online sexual chat with minors was charged with enticement of a minor for sexual purposes and sentenced to three to five years in a federal prison.

- A man caught masturbating in his car was charged with indecent exposure and received a year of probation.

- A man charged with two counts of indecency with a child received six years of probation.

- A woman who had sex with her sixteen-year-old son's friend was sentenced to a lengthy jail term.

All of these people were sex addicts who became sex offenders; none, however, were pedophiles.

I think I found child pornography on my husband's computer! How can I be sure? What should I do?

If your partner has had sexual contact with a minor, consenting or not, he or she can and most probably will go to jail or be given probation, depending on the state, risk level, and the circumstances of the crime. In the United States, the legal definition of someone who can be convicted of child pornography is this: "*Any person who knowingly mails, transports, ships, receives, distributes, reproduces, sells, or possesses any book, magazine, periodical, film, videotape, computer disc, or any other material that contains an image of child pornography that has been mailed, shipped, or transported by any means, including the computer...Shall be fined...or imprisoned not more than 10 years, or both, but if such person has a prior conviction...such person shall be fined under this title and imprisoned for not less than 10 years or more than 20 years.*"[6]

The legal definition of someone who can be convicted of child pornography may not capture all the material that an adult with a sexual interest in children may consider to be arousing. There are several categories of pictures that may be sexualized by an adult with an interest in children. For example, nonerotic and nonsexualized pictures of children in their underwear or swimming suits from commercial or private sources in which the context and organization by the collector indicates inappropriateness.[7] There may be pictures of children naked or seminaked in nudist settings. Another form is pictures of children in play areas or other environments showing their underwear or varied degrees of nakedness. These may not fall under the legal definition of child pornography but may nonetheless be indicative of an interest in children. The legal definition of child pornography has some different phrases in it that often lead to confusion and have been subject to some scrutiny.

As it stands, *child pornography* means any visual depiction, including any photograph, film, video, picture, or computer or computer-generated image or picture, whether made or produced by electronic, mechanical, or other means of sexually explicit conduct where

- the production of such visual depiction involves the use of a minor engaging in sexually explicit conduct;

- such visual depiction is a digital image, computer image, or computer- generated image that is, or is indistinguishable from, that of a minor engaging in sexually explicit conduct; or

- such visual depiction has been created, adapted, or modified to appear that an identifiable minor is engaging in sexually explicit conduct.

Sexually explicit conduct in the context of child pornography means

- graphic sexual intercourse, including genital-genital, oral-genital, anal-genital, or oral-anal, whether between persons of the same or opposite sex, or lascivious simulated sexual intercourse where the genitals, breast, or pubic area of any person is exhibited;

- graphic or lascivious bestiality, masturbation, or sadistic or masochistic abuse; or

- graphic or simulated lascivious exhibition of the genitals or pubic area of any person.[8]

More investigation on the sexual interest of children should be done. The current research doesn't take into account all the new technologies that have developed.[9] The lack of research into this important area can hamper our ability to help individuals and their families, and to distinguish between levels of risk.

The Internet Trap

A high percentage of partners first find hard evidence of questionable sexual behavior on their partners' computers. You may have also stumbled across other information, such as sexual chats involving young children, instant messaging, newsgroups, bulletin boards, or websites aimed at children. The following four areas indicate serious sexual online behavior.[10]

1. Possessing new or recent images or images associated with sex

2. Participating in an online community of offenders

3. Trading of images

4. Cataloging of images

There are also other types of "images" you may become aware of, such as the so-called model sites that have original photographs of scantily clad children. Or perhaps you have evidence of your partner looking at clothing catalogs or family nudist sites. Some of the images in online advertisements show toddlers wearing tight underwear or slightly older children wearing makeup and posing with feather boas.

In a recent *New York Times* article, more than 200 of these online advertising sites aimed at pedophiles were found. Most legitimate modeling sites are password-protected with access granted only to companies and casting agencies after a background check. The *New York Times* article exposed another site that claimed to be a company that helped children start modeling careers. There is, however, no identifying information on this company, and it was linked to as many as six other sites featuring little girls.

If you have discovered child pornography on your computer, it does not necessarily indicate your partner is a pedophile. It's possible that your partner opened up a site without knowledge of what was there. Pornographers use tricks in the recruitment of new customers. The following are some methods typically used to push pornography to new users:

- *Porn napping:* Purchasing experienced domain names and then redirecting the user to their own sites

- *Cyber squatting:* Purchasing legal domain names and putting explicit pornography on the site

- *Doorway scams:* Figuring out ways to use search engines to get their sites high on the search engine list when someone could be searching for perfectly legitimate information

- *Misspelling:* Taking domain names of legitimate sites and using the most common misspellings to get the user to their website

- *Advertising:* Using creative fake system-error messages that users believe they have to click, but in reality they are clicking on a pornography link

- *Entrapment:* Falling prey to any of the above scams depending on what was done at the porn site, whether an unintentional or intentional visit, a whole host of problems can be incurred

What if there is no indication of any computer usage or pornography, but there is a suspicion of interest in children, verbal comments, staring or looking at children, a history of sexual abuse of a child, exposure of genitals, past involvement in the criminal justice system, or admission of incest as a young child?

Once again, this doesn't necessarily indicate pedophilia. These behaviors can indicate other problems and should be evaluated by a trained therapist.

If you suspect any inappropriate behavior with children living in the house, get immediate help and do everything you can to keep the children safe. Contact the local authorities or a twenty-four-hour child abuse hotline to report suspected child abuse. If you're not sure what to do, get in touch with a professional who can immediately assist you.

Other common scenarios include interest in younger children and teenagers, sexualization of teenage girls and boys, and grooming activities that are often used to entice these vulnerable adolescents into consenting to sexual behavior because they "are in love" or see it as an escape for them. Usually a power differential, to make the child feel vulnerable, is a significant part of that relationship.

I'm so embarrassed. How do I get help?

Most partners are embarrassed, feel shame, and will not tell anyone. They may even want to protect their partners. There are stories in the media about people being caught in sting operations, going to jail, being beaten up, being ostracized and unable to live in certain areas, losing their jobs, or worse. Of course, you want to protect your family, your loved ones, or your status, and there doesn't seem to be anywhere to turn or anyone to turn to.

You may wish you could just make it all go away. Maybe you've done that before only to have the problem resurface. You're scared, feel guilty, think the worst, and wonder if you will be held culpable for not reporting this behavior or seeking help. You can't tell your neighbors, the police, your family, or even your best friend. You don't know whom to trust.

After the initial shock, confrontation, the guilt and shame, you might feel angry, furious, enraged, revengeful, depressed, hopeless, worthless, and traumatized. People may tell you that you seem different or suspicious, and you may go into rages or withdrawal or simply act crazy. You're not crazy, but you do need help. This cannot be dealt with on your own.

No matter how much your partner begs, pleads, threatens, or promises to change, you must tell a professional. It's important to know that if you tell a therapist your partner is viewing child pornography, the therapist is not a mandated reporter in that situation. The therapist is still required by law to maintain your confidentiality. This is not the case, however, if you partner is manufacturing child pornography or being sexual with a child. Creating child pornography is reportable and your therapist will be required to contact the appropriate authorities.

If you feel that by telling someone you will be in danger, make sure you are safe before you take action. There are organizations that can help find safety for you and your children. See the Resource Guide on page 259 for additional resources to help guide you in the right direction.

Making the Decision to Stay or Leave

Diane's Story

When Diane met her future husband, she instantly fell in love. Jack had been looking for the "love of his life." But after being married for only six months, the couple was asked to leave their apartment complex because someone reported that Jack had been exposing himself to young children. Diane couldn't believe it.

This could not possibly be the quiet, gentle man she knew and loved. Jack was arrested, given probation, and admitted into a treatment program for sex offenders.

Over the next year, Diane tried to understand and come to terms with Jack's behavior. What unfolded was devastating for her. While in treatment, she discovered Jack had been molested as a child and had been exposing himself to children since he was a young teenager. Jack's past revealed a significant interest in young children, and as a teenager he had been predatory in nature. His compulsivity extended itself to other forms of sexual behaviors, such as pornography, erotica, and collecting children's movies.

As time went on, the couple faced many hard choices. Although Diane remained married to Jack, she struggled with the decision. She felt like there was little support for her in group therapy since she felt different from most of the other women whose husbands had not committed a sexual offense. Jack wanted to develop a healthy sexuality and realized that his interests for children may always be there, but he could manage his behaviors. After soul-searching therapy, Diane was able to set boundaries for herself and was clear about her expectations in the marriage. The couple decided they would never have children, and Jack continued treatment and group therapy. Diane also continued psychotherapy. They both knew what the possibilities for the future may hold if Jack did not maintain his sexual sobriety.

As part of his probation, Jack submitted to polygraph tests. During a test, it showed deception. Jack had violated his probation by looking at child pornography. He was sent to prison for five years for violating his probation. When he left prison, he returned to treatment and Diane took him back.

But shortly after his release, Jack began visiting massage parlors and prostitutes, and viewing catalogs and pornography online at work. Although he had no hands-on contact with children, he was deceitful and violated the treatment contract established in group therapy. He had engaged in high-risk sexual behaviors and put himself and his wife in dangerous situations. Diane asked Jack to move out and is now deciding whether to stay in the marriage or get a divorce. Jack continues to work on his deviant arousal patterns and his sexually compulsive behaviors.

Each person must make their own decision about what to do about their partners' addiction. There is no right or wrong answer. You will hear others say, "I could never stay if my partner did..." No one actually knows what they would do in any particular situation. Sometimes you find the courage you never thought you had. Hopefully, what you are reading in this chapter will help guide you in making whatever decisions you need to make. The best advice is don't make any impulsive decisions and always ask for help. Immediate steps should be taken, however, if someone is in danger.

The Arousal Template

An arousal template starts to emerge between the ages of five and eight years. Because of this, events early in life can have a profound impact on the emergent sexual self.[11]

Early childhood experiences, family messages, influence from peers, the media, religious teachings, sexual experiences, and exposure to sexual stimuli as well as a variety of other factors go into an internal process called sexual arousal. Traumatic experiences, such as early abuse, can also have a tremendous impact on someone's arousal template. Arousal is a physical phenomenon; however, it's influenced by the thoughts, feelings, and beliefs we have about ourselves and the world around us.[12] Here are some examples of how an arousal template takes shape in childhood or early adolescence.

Nancy, forty-three, came into therapy because she was only able to have an orgasm while masturbating with the recurrent fantasy involving a teenage girl seducing an older man. It was apparent that this fantasy had been developed to give her some sense of control over a situation from her childhood where she had felt powerless.

John had grown up in a sexually repressive environment and didn't receive the affection and nurturing a child requires. He can recall soothing himself through genital touching while still in diapers. As John grew, when he was unable to deal with the stresses of life, he experimented with wearing diapers in order to access those old feelings of self-soothing. His use of diapers during masturbation quickly evolved into compulsive use, and he was unable to engage in sex with a partner.

Charlie came into therapy because he realized that his interest in teenage girls was inappropriate, and he was in a position where he had access to them. He realized that if he couldn't get his urges under control, he would have to leave his job. When exploring Charlie's background, it became evident that he had been sexualized by a female babysitter, and his attraction to teenage girls didn't change as he grew older. There were other factors that related to his fixation, such as feeling inadequate as a teenage boy, having low self-esteem, and growing up in a house with an alcoholic father and a mother who was codependent. He became fixated on young girls who he could manipulate and would encourage their "admiration" of him. He was married and had children of his own. Over the years, Charlie explored his arousal template but had not acted out with any teenagers. Charlie admitted there could have been acting out, but his use of his recovery tools and open and honest communication with his wife helped to avert any damaging behavior.

The Internet has had a profound ability to expand arousal templates. Old arousal templates can be changed or supplemented. In areas that are illegal or unhealthy, the Internet makes it possible for people to reinforce that undesirable behavior and strengthen an unhealthy arousal template.[13]

The hypnotic effect of the Internet, along with the vast array of sexual information available, can become a powerful tool for getting us involved in a world we never knew existed. Many people report feeling as though they are in a trance until somehow by chance or accident, they are abruptly pulled back to reality. Once they become aware of what they have done, they are dismayed by the fantasies, thoughts, or behaviors they engaged in, things they never imagined they would participate in. Anything can become part of an arousal template. Sometimes the unlikely pairing of two things can form an arousal template. For example, *Cheryl's sleep was often interrupted by her parents' fighting. They would scream and curse at each other. In order to soothe herself, she would masturbate. As an adult, she realized it was only when her partner would use profanity that she was able to reach orgasm. Arousal and profanity had become linked together.*

Objects, situations, and scenarios can become sexualized. Even anger can become sexualized. Our sexuality is comprised of many things and, hopefully, can grow in a healthy way. When we are affected by our environment and experiences, our sexuality can be influenced and become shameful for us. A healthy understanding of ourselves, our values, and our beliefs will open up a whole world where we can enjoy our bodies, our sexual uniqueness, and our fantasies and have sexual and love experiences that will become part of our arousal template.

What do I tell my children, neighbors, family, and friends?

This is probably the hardest of all. Whom can you really tell and who will understand? First, it's not your job to tell anyone. It's the addict's responsibility to tell the people in his or her life about what has happened. In a perfect world, your partner will not be in denial, will seek out help, and will understand how this addiction has affected others. However, we don't live in a perfect world and there are many occasions when that doesn't happen. You have to decide where to get support.

The people you tell today may be the very people who will judge you if you decide to stay or even leave the addict. The addict may even ask you to not tell anyone. Sometimes the anger is so over-whelming, you'll want to tell anyone who will listen. But once recovery begins, you may regret sharing such explicit information with others. Keeping all this in and handling it by yourself is also not the answer. If your partner does get into treatment, then the two of you can deal with these questions within the framework of the therapeutic process. If you're struggling with the questions raised in this chapter, be assured that you're not alone. Unfortunately for many people, the pain and confusion you're experiencing now is becoming more common.

Remember, you need a lot of support during this time. Reach out for resources in your community. Seek out others who have been through what you're going through. Explore local support groups. Find a qualified therapist. Addiction happens in secrecy; recovery happens in community. Shame is reduced by sharing your stories. Be thoughtful and kind to yourself. Get help and support. You do not have to do this alone.

Chapter Eleven:
How Does Sex Addiction and Infidelity Affect Gay Couples?

Robert Weiss, LCSW, CSAT-S

ℰℂℛ

It was like he took a knife and slashed my soul.
Everything I believed about love, relationships, and our future together got
twisted up into a frazzled mess that I am still trying to untangle.

— Seth, a thirty-four-year-old gay man,
after learning that his partner of eight years had been visiting
male prostitutes throughout their relationship

The inevitable hurt, anger, and disorientation that occur when relationship trust is betrayed transcend sexual orientation. Spousal duplicity unleashes a cascade of powerful emotions. These emotions are equally intense for people who are heterosexual, bisexual, and homosexual or something in between.

When a committed partner's faith in his or her spouse turns out to have been misplaced and that trust is broken, we all end up in the same place. Fear, remorse, rage, numbness, longing, and despair are basic elements of grief that are simply human, no matter the gender of our partner. And while it's useful to be aware of how the significant cultural differences between heterosexuals and homosexuals affect sex and relationships, it's more important to acknowledge feelings are feelings, loss is loss, and broken hearts aren't exclusive to a particular race, gender, or sexual orientation.

While this chapter will help illuminate the differing ways partner or spousal betrayal through sex can be viewed from a gay-male context, it's not intended to provide the sex addict with new ways to justify his sexual acting out under the guise of a gay identity. For

183

clarity, this chapter will first discuss accepted sexual and relational practices within the gay subculture.

How is sex addiction different in gay men?

Approximately 8 to 10 percent of all gay men today have a sex addiction problem, though this statistic may seem low in relationship to the amount of sexual activity readily witnessed in most gay-urban environments and in the gay media.[1] Even those who isolate themselves or rigidly compartmentalize their personal and sex lives still see a densely populated sex culture when entering the larger gay arena of gay online life, bars, street festivals, and the gay ghetto. And though many urban gay men today have a greater array of social and recreational options than ever before—such as volunteer and recreational groups, dating and social clubs, professional networking and spiritual organizations—many continue to tie their social lives to environments that reinforce either the use of alcohol and drugs, or the search for sex and romance.

The most well-known and profitable private local businesses in Western gay culture are bars, gyms, bathhouses, online porn, and partner-search sites and sex clubs. Gay publications and Internet venues prosper with dollars earned through advertising focused on working out and diet, sensual massage, prostitution, porn, casual hookups, and personals. Thus, the urban gay man's attention is inevitably yanked toward self-pleasuring and distraction. At the same time, he's told that he will find love only by achieving physical perfection through workouts, tanning, and cosmetic surgery. The Internet chat, sex club, GPS partner-search engine, bar, gym, and dance club scenes—which can be vital, meaningful reflections of the gay experience for some—also have a dark side, presenting those with restricted emotional resources and limited intimacy skills with a lifestyle that they may be ill equipped to handle.

Gay male sex addicts are not compulsively sexual because they are gay; rather their impulsive and compulsive sexuality stems from each individual's psychological issues and biological predisposition to emotional vulnerability and addiction. These are exactly the same set of symptoms presented by heterosexual sex addicts. Unfortunately for gay sex addicts, and even more so if they have a committed partner, the gay addict's destructive sexual behavior takes place against a cultural background of dramatically greater sexual freedoms than his heterosexual counterpart. The urban gay man is in some ways a prisoner of his freedom. He has fewer opportunities for self-examination and little support for behavior change should his sexual behavior become addictive or compulsive.

Likewise, gay partners will find little support or validation in the gay community for the hurt, loss, and confusion that comes with partnership betrayal. Ever vigilant to avoid reinforcing the larger society's image that being gay means being troubled, the public face of gay culture is cautious about showing negative aspects of gay sexuality in any form. Consequently, some gay men and gay media will tolerate and even celebrate drug use and sexual practices with the potential for clearly harmful consequences.

All Gay Men Are Not Equal

There exist generational differences among gay men in their concepts and values surrounding intimacy and monogamy. Pre-baby boomer men, who grew up in an era when homosexuality was considered a disease and homosexual behavior a prosecutable legal offense, learned to live their personal lives behind closed doors. Men in this period placed a high value on sexual discretion and secrecy, often living closeted and restricted lives with few chances for healthy partnering. Baby boomers, who achieved manhood during the wide-open sexual mores of the late 1960s through early 1980s, came to embrace their sexual freedoms as a banner of pride to be openly celebrated.

Yet what followed, the sex = death period of HIV/AIDS of the early 1980s through the end of the twentieth century, had a profound dampening effect on gay sexual enthusiasm. Tens of thousands of men who might have matured into gay relationship mentors and role models died before age thirty-five. Younger Generation X and Generation Y gay men came into their sexual prime during a period of much greater public acceptance and legitimacy of being gay, but these men have also been surrounded by a culture of "post AIDS" sexual conservatism and have demonstrated less of a need to "be different." This has evolved into a greater interest in long-term committed relationships, marriage, and raising a family than in previous generations of gay men.

Once devalued by gay culture as an attempt to "mimic" heterosexual relationships, gays are increasingly engaging in monogamous coupling, often including the ceremonial acknowledgments of marriage, adopting children, and living a more traditional lifestyle. At the same time, these men, along with the larger heterosexual culture, are faced with the evolving sexual and relational challenges presented by the Internet and social media. Overall, as gay men have moved from being rejected by the larger culture, to grudgingly being accepted by the culture, to helping to define it (in media, business, fashion, design, and music), they have embraced more traditional heterosexual relationship models, yet many have retained openness to sexual role and relationship experimentation.

Although the feelings generated by a betrayal of relationship fidelity are similar for all who expect a partner or spouse to be faithful, an unspoken expectation of fidelity is for many gay men a less closely held value than that of their heterosexual counterparts. Lesbian women, who typically have higher expectations of fidelity, rarely participate in sex addiction treatment, even though there are likely many lesbians having problems with compulsive sexuality. Thus, women are more likely to overtly experience the kinds of consequences that would lead them to seek help due to a relationship problem.

Broadly speaking, gay-male culture places less emphasis on monogamy and fidelity than straight culture does, and offers more extensive and accepted opportunities for men to have casual, anonymous sex. Many gay men of all ages comfortably view sex as a form of play or recreation—with sexuality or even romance not always assumed to be the defining factor or "glue" that holds a couple together. It's against this sometimes confusing background that gay sex addicts and their partners attempt to resolve the turmoil of their broken promises and turbulent emotions and attempt to get help.

Sexual norms in gay culture tend to be different and generally more permissive, tolerant of diversity, and open. Partners may have more difficulty characterizing or recognizing sex addiction or compulsivity in a spouse based solely on his history of sexual behavior. While it may be easier to detect sex addiction in a married, heterosexual man with three kids who secretly sneaks off to the strip club or adult bookstore, it's more difficult to assess addiction or compulsivity in a gay man based on the nature of his behavior. For example, having an Internet profile for hookups, wanting to experiment with a three-way, or going to a bathhouse doesn't necessarily mean your partner is a sex addict—even if you don't agree with or approve of those activities. The following is a list of indicators that your gay partner may have a problem:

- He lies to you about sex or keeps secrets about his sexual activities.

- He breaks promises or agreements made between the two of you about his sexual behavior.

- One or both of you have experienced specific negative consequences due to his sexual behavior, such as arrest, disease, job loss, or public embarrassment.

- Sex—in whatever form it takes for him—is or has become his primary recreational activity, superseding time with friends, time with you, hobbies, or other social activities.

- His sexual behavior is escalating, either in the amount of time he spends doing it or the intensity of the behavior he is involved with, or both.

- He has made repeated attempts to stop or reduce his involvement in some sexual behavior only to return to it later despite those problems.

If the themes described above of lying, secrecy, escalation, consequences, and loss of control are the primary concerns experienced in a partner, then it is very likely he has a sex addiction problem, whether or not he acknowledges it.

How is my struggle different as a gay partner?

While the recovering gay sex addict has much healing work to do to become sexually sober, including cleaning up the consequences of his sexual acting out and negotiating a newly experienced emotional life, his committed partner has even more challenging tasks ahead. Whereas the sex addict has known about his sexual behaviors all along, partners are often blindsided by the revelation of previously hidden sexual activity or the degree of activities that were occurring. Partners suffer from the fallout of the addicts' sexual and romantic exploits and, in a broader sense, from this new, unwelcome problem in their lives—one not of their own making.

Often, faced with a history of lies and betrayal by the person in whom they had placed the most trust, partners can feel traumatized and overwhelmed. They may find themselves mentally reviewing and questioning the entire experience of their relationships, looking back to figure out what they missed, what went wrong. For those who believed they had a monogamous relationship, the revelation of betrayal on a large scale causes questioning of what, if anything, is true about their relationship as a couple. Partners have a lot of confusion about how to proceed without trust.

Mark's Story

Mark, who had been fighting to maintain his own self-respect and dignity after discovering hundreds of sexual chats, emails, and sex-date plans on his husband's computer, didn't expect support from his gay friends or family. He didn't talk to anyone except a therapist about what he was going through.

> I didn't think people would understand how I felt, so I didn't bother reaching out. My friends are always talking about everyone they have sex with and how gay guys have sex with everybody they know anyway, so how can I expect them to support me? My guy cheated—"So what?" Honestly, it has been hard enough not to keep blaming myself for thinking that my relationship could somehow be different. And since my family has never supported my being gay anyway, I knew they wouldn't be there for me in a situation like this. I felt like it was better to just deal with it alone. Whose shoulder was I supposed to cry on? I grew up Catholic. It's not like I was going to get help from a local priest.

A heterosexual wife can feel confused and inadequate when her husband says, "Looking at a lot of porn and going to strip clubs, it's a guy thing. You couldn't understand, so leave me alone." Gay spouses face the same issue when told by a partner, "Hey, you know what it's like to be gay. We just do this; just look at all the gay porn online. Stop bugging me." It can be confusing to a gay partner to define exactly what he has the right to ask of his mate in terms of being faithful. And gay partners experiencing betrayal are also less likely to receive empathic support from peers and family.

Seth, whose quote begins this chapter, speaks further about his experience:

> *Discovering that my partner had lied to me for so many years was by far the greatest hurt. But when it all came out, I was nearly as shocked by how little support I got from gay and straight friends alike. It was almost as if everyone expected that a gay guy is going to cheat, lie, and keep secrets. Even people who knew us and loved us were only minimally supportive. Unlike my sister, who had family, church, and the law on her side when her husband left her for another woman, the reactions I received after expressing my hurt, fear, and sadness seemed to run the gamut from being called "reactive" to being told, "It won't be that hard to find another guy if this doesn't work out." And that was from people who love me and know us well as a couple.*
>
> *I spent eight years with him! Yet, because we are two men together, the violation I experienced didn't garner nearly the same consideration or sympathy from those around me as my sister's loss did. And though it was painful and sad for her, she was married for only three years. If that's not a rejection of who I am, I don't know what is!*

A lack of affirmation for gay male intimacy flows from the larger culture. Consider the gay man's challenges to marriage, lack of acceptance into many mainstream religious communities, and unequal legal status for male-male relationships and parenting. All of this contributes to the reality that gay-male culture tends to value relationship monogamy differently than heterosexual culture does.

Without a larger established cultural acceptance and few significant role models for gay relationships and intimacy, same-sex partnerships often have more room and permission to explore differing models of relating emotionally and sexually, but less support for attempting a monogamous commitment.

Mark shares some of his struggle with betrayal:

> *At first, I couldn't believe what I read on his computer screen. How could I have missed it before? I hated him and wanted him to leave. I raged at him and told him I thought I had been better off before we met. How he could say he loved me and be doing this at the same time? I doubted everything he had ever said. What's worse, his sexual craziness played into my already low self-esteem. I knew I could never compete with the endless array of hot-bodied guys he had been viewing online and hooking up with. Sometimes I got angry with myself and doubted my worth as a partner. What was wrong with me that I wasn't enough for him? And how could I not have known what was going on, how stupid could I be? Why didn't I ask more questions, voice my doubts and concerns sooner? And then there are the health issues still to be determined. It may be months before the HIV status of either one of us becomes clear—and I didn't have sex with anyone else!*

Mark's painfully honest account of his experience points out some commonalties among all partners finding themselves in this situation, straight and gay. His feelings of disillusionment, uncertainty, and self-recrimination are all too familiar to any partner of a sex addict. Much as someone who suffers the death of a friend or parent, he questions whether he could have said or done more.

As in heterosexual partnerships, shame and embarrassment over the betrayal and the sexual nature of the problem often prevent partners from reaching out and getting the support they themselves need. This isolation only adds to their difficulties.

Frank, a forty-three-year-old gay man who contracted HIV from his unfaithful partner, offers this:

Where are you supposed to go when your lover has betrayed and violated you on every level? There's nothing in the "gay manual" about that. And it wasn't something I was going to talk to my brothers about or my co-workers. Especially since I had spent the better part of four years telling everyone how well things were going in my relationship and that, yes, gay men could be happy together over the long term. I didn't know who to talk to about this or where to turn. I felt like maybe it was my fault, maybe I hadn't been a good enough lover, and it embarrassed me that others might think that as well. Instead I got hungry for information. So I went out and read every book I could on the subject of betrayal and sex addiction. I wanted to understand the problem so that somehow I could fix it on my own, make it right for both of us.

Gay Men and Monogamy

While most committed or married heterosexual couples would consider any sexual or romantic interactions taking place outside of their relationships to be in violation of their commitment, this is not the case among all gay men. As stated, gay men tend to have greater acceptance of the alternative relationship and sexual choices, monogamy being only one of them. *Open relationships,* where casual sexual involvement with multiple partners is integrated into an existing committed partnership, is a lifestyle choice more readily integrated into homosexual relationships than heterosexual ones. For some, an open relationship offers a negotiated way to "have your cake and eat it too." Agreements for non-monogamy can occur at any point in a relationship or not at all.

Some male couples never seek monogamy, some evolve into monogamy as their intimacy deepens, and still others who have spent many years together may later choose to "open up" their relationship to sex with others in one form or another. Others might also choose to be open to romance and sex with others, but this choice leaves both more vulnerable to "falling in love" with someone else, thus having a greater potential for harm and eventual dissolution of the relationship.

Some gay men may choose differing forms of non-monogamy, not based solely on sex. For example, one couple might agree to have emotional monogamy—meaning no affairs, no romances with others—but be open to sex outside of the relationship; while others may chose to be open to both.

Non-monogamous relationships work best when both partners are comfortable with their relationship being "open" and when both agree to well-defined rules establishing clear boundaries of the sexual arrangement. Once this agreement is made, one or both are free to engage in whatever sexual situations they have settled on as long as the rules are respected.

Some styles of non-monogamous relationships include

- Either partner may have sex and/or romance with whomever they want outside of the relationship and agree not to discuss it.

- Either partner may engage in sex and/or romance with whomever they want outside of the relationship but are committed to discussing their experiences.

- A partner may only engage in sex with other people when both agree in advance on that specific person or situation.

- The couple only has sex outside the relationship when both partners are present (threesomes).

- Partners can only have sex with people already known to them.

- Partners agree to only have sex with anonymous strangers.

- Partners only have sex with someone else one time; no ongoing romances allowed.

- Partners who live apart are monogamous when together, and free to do as they wish when apart.

Gay couples may experiment with differing forms of non-monogamy, but problems are likely to develop if

- Each partner has a different understanding of the rules.

- One or the other lies or covers up his sexual activities.

- One partner becomes emotionally dependent on someone else.

- One or the other isn't fully in agreement with the plan or is just going along with it to "make a partner happy" or "keep the relationship." (A common occurrence for partners of sex addicts.)

Misunderstandings of this type breed resentment, hurt, jealousy, and the kind of bad feelings that can severely damage an otherwise functional relationship. Couples that attempt non-monogamy may later discover that it has created more issues than it resolved, and if there were relationship troubles prior to ending monogamy, there are likely to be even more problems on the horizon.

Unfortunately, it can be difficult to go back to monogamy once this particular door has been opened. Some sex addicts have tried the open-relationship route in an attempt to manage a sex addiction problem, but even when offered non-monogamous relationship choices, they still found themselves embroiled in lies and broken commitments. This helps to determine that an addiction problem may be present.

Unlike non-addicted men who can define a sexual boundary and stick to it, sex addicts are "powerless over their sexual behavior." Once they start down a road of recreational sexual behavior, they are unlikely to be able to control where it will end. In cases where a couple has attempted non-monogamy only to end up with broken promises, disregarded agreements, sexual secrets, or betrayal, it may be that

- Non-monogamy isn't really emotionally manageable for them regardless of how appealing it was in theory.

- Sex with outsiders has taken the place of having sex with each other.

- One or both partners has a sex addiction problem.

- One partner has a hidden agenda; for example, the desire to pursue an outside relationship.

- Non-monogamy was introduced as a last-ditch effort to revive a troubled or failing relationship, a situation most often doomed to failure.

If the couple's problem is sex addiction, non-monogamy will not likely be an option. *The absolute key to a successful open relationship is mutual trust.* If one partner has been found to be lying, keeping secrets, and otherwise violating the boundaries of a committed relationship, open or monogamous, then essential trust is broken and not easily regained. Without mutual trust and complete honesty, open relationships are likely to end up disintegrating into bitterness.

My partner entered recovery and now he wants me to get counseling. Why would I need treatment?

Many partners of sex addicts resent being asked to go to therapy. And why wouldn't they? After all, the person who broke his promises, withheld painful secrets, and sexually acted out is clearly the source of the problem, not the partner who ended up victimized by the situation.

And while it's true that the gay sex addict has a great deal of work to do in addressing his compulsive need for validation and self-soothing through sex, and he alone is fully responsible for the consequences of his behavior, many partners also have emotional issues that need to be addressed—concerns often more subtle than the obvious behaviors of the sex addict.

Sexual betrayal is a form of emotional trauma, whether experienced by a man or woman. Being betrayed by a partner or spouse by finding out about his or her "secret" sexual or romantic life, potentially being presented with health, financial, and other unanticipated problems, is bound to produce a shockwave of emotions in even the most well-adjusted man or woman. It is important for the partner of a sex addict to seek support and guidance in working through these types of emotional and real-life concerns. Important questions need to be resolved: issues such as whether you should continue to sleep with him, have sex with him, live with him, treatment options, and getting the right kind of help. Although the mess created by the sex addict is not of the partner's making, it is still a mess and both of you are living in it. Research also clearly indicates that couples with the best chance of healing their relationships over time are those where both partners are undergoing some form of counseling.

Some men unconsciously partner with people with addictive personalities due to their own underlying emotional issues. It's worth the time and effort to examine why this is, once the initial shock of betrayal has passed, even if you don't remain together. Some partners of addicts can at times appear selfless and kindhearted to all, while beneath the surface they struggle with powerful abandonment fears. Unconscious though these concerns may be, they do affect who is chosen as an intimate partner and how the relationship is carried out.

Some partners of sex addicts feel most comfortable when being depended upon and can go to great lengths to become indispensable to those around them. Typically unaware of their own deep lack of self-esteem, these men seek out circumstances that encourage them to be givers, a childlike role learned in chaotic, problematic, or emotionally neglectful families. Some learned early in life that the ability to give, be a peacemaker, and consistently attend to the happiness of others above themselves were essential survival tools. And while being a giving person is a positive attribute, these men often give without enough regard for their own self-care or end up giving much to those who have little to offer in return.

Characteristically, these men will give and do more for others than is actually healthy. They may be overburdened and over-committed. Their greater focus is to ensure the comfort of those around them at all costs, avoiding conflict or dissatisfaction from those they value. Divested of their own emotional and sometimes physical needs, they invest and pride themselves on "being there" for others, often without being aware of the deep anger and resentment that lies beneath the surface. The dark side of the partner appears in his expressions of his resentments and feelings of victimization. Using blame, nagging, sarcasm, criticism, and devaluing to express anger and disappointment, he leaves those around him feeling guilty, hurt, or shameful without a clear path to restore harmony.

Ultimately these partners become angry and disappointed with themselves as well, not liking how negative they have become, but with little understanding of how they got there. Some become overly dependent on food, compulsive exercise, overspending, or other potentially self-destructive behaviors to help soothe unmet needs and frustrations. These patterns can set up lifelong struggles with body image, weight, or finances.

Frank, speaking again about his experience, relates:

> *I was angry and started calling him every few hours to check up on him, and I also did a lot of what I call "detective work." I constantly was going through his wallet, receipts, credit card charges, journal, and computer history. I thought that if I could just know everything, then somehow I would know if it all was going to be okay or not. Eventually, I got tired of the whole thing being focused on him: his acting out, his emotional problems, his shame and embarrassment. What about my loss, my pain, my fear about the future? I got tired of asking him about his meetings, how his sobriety was going, and if we were going to be okay. I found myself becoming more critical and unpredictable, expressing my anger sideways through sarcasm, nagging, and emotionally withholding from him. I started to dislike myself. That's when I finally decided to get some help for me.*

More Than Anger

It's not unusual for couples experiencing an addiction problem in their relationship to have to face other dysfunctions as well. Along with sex and drug addiction, *domestic violence is one of the most prevalent and destructive problems among lesbians and gays.* In sharp contrast to the popular cultural misconceptions of gay men as being effeminate or nonaggressive, gay men can have difficulty expressing their anger and frustration, and can resort to physical expressions of their feelings. *Anyone has the right to feel extremely violated and angry with a partner or spouse, but hitting your lover or being hit by him is never acceptable.*

The law is quite clear about these issues, and those who do lash out physically—gay or straight—can be arrested if reported.

The potential for violence in these circumstances is not exclusive to gay men. Some heterosexual female partners, who may have had no tendency toward violence in the past, have become physically or otherwise abusive when presented with the trauma of sexual betrayal. When confronted with truths they don't wish to hear and the strong feelings that go along with them, some sex addicts can also become abusive. A traumatized partner, particularly one without help and support, can become abusive in ways that were previously uncharacteristic of him. This only highlights the importance of partners getting support and seeking professional help for themselves. Beyond physical violence, there are other ways to shame and frighten a partner that are equally unacceptable. Throwing and breaking things, pinning someone to a bed or wall, refusing to let someone leave by blocking a doorway, or stalking and following someone are all forms of intimidation that indicate a serious problem that needs immediate attention.

Verbally threatening to kill or hurt yourself or your partner or spouse when upset also warrants immediate help. *Relationship violence and threats of self-harm should not be ignored.* If this is happening, you should find a professional to speak with immediately. Most urban mental health centers, gay and lesbian community centers, and trained private therapists can help.

What is my next step?

If your trust has been betrayed, you're right to feel mistrustful, distant, hurt, and confused. For couples that choose to remain together, it can take up to a year or more before relationship trust will begin to be restored. In the meantime, the betrayed partner is stuck with an unwelcome mess of emotional fallout and other consequences. And, unfortunately, if the couple chooses, as most do, to work through this period and remain in the relationship, there are no guarantees that an addict partner is telling the whole truth, even if he's in therapy, treatment, or a Twelve Step group.

Left with uncertainty about a relationship's past, present, and future, you need to take healthful actions toward your own emotional self-care. This might include asking the addict to sleep in a separate room, move out for a while, or even take *a time-out* from the relationship.

During this stressful and painful time, partners or spouses must take concrete steps to focus on their own emotional and physical needs, and let the sex addict get much-needed help through Twelve Step support and therapy. Below are some trusted do's and don'ts guaranteed to put a healthy focus on your own healing.

Partner Do's:

Do get tested for STDs, and not just HIV. Most active sex addicts are careless with their own sexual health and the sexual health of their partners. Later, seeking to hide their behaviors, they deny, sometimes even to themselves, the health risks they've taken in their sexually addictive behavior. And HIV is not the only concern. Sex addicts are frequently exposed to a variety of diseases, including hepatitis, venereal warts (HPV), syphilis, gonorrhea, and herpes.

Once a sex addict has disclosed his sexual acting out, *even if he says that he was "always safe,"* it's best for both partners to be fully tested to ensure mutual physical health. Some STDs like HIV and other viruses have an incubation period before tests can detect them, so even a first-test clean bill of health means getting reevaluated in about four to six months.

Do investigate your legal rights, even if you planning to stay together. You need to know your rights in the areas of potential separation, financial concerns, and parenting if you have children. Gay spousal rights to property, alimony, and so on vary widely depending on the status and length of your relationship and where you live. You need to know where you stand. Those in legal domestic partnerships or with shared property have specific legal concerns to be addressed.

Finding an informed gay-sensitive family attorney and gathering this information is vital—whether you plan to leave or stay. Much of the needed information is also available online. A simple online search, for example by entering the terms *same-sex, domestic-partnership law, Texas* (or whatever state you live in), will likely take you where you need to go.

Do learn everything you can about sex addiction. Read, go to workshops, and look online for informative, useful material. Like the partner of an alcoholic, you need to learn the facts about your partner's addiction and the recovery process, not merely to educate yourself or to understand your spouse, but also to help make informed decisions about your own future. Treat sex addiction as if it were a physical illness and get informed!

Do reach out for help. Sometimes sexual issues feel too personal to share with family or friends. Many gay men much prefer to talk about their sexual and relationship successes rather than their problems. Nevertheless, getting support both from trusted loved ones and from a professional trained in sex treatment is invaluable. Whether or not you feel like you have your own issues to address, you need help simply because you are deeply involved with an addict. This journey requires a level of support that goes beyond the life experience of most people. Find out about and attend S-Anon, COSA, CODA, Al-Anon, or a private therapist's support group. Don't worry if the other members are gay or straight, male or female. As long as you're welcome, go! Remember, others have been through this and survived. Find out what they have to say.

Do explore your own sexual and relationship history. Sex addicts can come in pairs and there may be life issues here *for you* to address as well. Partner and spouses can also uncover times that they themselves acted out sexually, typically in an attempt to please a sexually addicted partner, to keep him from going out with other men, or to keep him from leaving.

By considering your own history, it's easier to understand how you might have ignored or mistrusted your own past feelings about the relationship, an act you don't want to repeat going forward. This is the time to get your own therapist if you don't already have one. Let this professional guide you and act as your support when looking at your own past.

Do let him know about your anger and hurt. It is never your job to protect your partner from your feelings. Be assured that by expressing your feelings, you're not punishing him or pushing him back into acting out. In fact, the more fully the sex addict comes to understand how his sexual behavior has affected you and others he cares for, the better it is for his own long-term healing and recovery.

Do get help to functionally express your feelings. You're hurt and angry and this must be let out for you to eventually move on. But an endless barrage of criticism, withholding, giving the silent treatment, or looking down on your partner ultimately won't help anyone heal. Either the sex addict is going to embrace honesty and sexual behavior change or he isn't. A constant vigil to prod him into health by reinforcing fear, shame, and guilt is likely to backfire.

Do take an active role in your own healing. The sex addict is either going to work on taking an active role in his own healing or he isn't. Regardless of his choices, you need care, love, and support. You need to talk about what has happened with compassionate friends and family, and you need a stable support network. Exercise, rest, take time off, see family and friends, and make sure to take care of you.

Do trust your feelings and observations. If the sex addict isn't getting help for his sexual behavior problems, isn't attending therapy, or isn't going to support groups, it would be unhealthy to believe things are getting better. His promises to change or stop mean very little, but his concrete actions toward change mean a lot.

Do request and expect a full disclosure of his sexual acting out if you feel you wish to know. You have a right to know what you have been kept in the dark about during the course of your relationship. You should expect a disclosure fairly early in the process that will put all past secrets on the table. This process should be done with a well-trained sex therapist who can organize and manage this difficult but necessary process.

Partner Don'ts:

Don't have sex with him without protection for at least a year—no matter what he says about his past activity or recent tests. It doesn't matter. Even if neither of you are HIV-positive, there are a host of other potential problems, like herpes and hepatitis C.

Don't use sex or romance to make him or you feel better. Some couples will seek instant sexual intensity or romantic honeymoons to restore intimacy in their relationships following the disclosure of a sex addict's problem. It's not unusual for couples that have been having relatively little sex to suddenly start having a lot of it following some disclosure of betrayal and sexual acting out.

While sexual intensity may feel good for the moment, providing each of you with some feeling of reassurance, using sex and intimacy in this way actually moves you further away from healing the deeper, more troubling issues. Using sexual intensity to fix a troubled relationship is a form of mutual denial that is bound to fail. It's healthier, though less comfortable, to engage in a relationship cooling-off period, agreeing not to cycle into any sexual or romantic intensity, while in the early stages of working through the betrayal.

Don't make long-term decisions in the beginning. Life-changing decisions may include choosing whether or not to break up or permanently change residences. Wait until you have more clarity about where things are headed. Make no major changes for the first six months of the recovery/healing process.

Don't hold yourself responsible if your spouse sexually acts out. If he wants to act out sexually, he will. Nothing you do makes him do this; he always has choices. No amount of hurt or frustration expressed by a betrayed partner makes him do anything. The addict is always responsible for how he chooses to handle his feelings.

Don't go on your own sexual binge to get even or prove yourself. This is likely to cause more hurt, betrayal, or secrecy and will only make things worse. Getting even never works or feels good over time and usually creates more problems than it solves.

Don't randomly speak with others about the sex addict's behavior or his problems to humiliate him. It's a necessary and important thing for you to get the help and support you need by telling your story to others. However, telling his mother, boss, or best friend about his sexual behavior to embarrass or humiliate him is likely to cause unnecessary heartache.

Don't make threats you don't intend to carry out. Threatening to leave him when you're angry, but then taking it back when you feel better, only serves to reduce your credibility. Freely express your hurt, anger, and despair, but it's best to not make threats at all—unless you are well prepared to carry them out.

Where do I go for help?

Despite the embarrassment a wife may feel when seeking guidance in working through marital betrayal, if she reaches out, she'll find more abundant emotional, therapeutic, and social support available to her than most gay men will find. Unfortunately, many gay partners have fewer available resources and are less likely to turn to the same sources for help as might a woman in a committed heterosexual partnership.

Some heterosexuals may turn to their faith for help with family problems, but despite the increasing number of religious or spiritual organizations that are inclusive of gays and lesbians, a legacy of ongoing prejudice makes it less likely that a gay partner would turn to a faith-based guide for help with male-male spousal betrayal.

Similarly, most gay men are unlikely to turn to an older parent or even a sibling for direction in these circumstances. Especially if—as in Mark's case in the beginning of this chapter—they have previously experienced rejection and a lack of support from those family members, who are uncomfortable with having a gay son or brother.

Psychotherapists of both sexes, who are trained to provide a safe, healing environment to those in emotional pain, may not be as willing or able to provide the same empathic emotional support to a partner suffering from broken trust in a male-male relationship as they might for a heterosexual one.

Many well-meaning professional therapists, gay and straight, may offer less helpful responses for some of the following reasons:

- The therapist, consciously or unconsciously, has difficulty acknowledging a male-male committed relationship as having the same emotional depth or meaning as a hetero-sexual marriage, thereby underestimating the intensity of a partner's loss.

- The therapist, mirroring a culture that doesn't support gay marriage or equal rights for gay male couples, may not engage the couple to stay together or encourage the partner to work in therapy with the same intensity and involvement as he or she would if the couple were heterosexual or legally married.

- The therapist with unresolved, uncomfortable feelings when discussing the romantic and sexual details of gay men may avoid or miss important details. And frank, honest sexual discussion is especially important when working with sex addicts and their partners.

- A well-meaning, but underinformed therapist can be misled by the sexually addicted patient who frames his sexual acting out as being "what gay men do" or "how gay men are."

- The therapist who holds an underlying belief that by being a gay man, you will inherently have sex and relationship problems may dismiss the partner's or spouse's expectations of fidelity or discount the reality of a sexual addiction problem.

- Gay therapists unfamiliar with sexual addiction assessment, diagnosis, and treatment methods may naively attempt to normalize the sexual acting out, thereby missing the problem altogether.

Ideally, the best setting for a sex addict's partner to get help is in the same place where the addict receives it, with a counselor or psychotherapist who supports gay rights and is trained in the treatment of addictive disorders and sex addiction. While you are well served by being in individual therapy, you should expect to have some involvement in your partner's treatment as well. His treatment and recovery process should not be a mystery or a secret.

You need to understand what his problem is about, along with how it affects your relationship as a couple. You need a place where his secrets will be honestly disclosed to you, along with a clear-cut plan for recovery. Perhaps most important, you need to hear what other partners just like you are going through. Thorough and thoughtful treatment for couples with sexual addiction problems will do the following:

- help educate you about sex
- provide couples therapy
- offer a disclosure process
- provide a partners' group where you and others can express your feelings and provide mutual support

Though it can be difficult to find all this in one treatment setting, well-developed outpatient sex programs are increasingly available in most large cities. See the Resource Guide on page 259 for a list of specific resources. The good news is that you don't have to limit yourself to groups focused solely on gay partners. In fact, sex treatment ideally mixes both gay and straight addicts together in the same therapy group. It's equally helpful to give gay and straight partners a chance to learn from each other.

This kind of setting brings you together with other men and women who share the same pain, loss, and confusion about their betrayals as you do about your partner. Groups like this are validating and offer you the chance to hear how similar your emotional experiences are to those of other people. You may be surprised how much you have in common with a wife of a sex addict, even though she may have been legally "married" and will likely have the support of church and family.

Interestingly, it also helpful for female spouses in a betrayal group to hear a man's perspective of sex, something they very much need to understand. One woman in a mixed spouses group put it this way:

> It wasn't until the gay guys joined our group that the women realized that men really do feel differently about sex than we do. Up until then I kept looking at my husband thinking, "How could you so casually separate sex and love? How can you tell me that your sexual encounters didn't mean anything to you when, for me, having sex always means being connected?" I was floored when some gay partners explained that they really did understand how sex could be casual in that way because they, too, at times had had sex like that.
>
> Yet seeing the gay spouse's sense of betrayal and violation, so similar to mine, surrounding the lies and secrecy of their sexually addicted partners, helped me realize that my husband's sexual behavior really wasn't about me at all. It helped me see that men in general are more able to separate sex and love than women are and that my husband's betrayal of me has more to do with his own willfulness, dishonesty, and double life than it had to do with any other woman in particular or with our sex life.

If therapy is just not for you, it's important to still consider finding support in other ways. There are many partners who have found needed answers and support by thoroughly reading about the addictive process and involving themselves in Twelve Step partner groups like Al-Anon, CODA, COSA, and S-Anon.

These support programs offer partners the same safe haven, fellowship, and direction as the Twelve Step sex programs SAA, SCA, SLAA, and SA offer to the sex addict. And though it may be a challenging step to get yourself to that first group or meeting, partners who stick with this process report that despite the crisis that initiated their attending, over time they themselves grew in unanticipated ways, becoming more like the men and women they had always wanted to be.

Chapter Twelve:
Straight Guise: Is My Partner Gay?

Joe Kort, MA, MSW, CSAT

∽∾

Ten years ago, tapping a key to bring the family computer to life, Diane, a forty-two-year-old Detroit bank teller, found herself staring at an image she came to wish she'd never seen. It was a photo of two men having sex. Checking the computer's history, she discovered this wasn't the only gay porn site someone in her family had visited, and someone had been cruising these sites for some time.

It had to be one of her sons—either Jason, thirteen, or Ryan, fifteen. She spent an anxious day waiting for her husband Mark, a forty-four-year-old real estate agent, to come home. Married for nineteen years, Diane and Mark were very close. They lived in a conservative Detroit suburb, were heavily involved with their sons' schools, and went to church each Sunday as a family. "It's probably Ryan, don't you think?" she asked Mark when they finally had a moment alone.

"Yes, you're right. It must be Ryan," Mark said.

Diane was devastated. "We have to see a therapist," she said. "I have no idea how to deal with this. I'm going to call someone tomorrow."

"Slow down," Mark said. "Let's not act too quickly."

But Diane couldn't wait. "I'm going to talk to Ryan about it."

"Not yet. That's not the best way to handle it," Mark replied. They went back and forth like this for days, talking about it every evening, usually ending up in a fight. Finally, when Diane could no longer take it, she told Mark that she was going to confront Ryan with what she knew. "You shouldn't do that," Mark said.

"You're always trying to stop me," Diane cried. "But not this time. I should have done this a week ago."

Only then, when he realized that his wife was a few moments away from confronting their older son, did Mark admit the truth: the photos were his.

Diane was too shocked to speak. In tears, Mark admitted he had been visiting gay chat rooms and porn sites for more than a year. Not only that—he'd met men through the Internet and had had multiple sexual encounters with other men. "But I'm not gay," he told her, insisting that these were only sexual encounters, that he had no emotional feelings or ties to any of the men he'd had sex with.

Diane was mortified. She wanted to know when all of this began. Though confused, Mark confessed that he'd always had fantasies of men orally pleasing him but never felt the need to act on it until last year when he began visiting gay chat rooms.

"Why then?" she asked. Mark said he didn't know.

By the end of their talk, Mark promised to get help—and he did. He began seeing a therapist and taking antidepressants. Together, they agreed that Mark had been depressed. They also agreed that Mark's difficult relationship with his father had left him seeking male affection through homosexual sex. But that did not mean he was gay. Mark also promised Diane that he would stop surfing the Internet and meeting men for sex. Mark kept his word—for a year. Then he found his way back to his favorite sites. Only this time, he used his work laptop, which Diane didn't have access to. In an online chat room, Mark met Steven. The two fell in romantic love, something Mark had never counted on. He became preoccupied with Steven, wanting to be with him all the time, thinking about him obsessively when they were apart.

Like many other closeted gay men, Mark finally realized he might be gay when he fell in romantic love with another man. This realization ignites the coming-out process, as Mark was discovering. But he wasn't quite ready to embrace that process just yet. Mark invited Steven to his home to meet Diane and introduced him as a friend. In doing this, Mark hoped that Diane wouldn't be suspicious about his whereabouts and activities.

But Diane knew something was going on, mostly because Steven didn't like her. When she mentioned this to Mark, he dismissed it. "You're imagining things," he said. This made her even more suspicious. She began checking Mark's cell phone and saw that he made many calls each night to Steven's number. Feeling tormented, she eventually called Steven and asked him what was happening. Steven told her everything. This revelation drew Diane and Mark to therapy. And only then did Diane find out the truth—that her husband had been cheating on her again.

"So you lied to me?" Diane exclaimed. She was in tears.

"You never asked," Mark responded. He was crying too, despondent over the thought of losing Diane.

"I didn't think I had to ask! You told me that it was a fluke thing and that it was over!" she cried.

"I thought I could manage the urges," Mark said quietly. He thought that if he kept it quiet enough, he'd never have to tell Diane about his true feelings. He didn't want to hurt her; he loved her. And he still didn't believe he was gay, only that he had homosexual urges. To Mark, "gay" was an affirmative identity, something that made you want to be in gay pride parades and tell the world who you are. That was never his experience. He was a happily married man with two kids and a successful career who simply felt compelled to have sexual relations with men.

Mark was also very much in love with Diane, which complicated his identity issues. *How could he be gay if he loved his wife? Maybe he was bisexual. Or maybe he just liked having sex with men.*

That rationalization had served him in the past, but no longer. He couldn't deny his love for Steven. Yet he'd never thought what it would mean to live the gay lifestyle or come out to his family and friends. Inside, he was mortified that he'd hurt his wife so deeply. He knew that he wanted the marriage to work. As he sat weeping, begging Diane's forgiveness, pleading with her to take him back, promising that he wouldn't act out homosexually again, something else very profound was happening: Mark was in the early stages of coming out as a gay man. Falling in love with Steven had only accelerated the process.

Over the months, it became clear to Mark that he was gay. He came to accept that he'd spent most of his life repressing his homosexuality. Now he felt enormous guilt for all he had done to his wife and to himself—not to mention his children. Mark insisted he didn't want to change his life. He loved Diane, their children, and their life together. They'd always had good sex. In fact, since Mark had decided not to pursue acting on his gay identity, sex had become even better, which confused them both even more.

Yet things were complicated. Diane was adamant that she didn't want to be married to a gay man who was sexually active in any way with men. Mark wanted to assure her that he could be sexually exclusive to her, but he could not make that promise. He began negotiating with her about using porn or going into chat rooms, but Diane said that was unacceptable. She was concerned that he'd start seeing men again. "I'm not going through this again," she protested. Eventually Mark and Steven broke up, but Mark and Diane also separated so that Mark could live as an "out" gay man. This was extremely difficult for both of them. Neither wanted to see their marriage end and both were very much in love with the other. But they couldn't find a way to make it work.

This case illustration is an example of a phenomenon that is increasingly common in our society. The shock and pain of discovering your husband is having sex with other men can be overwhelming. This relationship dynamic has become surprisingly common in recent years. Consider the following statistics:

- According to the Centers for Disease Control and Prevention, more than three million women are involved with men who secretly have sex with other men.[1]

- The Straight Spouse Network, a national organization with support groups for mixed-orientation couples, estimates that at least two million gay/bisexual people are married to straight partners. This figure also includes men married to lesbians.[2]

- According to the Family Pride Coalition, 20 percent of all gay men in America are in heterosexual marriages.[3]

- Additionally, a New York City survey found nearly one in ten men say they're straight and have sex with other men.

They also found that 70 percent of these straight-identified men having sex with men are married. In fact, 10 percent of all married men in this survey reported same-sex behavior during the past year.[4]

The research findings include the following:

- Straight-identified men who have sex with men reported fewer sex partners than gay men.

- Straight-identified men who have sex with men reported fewer STDs in the past year than gay men.

- Straight-identified men who have sex with men are less likely than gay men to report using a condom during their last sexual encounter.

This chapter will help the partners of these men, first by separating the two types of men: men who are gay and bisexual; and men who are heterosexual who seek sex with other men. The difference is one of sexual orientation versus sexual preference. It will also help women develop a deeper understanding of their partners' behaviors and recognize that it can have many meanings, and that it may not mean the relationship has to end.

What does it mean when men seek sex with other men?

Not all of men who have sex with men are gay—in fact many are not. There are many reasons men have sex with other men, only some of which have anything to do with homosexuality or bisexuality. These men will be called SMSM (Straight Men Who Have Sex with Men). Just because a man is sexual with a person of the same gender doesn't necessarily reflect sexual/romantic orientation. He can be heterosexual and enjoy the act of sex with another man. There is a difference between sexual identity, orientation, fantasies, and behavior.

It's not up to a therapist or a spouse to make the judgment whether an individual is gay or bisexual—it is up to each man to identify this for himself. Personal judgments and feelings too often enter into the marriage in a rush of reactivity and complicate the situation. What follows is men lying to and cheating on their wives rather than being able to talk it through. The shame of homosexuality causes these men to not even tell their therapists, so they work on it alone. Although the spouse may have difficulty honoring that this is an individual decision process, this is really the only course of action.

What are the differences?

There is a difference between sexual behavior, sexual fantasy, sexual orientation, and sexual preferences. How does one know ultimately whether he is heterosexual, gay, bisexual, SMSM, or something else? Sexual preference takes into account the desired actions and fantasies with a partner. Sexual orientation encompasses a sexual identity—with all the feelings, fantasies, and emotions that excite us sexually. Thus, there is a distinct difference between a gay man and a "male seeking male."

A gay man's sexual orientation is characterized by lasting aesthetic attraction to, romantic love of, and sexual attraction exclusively for his same gender. His sexual thoughts, fantasies, and behaviors are aligned exclusively or largely toward men. While some gay men can enjoy women as part of their sexual fantasies—even behaviors (for instance, being sexual with a woman while also with her husband)—they are mostly, if not totally, attracted to men. If a gay man were walking on the beach, he would notice only the half-naked men; he would not notice women in the same way.

On the other hand, an SMSM might consider sex with a man for sexual gratification. But at the seashore, he would be ogling women. He's a heterosexual who engages in sex with other men for a number of reasons. His same-gender sex acts arise to achieve physical release, not from attraction to or desire for other men. Many SMSMs are left cold, even turned off by images of naked men, but they get sexually aroused by women.

Often these men want to bond with—and get affection from—other men. Their behavior may also reflect a desire to experiment, or to express conflicts with their sexual feelings and desires, which have nothing to do with being gay. For SMSMs, same-sex encounters are not about romance or desire, but about sexual and physiological arousal with another who happens to be male. A discussion follows on the differences and similarities.

- A homosexual is a male who understands he is sexually attracted to other males and may or may not have some romantic interest in males as well but is not interested or has not yet come out of the closet toward gay-identity development. This man may never come out of the closet or may never act on his impulses. This man is not affirmative about his homosexuality, and if he does move in that direction, may not build a life around it.

- A gay man is a male who is sexually and romantically attracted to other men. He wants to and does develop his life to support his gay identity. He starts his identity development by self-identifying as *homosexual* but moves toward a positive and affirmative identity as *gay*. A gay man's sexual orientation is characterized by lasting aesthetic attraction to, romantic love of, and sexual attraction exclusively for others of the same gender. A gay man's sexual thoughts, fantasies, and behavior are aligned. It's an identity based on affection and emotional, spiritual, psychological, and sexual feelings exclusively or mostly toward men.

- A SMSM is a heterosexual male who has homoerotic and same-sex attractions to sexual behaviors with other men and who may or may not act on them. Again, he is not attracted to the man himself sexually or romantically, but only seeks sexual release. He doesn't have romantic interests in other men whatsoever. These men do not notice other men erotically; rather, they are sexually and romantically interested in women only.

- A bisexual male is a man who is sexually, emotionally, and romantically interested in other men and women. He may have a stronger desire toward one gender or the other, but understands his identity could go either way.

One's sexual preference takes into account the desired sexual actions and fantasies with a partner. Sexual orientation encompasses a sexual identity with all the thoughts, feelings, fantasies, and emotions that cause us to become sexually excited. Thus, there is a distinct difference between a gay man and a SMSM.

What are some reasons men have sex with other men?

Assessing all the possibilities, such as homo- or bisexuality, sexual addiction, bi-curiosity, homoeroticism, sexual abuse and more, will help you understand your situation. It's important to note that these categories are not mutually exclusive—some individuals may fall into more than one category.

Hetero-Emotional, but Homo-Sexual

These men are romantically attracted to women. Usually heterosexually married, they can be sexual with the women they love, but are predominately aroused and driven by desire for sex with other men—not romance. They see themselves as heterosexuals with only sexual interests in men.

Sex Workers/Male Escorts

These heterosexual men engage in sexual behavior mainly for financial reward. They lack desire for the other men and are aroused by the behavior, not the client.

Shame Seekers

These heterosexual men feel strongly compelled to seek intensely arousing but shameful experiences—dildo sex, bondage, and various sexual experiences and preferences that would typically be labeled as homosexual. To avoid having females identify them in this way, they seek out men whom they perceive as nonjudgmental.

Sexual Experimenters

Heterosexual boys often experiment with other males, usually during adolescence and up to age twenty-five, out of sheer curiosity. A heterosexual male might be interested—particularly while intoxicated—

to experiment sexually with another man. However, it is simply experimentation and may not happen again. When women experiment with other women, they may see the behavior as only experimentation—often for the arousal of heterosexual men. They are usually not labeled lesbians.

Sexual Addicts

"Gay" behavior can also result from sexual addiction. Sometimes the escalation of sexual behaviors can compel a man to be sexual with another man for another level of his "sexual high" or to provide him with a sexual opportunity because he is so driven to act on his urges.

Opportunists

These straight men have high sex drives and are aroused easily. They connect with men for quick and easy release, avoiding emotional engagement. Heterosexual patients tell me they have done this to avoid having to "wine and dine" a female partner who they perceive won't provide sex without a relational experience, whereas most gay men will. This is not a comment on homosexuality as much as it is about males, as this kind of "quickie, anonymous" sex does not occur with lesbians like it does with gay men.

Father-Hunters

These heterosexual men lacked affection and attention from their fathers, and now seek sex with men as a way of finding that nurturance and male acceptance. These clients will often admit the sex was not enjoyable—and certainly not as enjoyable as with women. They wished they could have sat, talked, and just be held by the man they hooked up with. It's an attempt to satisfy their "father hunger."

Narcissists

These self-absorbed straight men have a constant need for attention and acceptance. They use sex as a lure to be worshipped and adored. Here it is not about the other man; it's about an experience for himself using the other man for his own sexual gratification.

Dominants/Submissives

Sometimes during the practice of bondage and sadomaso-chism, there is erotic play between two men. Occasionally it is with women present. Sometimes it's about availability, where a man wants to act out his fantasies and women are not interested or around.

Cuckolds

These are men who enjoy fantasies of—or the reality of—their wives or girlfriends having sex with other men in front of them. The proximity of the sexual experiences can be close up or far away, as long as they have the knowledge of where and when it's occurring. They're often sexually aroused by feeling humiliated that their female partners are being pleased by another male whom they see as more potent or better endowed. Cuckolds are also men who enjoy being sexual with other men's wives in front of the husband. Both of these scenarios may also include sexual contact with the man but only in the presence of the wife or girlfriend.

Homosexually Imprinted

If a heterosexual boy is molested by a male, he may keep reenacting the sexual abuse to defuse and desensitize his emotional pain. If unresolved, this may occur into adulthood. When his original trauma clears up, he may stop reenacting his molestation. At first glance, these men appear to be in early denial about their homosexuality. As a result, many clinicians reassure clients that once their sexual abuse issues are resolved, their same-sex behaviors may evaporate. But this doesn't always happen, particularly if the client is innately gay, lesbian, or bisexual.

Again, homosexual behavior doesn't mean the man is gay or even bisexual. He can simply be left with an imprint to reenact his abuse and find "pleasure" in what was inflicted on him as a child. This really isn't pleasure at all, but trauma turned into orgasm. In their book *Male Victims of Same-Sex Abuse: Addressing Their Sexual Response*, John M. Preble and A. Nicholas Groth write:

> *This may actually reflect an effort at mastery of the traumatic event…When he was being sexually victimized, someone else*

was in control of him sexually. During masturbation he is literally in control of himself sexually, and this may be a way in which he attempts to reclaim mastery over his own sexuality. Likewise, his participation in consensual sex reflects his choice and decision.[5]

The authors go on to say that "the fantasy thoughts are prompted by fear more than desire, by anxiety more than pleasure." In other words, they become a way of managing fear and anxiety.

SMSMs who suffered childhood sexual abuse that may have caused homosexual-behavioral imprinting may have strong, recurring same-sex fantasies and behaviors that may indicate a deeper social or sexual need. American culture doesn't give permission for men to touch or have affectionate feelings for one another. Oddly enough, sexual contact can become the only way men can display affection for one another and keep it a secret to avoid being shamed by others.

When men are struggling with their sexuality, they're looking for answers about whether they are gay, bisexual, or straight. They're usually hoping a therapist will detect something in them that's worth preserving and encouraging, saving any hope of heterosexuality. Typically, such men are at the questioning stage about their sexuality and are trying to find explanations for what they're thinking, doing, and feeling. In fact, there can be many answers that don't involve the client being gay or bisexual at all.

What is erotic intelligence?

Emotional intelligence has become an increasingly popular term to help people improve performance in the workplace and in educational settings. Employers and teachers recognize that emotional intelligence plays a role in understanding people. Similarly, *erotic intelligence*—what men and women do and fantasize about sexually—reveals quite a bit about them. Your sexual fantasies are a result of your psychological makeup. Your libido is not separate from who you are. In fact, much of one's identity is embedded in his or her erotic life. Just as you can tell much about people from the friends they keep, so you can tell a lot about anyone by understanding his or her sexual desires.

SMSM's arousal templates have prompted them to be sexually drawn to encounters with other men. Erotic intelligence is not so much about sex, but it is expressed through sex. One's childhood and past experiences become linked and embedded in one's arousal template through sexual fantasies, desires, and behaviors.

An arousal template is what turns us on sexually, whether it's role-playing, fantasy, or sexual positions. Our love and sexual-preference "map" is determined during childhood. At this stage, we're imprinted with family beliefs and societal norms. Imprinting is the psychological process through which specific types of behavior are locked in at an early stage of development. All of us, gay and straight alike, are conditioned to think, feel, and act the way our early childhood caretakers nurtured and taught us. We observe and internalize how others love us, neglect, or abuse us.

Here is where it's crucial to differentiate sexual orientation and sexual preferences. Sexual mapping and imprinting shapes sexual preferences, not sexual orientation. There are those who believe that one's sexual orientation—how one self-identifies in terms of gay, straight, bisexual—is learned in childhood. In reality, we are born with our sexual orientation and our preferences are learned.

These arousal templates are about more than just love: They enter our erotic minds as well. But most people—male and female, gay and straight—don't need to examine their sexual behaviors and fantasies that aren't interfering with their lives. As a result, they have healthy sexual behaviors and can relate well with sexual partners.

Why did I marry a gay man?

You may be asking yourself, *How could I not know?* Some women, consciously or unconsciously, gravitate toward gay men or SMSMs. This happens for a variety of reasons—most of which are unconscious and subtle. While there are many women who knowingly marry gays or SMSMs, the majority have no conscious awareness of this. Some women in this situation find themselves in a disempowered position, allowing their spouse to continue his behavior and feel unworthy and powerless to confront it even after they realize it has happened.

You may be unconsciously drawn to men who might betray you. Perhaps while growing up, you experienced lies and witnessed emotional boundary violations that remained unresolved and left you traumatized. Perhaps there was infidelity in your family of origin. This could turn you into a partner who unconsciously seeks a "familiar" man who violates your trust all over again. Some women are drawn to men who aren't anything like their macho, patriarchal, abusive fathers in the hope that their partners will not sexually or otherwise overpower them.

Another common reason women marry men with sexual interests in other men is the desire for sexual and emotional distance within the relationship. You may have sexual issues yourself that have not been addressed and are attracted to men in similar situations. It's so ingrained in women to not explore their own sexuality and fend off the predatory nature of most heterosexual men that there's a tendency to lack awareness of their male partners' sexuality as well.

For many partners there's an underlying psychological process at work that deserves investigation. While straight spouses might not have consciously known their partners were gay, it's not an accident, for example, that these spouses married people who couldn't completely commit or be intimate and available to them as a straight spouse could have been. No matter what the case, it's normal to feel genuine love for your spouse and vice versa. Despite the initial reasons for their attraction, it's important to stress that most of these marriages are built on love.

What does my family history have to do with this?

There may be issues in your family that laid the foundation for you to select a partner who is gay. For example, you may have been wounded and traumatized by your father. Perhaps he was abusive emotionally, sexually, or physically; had affairs; or was neglectful. You may have decided, consciously or not, to minimize or block any type of sexism or form of abuse coming your way. Or on the opposite extreme, you married a man whose sexual power is distant or troubled, or he may be a sex addict or have a problem with impotence, or be a gay man struggling to squelch his homosexual impulses. This might be your way of protecting yourself from straight men's sexual aggression. Gay men will make women like this feel safe, especially if sex is kept to a minimum. Most often the reasons for choosing a gay partner stem from dependency needs and fears of being vulnerable. Women who surround themselves with gay men always say they appreciate not feeling judged as harshly as they are by straight men.

Another reason straight women marry gay men is because, in general, gay men tend to honor women for who they are. With less sexual tension between them, gay husbands can be more sensitive to their wives' needs and be willing to overlook physical distractions, such as weight and appearance, that straight men might not. This may be a welcome relief for a woman shunned or rejected sexually or romantically by straight men.

So why do straight spouses stay in relationships with gay or lesbian partners? When these straight spouses look back, most will say they picked up signs that something was missing from their gay spouses, but they paid little attention. They will admit there were times when they began to wonder about certain things that were happening—or not happening—in their marriages. Straight spouses might make excuses for the red flags they noticed in the past. For example, you may have realized your partner was less gender-conforming than other men or women. Denying these warning signs is how someone can unconsciously maintain a distant, low-intimacy relationship with his or her partner throughout the relationship. One straight male client who discovered he had a lesbian wife said,

> *I had no idea. My friends and I felt as if I had died and gone to heaven to have a wife so interested in sports. She would watch more football than me and could kick my butt at basketball. I loved it!*

He never attributed his wife's interests to the possibility that she was a lesbian. Instead he believed he had found a woman who shared his passion for sports. He reported that she always had gay and lesbian friends and he considered her open-minded.

Understandably, straight spouses will usually deny their own personal stories, particularly at first. Feeling hurt and betrayed, they blame the gay spouse. The initial revelation only aggravates the feelings of betrayal. This is hardly the time for the straight spouse to examine his or her part in the drama. But over time, these straight men and women are often able to make sense of their actions and understand why they chose to marry gay spouses.

Less is written and known about the men who marry lesbians or bisexual women. Some men in this situation might like that their wives occasionally enjoy sex with women, finding it erotic, and they may not equate it with lesbianism.

Some straight spouses may have been sexually abused themselves, which influences them to marry someone with similar sexual problems. In other words, if you have been sexually abused, you may be struggling with your own sexual conflicts about the unresolved abuse. Consequently, you may unconsciously look for someone who is also struggling with sexual conflicts. Author Dr. Patrick Carnes's research with sex addicts shows a high incidence of sexual abuse in the history of both partners.[6] Understanding sexual abuse in your past and determining if this abuse influenced you to marry a gay or lesbian partner can help you understand how your past impacted your choice of a mate.

Why do gay men marry straight women?

While some women find themselves in relationships with SMSMs and can salvage those relationships, others end up in relationships with men who, over time, discover that they truly are gay and want to build a life with another man, as in the case example of Diane and Mark. If your spouse has begun to come out or identify himself as gay, you may be wondering, *Why didn't he discover this sooner, before getting married?*

Homosexuality is still, by and large, stigmatized. Young people often don't feel comfortable exploring anything but heterosexuality. Thus, it makes sense that gay men and lesbians marry heterosexually, both for conformity's sake and because this type of relationship is all they've ever known. Either they hope their urges will go away or, more often, they're genuinely unaware they're even attracted to their own gender. If these men are aware of their same-sex attractions, they would not label it as gay but "kinky," and not self-identify as gay. Most of them truly love the women they fall in love with and marry. They want children and the American dream.

Some gay men will marry a woman who will take care of them, to bond with a mother figure; as a cover for their gay activities; or in hope that straight sex will "cure" their desire for men—or at least keep that desire strictly sexual. However, there are many negative psychological consequences to staying in the closet while married, for both the gay and straight spouse, such as decreased sexual fulfillment and reduced intimacy.

Paradoxically, some husbands act out in addictive ways to avoid dealing with their gay identity. Like drinking too much, sex becomes their way of evading the issue. It also serves the same function as any other time-consuming addiction: a way of burning off extra energy that might otherwise lead to introspection. They may make excuses—which many men may actually believe—including, *"I'm just doing research for a novel," "It's an assignment for my art class in anatomy,"* or *"A friend at work is gay, so I was curious."* On the other hand, some men become flatly asexual. Still others distract themselves from sex by throwing themselves into sports, work, or hobbies to suppress unwanted impulses.

Often, these men have no one to confide in, not even a priest, minister, or rabbi. They have difficulty finding comfort in organized religion and support groups like AA, as struggling straight people would. Without anyone to help them articulate their innermost feelings, these feelings and fears stay bottled up inside, impeding the coming-out process.

Before they consider being honest with themselves and their wives, gay men typically want to have their cake and eat it too, believing they can keep a wife and a boyfriend while keeping quiet about the latter. They change the definition of what they're doing, from cheating to "not wanting to hurt her." Arrangements like the so-called closed-loop clubs, where the boyfriend knows about the wife but she doesn't know about him, damage both relationships and are nothing but a recipe for disaster.

Changing behavior is possible; changing orientation is not. For some men, the process is gradual and may take many years. As in the case of Mark and Diane, some men don't recognize they might be gay until they fall in romantic love with another man. Given this, it might take years before he knows for sure whether he is gay and wants to come out. Unfortunately, this process is usually done privately, completely unbeknownst to the female partner.

How can I come to terms with disclosure?

Many straight spouses react to the news that their partner is gay by going into the very closet their gay spouse is in the process of leaving. Once they acknowledge they knew or suspected on some level their spouse was gay, they then have to deal with their own denial or, in some cases, their secret homophobia. Other straight spouses feel embarrassed, cheated, fooled. They worry about being judged by others. They're not sure how to move forward—who to tell, how to tell them, and when to tell. Some straight spouses grow enraged and bitter, never to examine themselves and the situation from any other point of view. Instead, they turn their kids against their gay ex.

Often the straight spouse struggles with feelings that he or she could have been more of a "man/woman" for the gay/lesbian spouse in order to keep the marriage together. It's important to know that this isn't the issue; the split has nothing to do with one's performance as a spouse. As a matter of fact, the truth is that your gay partner's sexuality has nothing at all to do with you. You simply married a partner with sexual conflicts.

On some level, I feel as though this is my fault. How do I keep from blaming myself?

Sexual acting out, straight or gay, often results from one or both partners' inability to achieve and keep intimacy. While these factors affect many heterosexual marriages, frequently the SMSM's motive for "straying" is to explore his true identity and reveal it to himself. SMSMs typically cheat or act out because they're repressing part of themselves. Their conflict is about their "identity," not about their ability to love and bond with their partner. It is not the result of marital problems.

Sometimes the woman feels as though she did something to cause her partner to seek out affairs with men. As readily as she claims total responsibility for the state of her relationship, her SMSM partner is willing to blame her as well, often claiming that she wasn't responsive to his needs. Once both partners understand the acting out is probably about issues of identity, not dissatisfaction, and once the man begins treating his female partner as a partner rather than as an adversary, they can begin to resolve their relationship. Both partners need to understand that neither gay partners nor straight partners are 100 percent responsible for the crisis in the marriage.

Now that I know, where do I go from here?

Some straight spouses want to stay married, even if they feel embittered and betrayed. Often, this only perpetuates a bad situation. If you find yourself in this situation, examine your reasons for staying and any possible underlying dependency issues. Sometimes the fear of being alone can be overwhelming. It might be helpful to consider your reasons with a nurturing therapist who can help you question some of these very painful issues.

Some straight spouses, however, feel relieved. They may have blamed themselves for the problems in their marriage—especially sexual problems—only to now realize that they were not at fault. Others are happy to feel released from having a sexual relationship with their spouse and grateful to enjoy a continuing emotional relationship.

Society typically supports the "betrayed" ex-wife and blames gay men for marrying in the first place. You may find this is initially comforting when you are hurt and angry. However, it can also perpetuate feelings of victimization. It represents tremendous growth for a spouse in this situation to move from blaming to examining her role in the situation. Healing involves moving from victimization to empowerment.

This chapter will help partners of men who have sex with men understand that such infidelity means something different than in "traditional" marriages. In marriages when both partners are straight, an affair can be an expression of a problematic marriage as well as hostility toward the spouse. In couples where the male partner seeks sex with other males, on the other hand, the adultery is often about the man's personal identity and can have little to do with the health of the marriage. The roots of these behaviors are more complex than simply gay-versus-straight, homosexual-versus-heterosexual. A man does not always need to make a choice between the two; it's possible to reconcile a gay arousal template with a heterosexual identity. Determining if the sexual acting out is about orientation, opportunity, sexual abuse, or addiction is critical to understanding these men and these couples.

Mixed-orientation marriages—where one spouse is gay and the other is straight—and marriages where men are discovered to be sexual with men frequently end in divorce. Yet these marriages do not have to end. It demands the willingness of both partners to communicate calmly and effectively about the sexual behaviors and understand what it means. Only then can they decide how to proceed with the marriage. Some of these relationships can be salvaged and eventually turn into vital and successful partnerships.

Chapter Thirteen:
I Have Decided to Go. What Do I Need to Know?

Caroline Smith, CSAT-S
Stefanie Carnes, PhD, CSAT-S

ℰᏆᏟᏜ

You have most likely made this decision after much soul searching, wisdom seeking, and painful deliberation. Most partners betrayed by a partner or spouse have never imagined being in such a position. The decision to leave is enormous, but it is only one of the many you will be required to make. This chapter was written to provide you with practical "need to know" information on what to do and what *not* to do after making the decision to leave your partner.

You may be comforted to know that others have struggled with some of the same issues that you are dealing with now. Consider the situation between Ken and Barbie. While their story is most likely not similar to yours, you may nonetheless relate to certain aspects of it. The following story of a sex addict, Ken, and his wife, Barbie, illustrate the many struggles found in relationships besieged with sex addiction. See if you can identify with any of the warning signs Ken and Barbie probably missed while living out the painful drama created when active addiction is an uninvited third party in a relationship. While reading this story, you may even identify with some similar themes.

Ken and Barbie met in college. Ken was a dashing upper-classman and Barbie was a naive freshman. They fell instantly in love, so instantly, in fact, that after dating just one month, they became engaged. Ken finished college and took a job as an assistant minister at a large church. Barbie, being the dutiful wife that her mother had instructed her to be, left college, moved with Ken to his new church assignment, and went about creating their own family. Barbie soon found that she was expecting their first child.

227

During this time, Barbie tried to create a happy life but became increasingly sad and confused. Ever since their wedding, Ken seemed to be distancing himself from Barbie. He wanted sex a lot, but would not be intimate, caring, or close. Life with all of its complexities went on, so Barbie tried to rationalize that if she just tried harder to make Ken happy, all would be well. When some of the teen girls in the church complained to their parents that Ken had been flirting with them, Ken left the ministry denying any wrongdoing. Since Barbie was expecting their second child, this incident was soon forgotten.

After a few failed attempts at other occupations, Ken finally found a career he was good at—sales. He joined a large firm, quickly became their top salesperson, and was consequently promoted to management where he was making about $500,000 annually. Every now and then, Barbie heard rumors from other wives that Ken was seeing other dolls. When confronted, Ken blew up at Barbie, telling her she was crazy. Barbie began to think that maybe she was crazy.

Ken and Barbie's family looked perfect from the outside. Their children attended the best private international school money could buy. They took annual ski trips to the Swiss Alps, vacationed on safari in Africa, swam in the Dead Sea of Israel, took shopping trips to London, Rome, and Paris, and lived on the greens of an exclusive private country club. Ken drove the latest and most expensive Mercedes, wore thousand dollar suits, and had a private masseuse and sports trainer. Everyone loved Ken, and Ken loved everyone, especially women.

However, Ken was becoming increasingly distant from his family. Barbie bought into Ken's comments that she was no longer very attractive. So trying desperately to regain Ken's interest, she underwent some "surgery on her plastic." But not even those drastic attempts to please Ken made any difference. Barbie resigned herself to being a good mother, playing tennis well, and hosting exquisite dinner parties for her country club friends.

Barbie made Ken look good in business and social situations. In turn, Ken provided extremely well financially for the family. Barbie knew something was missing in her marriage and even convinced Ken to go to marriage counseling with her. Ken agreed to see a therapist on one condition—that Barbie would not say anything negative about him to the therapist. That attempt at marriage therapy failed miserably.

On her fortieth birthday, Ken threw a huge party for Barbie; he even surprised Barbie with a long-distance special guest—her sister who also was her best friend. At dinner, he gave Barbie a birthday gift, a piece of jewelry worth over $20,000. The party was magnificent and the gift was amazing. Barbie felt sure that she must still have a place in Ken's heart. However, all that changed just one week after the surprise birthday party. Seemingly out of the blue, Ken asked Barbie if they could still be friends if they divorced. He then proceeded to tell her that he had fallen in love with another woman and added that he probably never had really loved her to begin with.

Understandably, Barbie was devastated. She called her sister and poured out her anguish and disbelief. Barbie was desperate to try and work things out. She lost eighteen pounds in one month off her already slim figure. She cooked Ken's favorite meals, kept the house spotless, tried not to cry in front of Ken, and took Xanax to keep going. Ken would not tell her who the other woman was; he only said that he was having the best sex he had ever had and that he believed this woman when she told him that she could make him happier than Barbie ever could.

To Barbie's extreme horror, she discovered the person her husband was having an affair with was, in fact, her own beloved sister. Barbie wanted to die. She prayed that God would kill her. She didn't want to commit suicide and leave that legacy for her kids, but she saw absolutely no reason to go on living. As it turns out, God did not want Barbie in Toyland just yet. Instead, he wanted to gently guide her into her own recovery from the devastation of her husband's betrayal and her own self-defeating behaviors.

Barbie came to realize that even if she were Marilyn Monroe and Mother Teresa rolled into one, it still would not have been enough to keep Ken from his addictive behaviors. Barbie found out that it is useless to think you can be stronger than someone's addiction. She learned to "detach in love." At one point, Ken suggested that Barbie have an affair of her own. So she did. She chose to have an affair with herself, to discover who she really was, to provide for and cherish herself. After years of pain and struggle, Barbie decided to file for a divorce. There was so much she needed to know . . .

The word *divorce* comes from the Latin word *divortium* or *divertere* meaning to divert. The *American Heritage Dictionary* defines the word divert as: "To turn aside from a course or direction." When someone has finally made the decision to go, that person has "turned aside from one course or direction" and is now choosing a new course and a new direction. This new direction often requires finding resilient ways of surviving and moving beyond the unthinkable wreckage of the past, embracing enhanced opportunities for self-discovery, and creatively constructing a new life rich with meaning and purpose.

No matter how you came to the decision to leave, you went through three different phases before you got there. For some, this three-phase process may have taken years. For others, it may have been just a few days. As you move forward, it is helpful to put a name to each of the three phases that you experienced before leaving your relationship. Here are the three phases:

Phase one: Denial. This is the time period leading up to the moment when you really contemplate leaving. This phase is marked by attempts to ignore the problems in the relationship. This phase can last months or many years depending on the risks associated with leaving. Risks such as financial insecurity or pain to the children often lengthen this denial stage. In Barbie's situation, she was in denial about the teenage girls at the church and later the women her husband worked with.

Phase two: Deliberation. After moving from the denial stage, the partner begins to move into the deliberation phase. It is a stressful and anxiety-ridden phase; it is critical at this time to obtain support from others. Oftentimes, when partners evaluate risks, they overinflate the risks due to a sense of paralyzing fear and dread. Many partners who chose to leave did so when they could see either that the addict was not serious about recovery or they recognized that the relationship was unsalvageable. Barbie participated in this phase when she spoke with her sister about her husband's behavior, asked her husband about the affairs, and attempted to mend the relationship through marriage counseling.

Phase three: Decision. The root of the word *decision* comes from the Latin word for *incision* or cutting away. When we make a decision, we often have to let go of something, and that is why it can be so difficult. Facing this can feel insurmountable at times, yet you may know at some level that facing the pain, grieving, and moving on will be better for you in the long run than hanging on to a relationship that has no future and is unhealthy for you. We have a right and responsibility to take action, to create emotional safety for ourselves and our children too, if they are involved. Over time, you will likely realize that many of the concerns you had about leaving the relationship were challenges that you needed to face and could conquer.

Where do I start?

A simple list of "do's and don'ts" will at least give you a place to start as you begin to make some positive changes in your life.

DO

Do obtain professional divorce representation.

Do find a therapist and attend therapy sessions.

Do take care of yourself physically, emotionally, and spiritually.

Do show your anger in appropriate ways.

DON'T

Don't share with your children.

Don't bad-mouth your partner in public.

Don't make the addiction about you.

Don't jump into another relationship right away.

Don't use alcohol, drugs, or food to replace your lost relationship.

Do obtain professional divorce representation

Divorce can be a blessing that helps you move forward with your life; however, it can also be an emotionally and mentally taxing process. It's good to ask for help when you need it. Hiring an experienced attorney who specializes in divorce is a good first step to piecing your life back together. Take the time to find an attorney whom you can trust and feel comfortable with. Ask divorced people whom you respect about the attorneys they hired and what their experience was like. In addition to the emotional impact of divorce, there are usually huge financial implications too. Getting a divorce involves a great deal of paperwork, so begin organizing your finances, legal papers, and receipts right away.

If you have children, a divorce can become even more complicated. You may want to keep the sex addict away from the children by seeking full custody and supervised visits. Many partners worry that the sex addict will be a poor influence on the children, expose them to sexualized material prematurely, or worse, actually sexualize the children themselves. It will be important to thoroughly discuss this issue with a qualified therapist and seek an evaluation for the addict if possible. Many sex addicts, especially those in recovery, do not pose a risk to their children. It is important to consider that the children will also suffer if kept away from their parent. Of course, if the addict poses a true risk to the children, then seeking supervised visits is appropriate. Again, seek support and advice from a skilled therapist to try to tease out these complex and difficult issues.

Do find a therapist and attend therapy sessions

Most humans are born with a desire to be intimately known and accepted. However, if we fail to understand the underlying fear that causes us to run from emotional intimacy, we are doomed to create future relationships that mirror our past relationships. To put it simply, if nothing changes, nothing changes.

Find a therapist who specializes in treating sex addicts and their partners. Even if you are not in couple's therapy, choosing a therapist who has expertise in this area will be beneficial. If you have children, you will want to find a family therapist they can talk to as well. Being involved in a therapeutic process to review our own role in our past relationship can be an important part of the healing process. As long as we are breathing, we have the capacity to change. Our brains are like wet cement—we can make fundamental changes. The cement is not "set" until we breathe our final breath.

Through therapy you can begin achieving balance in your life and fostering self-care. If you don't come to your own assistance to take care of yourself, your health, and your financial life, nobody will do it for you. You will find you will go from a difficult situation to something worse, compounded by your own self-defeating behaviors. This is the time to put on your game face and rise to the occasion to take care of you! Here are some things to consider in therapy:

- Take your past relationship wounding as seriously as you would cancer. Recovery will take time, energy, and resources. Become willing to go to any lengths to recover.

- Begin to channel the energy and effort that was formerly spent on trying to change someone else and spend it instead on understanding and changing yourself.

- Change your self-talk. If we want to experience meaningful change, we must listen to what we say to ourselves. If faulty thinking or cognitive distortions are present (which they certainly are), we must go through the challenging process of changing our thinking. This is important because our thoughts influence our feelings and our feelings impact our choices. If we wait until we feel differently, we will never change or fully recover.

- Recovery from a broken relationship is demanding mental and emotional work that requires that we surrender old and often dearly held beliefs. We may be tempted to hold on to feelings of resentment, self-righteousness, and/or piety. None of these feelings are constructive to our well-being and, if left unchecked, these beliefs can actually impede our growth and thwart our goal of self-discovery.

- When we struggle to detach from dishonest, exploitive, and dysfunctional relationships, it can indicate that we are subconsciously attempting to work through old unresolved wounds. For example, you may have been in an exploitive relationship as a child and are repeating that dynamic in your adult relationships. By holding on, you may be attempting to gain mastery over the past. When these old wounds are triggered, it may cause intense anger, reactivity, shame, fear of rejection and abandonment, loneliness, guilt, or pain. The thought of fully detaching from our ex-partner can feel like we are forfeiting a uniquely valuable opportunity to finally obtain that which has always been missing.

- No relationship can save us from our past wounds. Until we acknowledge the pain, shame, fear, and loneliness of our past and become willing to walk through all of our emotions without mood altering drugs, we will simply repeat our history.

- Life has a way of persistently presenting our lessons until we learn what we need to learn. To facilitate this experience, we will continue to encounter others who will embody the opportunity for us to learn our most imperative lessons. Therefore, we can become grateful for all those people who have been our teachers.

- When we experience gratitude for our lessons, our affirmations will reflect our desire for spiritual guidance and growth rather than self-willed demands.

Most of the insanity and despair we experience comes directly from trying to manage and control what we cannot. Serenity is achieved when we accept the reality of a situation and let go of our misguided attempts to control.

Do take care of yourself physically, emotionally, and spiritually

Take some time to take care of your needs, discover yourself, accept your situation, and do some soul searching. What that will look like for you depends on your individual situation. Start loving yourself enough to say no to others so you can say yes to yourself. Be selective about where you spend your time and energy. Start a relationship with yourself; discover who you really are and what makes you truly happy.

Do show your anger in appropriate ways

The anger we experience, as startling and frightening as it is, does bring us a treasured gift. The gift of anger is additional energy and determination. It helps our self-esteem when we spend this energy, the by-product of our anger, on making the changes that enhance our own recovery. Don't waste your anger with rage or resentment, but rather use it to come to your own assistance and to honor this new chapter in your life.

Anger usually peaks once we begin to fully grasp the reality of the betrayal and the overwhelmingly complex issues now facing us. A common reaction to betrayal is bitterness, jealousy, and resentment. When we continue to ride on the raft of these emotions, we do not allow ourselves to move on. We may physically leave but emotionally we stay behind. Hate bonds us to the other person. We have a choice to make: we can choose to be bitter or we can choose to let go and get better. Jealousy is victim anger; we feel angry and helpless when we value something and sense that we may be losing that which we value. We are indeed powerless over other people, their choices, and their behaviors. Resentment has been defined as "anger in a party dress" but it's not pretty. Bitterness, jealousy, and resentment are not enjoyable emotions, and if entertained they will stay.

The process of leaving is about leaving both physically and emotionally. Your goal is to actually leave once you have left. Many people have been physically divorced for many years but have not found a way to divorce emotionally. Do you secretly hope your former partner will be miserable, that your children will despise him or her, or that he or she will want you back, beg for your forgiveness, and plead for reconciliation? One indication of healing is that you rarely find yourself thinking about this person, and if you do, it is with all mental sincerity that you wish him or her well in creating a new life, one without you. When we continue to hate or strongly dislike someone, we are giving that person our power and serenity. We are inviting the individuals to shape our future for us.

If we have decided to leave, we owe it to ourselves to actually leave. This does not imply that we should not be angry. Anger is a gift if used wisely. It gives us the energy needed to make change. Rage, on the other hand, is not an expression of anger; it is a volcanic eruption of shame and frustration. Rage brings a temporary feeling of power and intensity, but if you give in to it, you will be left with collateral damage and an emotional hangover. Jealousy, bitterness, and resentment are ways we internally rage against ourselves. Letting go of the past is a gift given to ourselves.

Don't share with your children

No matter what the situation is, your partner is still the parent of your children. If you begin bad-mouthing your spouse, it is your children who will suffer. Kids will often feel as though they have to choose sides, remain loyal to one parent, or act out their parents' anger for them. They often internalize parental disagreements and interpret them as somehow their own fault. Children are also infamous for replicating their parents' mistakes when handled in an unhealthy way. As hard as it might be, do your best to leave your kids out of the conflict. Try to speak positively about the addict, and give them permission to love their parent. Involving them in the conflict is unfair to them and will only cause them to suffer.

Don't bad-mouth your partner in public

Dragging mutual friends into your conflict with the addict will also make the people in your life feel as though they have to choose sides and may alienate you from your support system. Of course, it is important and reasonable to get support for yourself with close friends, therapy, and support groups, but keeping boundaries with mutual friends is usually in your best interest. Taking the higher ground in this situation may help you maintain some of your friendships during this transition, friendships that you can bring forward into the new chapter of your life.

Don't make the addiction about you

In the Barbie and Ken example, it was hard for Barbie to understand that Ken's infidelity was not about her. This was especially difficult because one of Ken's affair partners was her sister. This cut Barbie to the core and made her feel inadequate in comparison. Ken's report that he had "the best sex in his life" left Barbie feeling that if she had tried harder to please him sexually, this wouldn't have happened. She didn't recognize that Ken's behavior was about Ken and not about her. She left the relationship feeling emotionally damaged, socially humiliated, and terrified about the future. If we take on the lie that somehow it is our fault (that we aren't pretty, handsome, sexy, rich, sweet, enough), we feel flawed and inadequate. This rejection by the person who swore to honor and love us until death do us part can shatter our world, even our sense of self.

It's important to recognize that the addict is afflicted with a disease. Part of the progression of this disease, is seeking empty sexual experiences at the expense of real intimacy in relationship. No change in your behavior could have altered the course or the path of the development of this disease. Believing that you could have caused or controlled the addiction is not realistic. This is not about your inadequacy, and it is important to continue to remind yourself of this fact.

Don't jump into another relationship right away

It can feel as though we are left to float adrift on a small island shrouded by the darkness of profound loneliness and shame. Therefore, it only seems logical that we would seek a life raft away from that much misery, right? Often the first raft to show up to rescue us is our desire for a new partner, one who will love us and not leave us. Another relationship will never truly take us off the island of loneliness and shame. It is only island hopping. It takes the sweet confinement of aloneness to build and remodel our internal home.

This requires sacred space to heal our wounds and sufficient time to support the process of falling in love with ourselves—maybe even for the first time. It is important to remember that the best relationships are those in which our love for someone exceeds our need for them.

Jumping into another relationship can provide a self-esteem boost and a deflection from our pain. We may feel worthwhile, sexy, and desired by another person in a way we didn't in our previous relationship. It can ease the sting of rejection and mask the pain. However, when we seek to boost our self-esteem through a relationship without doing our own internal work, it is a recipe for disaster. Betrayal does open profound needs within and we are the only person capable of truly meeting those needs. It's an inside job. No one can do for us; we must do for ourselves.

Give yourself this gift of time for a minimum of twelve months before you even think of beginning another romantic relationship. Most grief experts advise the bereaved not to enter another relationship during the first twelve months following the death of their spouse. It takes time to heal. Since divorce is also a death, a death of the past relationship, you deserve the same protection and provision. Allow yourself this space in time for introspection.

Becoming involved with another person too soon is the most costly of mistakes. It ensures that we will relive our painful past again and again. We deserve to find meaningful acceptance and relational intimacy, but before this can be achieved, we need to understand the dynamics of our past relationship. Helen Keller once said, "Although the world is full of suffering, it is also full of the overcoming of it." One effective way of overcoming suffering is to gain insight about the past. Understanding our past relationship will shed light on how we view ourselves in the context of relationships. Having this knowledge is critical if we are to change our course and rebuild.

Don't use alcohol, drugs, or food to mask the pain you are in

The pain of betrayal can be so severe that attempting to medicate it becomes a natural response. However, medicating just further perpetuates the pain and compounds the problem. It may be tempting to ease your pain with things such as prescription drugs, alcohol, eating too much, spending too much, working too much, or sleeping too much as you attempt to avoid being annihilated by your excruciating, unrelenting emotions. You may even engage in self-harm behaviors such as hitting, cutting, or burning yourself.

Recovery from relationship trauma must go hand-in-hand with recovery from any and all self-defeating behaviors. A vicious cycle is created when dependence on a substance or compulsive behavior is exacerbated by the stress of an unhealthy relationship. The pain of severing the ties of your relationship can be intensified by the chaotic feelings engendered by self-defeating behaviors.

We use the betrayal to explain and excuse our destructive behaviors. Conversely, our continued use of these behaviors allows us to tolerate unhealthy relationships by numbing our pain and robbing us of the motivation necessary for change and healing. We blame one for the other. We use one to deal with the other. As a result, we become more and more hooked on both. Our blocking attempts may seem easier than facing the formidable tasks before us, but numb never equals recovery. Numb only delays, debilitates, or destroys our ability to move beyond our unthinkable circumstances and heal our wounds.

Take It One Day at a Time

The world is full of people who leave bad relationships, but never really do the emotional grieving and therapeutic work needed to move on. Instead they hold on to the past, drag others into the conflict, and make others miserable. Don't let this be you! Seize the opportunity to charter a new path for yourself and discover new hopes and dreams. Practice meticulous care for yourself—legally, financially, spiritually, and emotionally—because nobody will do it for you. Know that you deserve a life filled with peace and abundant love. Determine that you will live your own life, one decision at a time, one thought at a time, one choice at a time, and one day at a time. String enough of these days together and you will indeed find happiness.

Chapter Fourteen:
Can We Make It as a Couple?
A Couple Talks about Long-Term Recovery

Virginia Hartman, MA, LPC
Paul Hartman, MS, LMFT

ℰℛ

There is good news and bad news for couples in recovery from sexual addiction. The good news is recovery for the couple is possible. The bad news is couple's recovery requires hard work, commitment, and patience. Still, the effort is worth it.

This chapter reflects the personal experience of the authors, a sexual addict and partner. We talk about how we achieved recovery and how we sustain recovery. While we focus primarily on long-term couple's recovery, we also refer to our individual recoveries, because our couple's recovery depends on individual recovery. We began our recovery journeys more than thirty years ago. As of this writing, we have been married more than forty-five years. We hope to share how a long-term recovering relationship can be fulfilling, satisfying, passionate, romantic, and fun.

Before we answer some of the questions couples face, we'd like to review the stages of recovery and discuss how these apply to the relationship.

The Six Stages of Recovery for Partners of Sex Addicts[1]

1. **Developing/Pre-Discovery:**
   Partners start to see that addiction is present.

2. **Crisis/Decision/Information Gathering:**
   Partners realize they can no longer tolerate the problem.

---

continued on next page

continued from previous page

3. **Shock:**
   Partners see how bad things are and go to therapy.

4. **Grief/Ambivalence:**
   Partners profoundly understand their losses and pain.

5. **Repair:**
   Partners reconstruct how they interact with themselves and others.

6. **Growth:**
   Partners experience a new depth in their relationships.

In our experience, these same stages apply to our relationship as a couple. For example, in the developing stage, we both knew that we were dissatisfied and unhappy in the relationship. We did not know specifically why. The crisis decision stage begins when the partner discovers some of the addict's sexual acting-out behaviors. *[Virginia]* As the partner, my thoughts were

- *This is too much.*
- *This is the one thing I can never forgive or accept.*
- *This is the end of the marriage.*

At this point, many partners seek help from an attorney. Divorce is usually the result. Looking back, I feel fortunate and grateful that I sought help from a therapist instead. Back then, there were few if any therapists who specialized in just sex addiction. I was already attending Al-Anon meetings. From recommendations there, I found a therapist who did group therapy, had expertise in multiple addictions, and could refer me to Twelve Step meetings as part of the treatment plan.

Even with help from a therapist, I did not believe that I could stay in the marriage. We had three young children, so part of me wanted to keep the family together. However, another part of me felt so betrayed that the thought of staying in the relationship seemed impossible. I needed time apart from my husband, the sex addict.

My therapist agreed. She recommended a clinical separation (sometimes called a therapeutic separation) rather than a legal separation. One of the most important lessons I learned then was that I did not have to make long-term decisions. I had to learn to live in the present moment. My therapist kept reminding me that over time—in my case, about six months—I would get through the pain of betrayal and loss, and my own inner wisdom would know what to do about the marriage. Instead of obsessing about my partner and whether or not to divorce, I learned to focus on me. My main tasks were to learn and practice self-care, reduce shame, stop blaming myself, build self-esteem, and stop obsessing.

While all this was happening, my addict partner felt tremendous shame, humiliation, remorse, fear, and hopelessness. In recovery language, this state is sometimes referred to as "hitting bottom." Even today with all the advances in addiction medicine, hitting bottom still seems to be a necessary part of the recovery process for addicts.

In this condition of hopelessness and surrender, the addict begged for another chance, saying *I will do anything.* That turned out to be an exaggeration. The therapist recommended inpatient treatment that would take at least four weeks, maybe longer. The addict refused. The addict used the excuse that inpatient treatment took too long and costs too much. Those are very common excuses. The real reason was my partner was still in some denial about the disease and lacked willingness. The addict did agree to some things that proved to be essential, including group therapy, attending Twelve Step meetings, and the clinical separation. Many addicts identify with the phrase "recovery is doing the things you do not want to do."

Primarily because we both had the help of a good therapist, we progressed to the third stage of recovery—shock. We both knew that there once had been a time when we truly loved and trusted each other. We could not believe what was happening to us. We both began the recovery process as victims. Without therapy and a Twelve Step program, we would have continued to recycle through the dysfunctional roles of victim, rescuer, and persecutor. Only because we had the willingness to seek and accept help, we learned to move from victim to choice maker. We learned that we were not bad people. We were people struggling with the disease of addiction.

What does the addict need to share and what does the partner have a right to know?

Our therapist assisted us with the disclosure process. (See chapter 2 for more information on disclosure.) This crucial step has the potential to lead to disaster when mishandled. Remember that the addict and partner are both trauma survivors. The disclosure process itself can be trauma-inducing. When couples attempt to do disclosure on their own, each of them risks being re-traumatized. The partner often demands detailed information about the sexual acting out. Some therapists refer to this as *pain-shopping*. If the addict gives in to the demands for too much detail, those details may become imprinted into the brain of the partner and make recovery virtually impossible. The addict often attempts to disclose only what the partner already knows and withhold everything that might successfully be kept secret. This dishonesty during disclosure reinforces the partner's belief that the addict can never be trusted.

A skilled therapist will coach the partner into waiting for disclosure until the partner is strong enough to hear it without the risk of being re-traumatized. The addict needs to become willing to be "rigorously" honest. The addict will sometimes withhold information out of fear that the partner will leave if she or he knows everything. Attempts at information management set up a power imbalance with the addict one-up and the partner one-down. Mutuality cannot exist from this dynamic. Thus, couples recovery cannot happen.

Keep in mind that disclosure is not a one-way street. In an attempt to get unmet needs met, the partner may have also lived a secret life. The rules of no secrets, no information management, no inappropriate detail, no dishonesty, and no unnecessary trauma risks apply equally to the addict and the partner.

My partner is the addict with the despicable behaviors. Why do I have to join in the work?

Details of individual recovery exceed the scope of this chapter. We simply need to emphasize that both addict and partner need their own recovery before there is any hope for recovery as a couple. Two wounded people cannot form a functional relationship as a couple. Sex addiction exceeds behavioral problems. Addiction is a brain disease. Recovery means healing the brain, healing core wounds, and changing behavior. Partners need to heal their own wounds of betrayal. They have their own symptoms and core issues. We both believe that we are together today because in the beginning of the recovery process, we experienced the miracle of self-focus. Twelve Step recovery is all about self-examination.

Why not just move on and not do the work? Is it worth it?

If we did not have children, we don't know if we would have chosen to stay together and work on our relationship as a couple. Our therapist encouraged us to work on the relationship even before we chose to stay in the marriage. The therapist taught us that we could divorce and become ex-spouses, but that we would never be ex-parents. Our original goal was simply to become friendly co-parents. We embraced the idea that a successful marriage is not the result of finding the right partner. A successful marriage is the result of learning how to function in a relationship. We agreed that if we were going to do the work of learning how to behave in a healthy relationship, we might as well learn with each other and see what happened.

Many couples caught up in the pain of sex addiction do choose to move on without doing this difficult healing work. Many of them go on to new relationships only to experience the same problems all over again with the new partner. This is an example of "first-order change": "The more things change, the more they stay the same."

How is it possible to be a couple again?

It is possible, but you'll need some tools to make it work. Visualize a three-legged stool. Two legs represent both partners and the third leg represents the relationship of the couple. We learned to view our relationship as a couple as "the third entity." Just as each individual needs to do his or her own work, the third entity requires marital therapy, couples group therapy, and the Twelve Steps.

When we began this work, Recovering Couples Anonymous (RCA) did not exist. We found a culture of support through other couples in Twelve Step recovery. Our relationship as a couple suffered some of the same wounds as the individual addict and partner, which included leading a secret life, couple shame, and couple trauma. Slowly we both came to see that we had problems that could not be fixed by simply changing partners. We began to see why so many people divorce only to perpetuate the dysfunction.

We believe that we did not fix the old relationship. The old relationship was so damaged by sexual betrayal and other traumas that it was beyond repair. Rather we chose to build a new relationship with each other. We sometimes joke that this is our second marriage. Actually we have only been married once, but we are in relationship with a brand-new person as the result of recovery.

Is this really going to work?

The following statement reveals itself most vividly in the process of trust building and forgiveness: *Whether you believe you can or believe that you cannot, you are right.* Both the addict and the partner often begin the process believing they cannot do it.

The reality is that the behavior of many sex addicts is so despicable that it is understandable for the partner to think, *I can never trust or forgive.* And on our own, most could not. This is one of the reasons we must become part of a culture of support. We need the experience of seeing others do that which we think cannot be done. This is difficult, but not impossible. Thousands of recovering couples have done it. If our goal is to have a successful relationship as a couple with our current partner, we must surround ourselves with others who are doing so as well.

Will I ever be able to trust my partner again?

Trust building for the partner falls into the category of "life is not fair." The addict's behavior broke trust, and the partner must be willing to do part of the work to rebuild that trust. Believing that trust can be restored is difficult for the addict as well. Often addicts are so shame-filled from the double hit of childhood trauma and current compulsive behavior that they believe no one, including themselves, will ever see them as trustworthy. Trust becomes the foundation of the new relationship that needs to be built. We must both choose to believe that we can build trust with our partner.

Fortunately, there is a formula for trust building. Al-Anon has an expression for such a formula: *Talk's easy, work's hard.* **Consistent** *trustworthy behavior over time equals trust.* Notice the word *consistent* is emphasized. Consistency is the key to the process. This becomes an even greater challenge because "addiction is a disorder that is characterized by relapse."[2] Left to his or her own devices, the sex addict will relapse. However, research informs us that addicts who do the work and live a Twelve Step recovery can live a life free of slips and relapses. Consistent trustworthy behavior is attainable even for a sex addict. The partner's role in all this starts with choosing to believe that it can be done, even though all the partner's experience points to the contrary.

The words *over time* in Al-Anon's formula emphasizes that even with all the recommended recovery resources in place, this process takes a long time. And it always takes longer than the addict thinks it should! In SAA meetings all over the country, newly recovering sex addicts can be heard whining about how they have been good for so long and their partner still doesn't trust them. Often such complaints can be heard after only a few weeks of abstinence from the compulsive behaviors that broke trust in the first place. Trust cannot be rebuilt in days or weeks; it takes months and years. The addict needs to bring patience to the process. The addict's core belief needs to be, *I can do this and it will take time.* Every time the partner expresses distrust or fear and the addict reacts with impatience and anger, the couple's relationship experiences a setback and the trust-building process suffers.

Even now, after all our years of recovery and relapse-free behavior, the partner can still experience triggers that provoke doubt, suspicion, fear, wonder, or painful memories. When the addict reacts with gentle, loving, reassuring messages, we move through these experiences with barely a hiccup to our relationship. Addicts can respond from recovery rather than dysfunction when they remind themselves that the trigger is often the result of the scar tissue from the old wound of sex addiction.

Accountability is another part of the trust-building process. Addicts must be willing to give their partners access to information needed for reassurance. They also need to take responsibility for sustaining their own recovery. For example, the addict may need to change jobs in order to discontinue the need to travel on business if that is a threat to his or her recovery. The partner may need the addict to stop going certain places or spending time with certain people. Remember this quote from Alcoholics Anonymous: *"We must be willing to go to any length to get it."*

Obviously, this is not legal advice for couples going through divorce. Protecting yourself in a divorce action is a totally different process than the process of building a relationship. Helpful self-talk at this point is, *This is difficult, but it is worth it.*

We use one other resource for trust building: Be impeccable with your word.[3] Many of us grew up in dysfunctional family systems where we learned to distort the truth as part of our survival system. In recovery, we must say what we mean and mean what we say. To live in recovery, we must become people of integrity. When we live from integrity, our actions match our words. We become trustworthy.

Can I ever truly forgive?

Another cornerstone for the foundation we are building is forgiveness. Like choosing to trust, this is another very tall order. The tools we learned for trust building help us in the forgiveness process. It starts with choosing to believe that you can do it. Again, this is true for both the addict and the partner. Sometimes the partner learns about betraying behavior and retaliates in ways that are inappropriate, hurtful, and vengeful. Sometimes partners act outside their value system in an attempt to get their needs met. In these cases, the addict and partner must both choose to forgive.

The strongest case we can make for forgiveness is to look at the alternative. What happens if we do not forgive? In Twelve Step recovery we learn that the opposite of forgiveness is resentment. Resentment is sometimes described as taking poison in hopes that the offending person will die. Choosing resentment does not work. It only hurts the person holding the resentment. Does this mean that forgiveness must always be granted? No!

Many of us come out of a faith system that teaches us that the betrayed must always forgive. Whatever our religious background, many of us have heard the instruction, "Turn the other cheek." Janis Abrahms Spring's *How Can I Forgive You?* provides excellent guidance for both the offended and the offender on this topic.[4] She emphasizes that the offender must earn forgiveness in contrast to the offended, who must grant forgiveness. We found this to be an excellent model for healing the couple's relationship from the betrayal of sex addiction. We learned that unconditional forgiveness and resentment are the opposite extremes on the forgiveness scale. We strive for the healthy middle of acceptance or genuine forgiveness when earned. When resentment remains buried and hidden, author Spring calls this *false forgiveness*. The unresolved resentment may surface years later. Resentment blocks healing for the couple's relationship with each other.

Twelve Step recovery provides another resource for earning forgiveness. Step Nine instructs us to *make amends* to people we harmed. We learn that the main people we harmed were ourselves and our family. Making an amend goes way beyond saying, "I'm sorry." Many addicts have said sorry so many times that the word becomes meaningless or even annoying. If we really mean we're sorry, Dr. Joe Cruse suggests using these five parts in the apology:[5]

1. *I was wrong.*
2. *You didn't deserve that.*
3. *I'm sorry.*
4. *Please forgive me.*
5. *I love you.*

When delivered with sincerity, these words can be a means for earning forgiveness. *Amend* means change. The best way to earn forgiveness is to change behavior. The entire recovery process helps us achieve real and lasting change. Many of us have heard the phrase "forgive and forget." If we embrace this approach to forgiveness, we may wrongly conclude that forgiveness is not possible for us because we know that we cannot forget. Our experience teaches us that we can choose to forgive even though we may never forget.

The bottom line is that recovery of our relationship as a couple requires forgiveness. You can't fake forgiveness. Working the Twelve Steps and committing to therapy helped us work through and let go of resentments. Getting to the belief that our partner was trustworthy and that we each could forgive the other, took us significant time. Neither of us remembers exactly how long. We both agree that this part of the healing process took not months, but years.

Will I ever feel safe enough to be vulnerable with my partner?

We weren't able to express vulnerability with each other until we reached the fourth of the six stages of recovery for partners of sex addicts—the grief stage. We both reached this stage earlier in our individual recoveries. With the help of the Twelve Step program and therapy, we separately acknowledged the losses we experienced over a lifetime. We learned to grieve those losses. John James's book *Grief-Recovery Handbook* provided invaluable help with this process.[6]

Remember, we are working in a model that recognizes our relationship as a couple as the third entity (think of it as that three-legged stool). So even though each of us had grieved separately, we needed to grieve our losses as a couple. Couples can only do this when they feel safe enough to be vulnerable with each other. Grieving is an emotionally intense encounter. This cannot be done together until trust and forgiveness have been established.

We will share one example of a loss that was both an individual and a couple's loss. After the birth of our second daughter, we experienced our third pregnancy. That pregnancy ended in a late-term miscarriage. That child who died before birth was a son. At the time of the miscarriage, we barely acknowledged the loss. We were both too caught up in the busyness of our lives at the time to grieve the loss. With help, we learned to face our losses together and grieve together.

We named our unborn son, talked about how our life as a family would have been different if he had survived, cried together, and continued to talk to each other about him whenever either of us thought of him. Grief is a process of healing. In addition to healing our relationship as a couple, grief also provided us with our early experiences of emotional intimacy.

Can we ever stop blaming, attacking, and defending?

We both needed to admit that we didn't know how to talk or listen to each other. Like most people, we learned couples' communication by watching it modeled by our parents when we were young children. For both of us, our parents modeled dysfunctional communication. Also, our resentments toward one another made respectful, intimate communication very difficult. Once again, we needed therapy to teach us how to do it differently. Recovery Couples Anonymous gave us opportunities to watch recovering couples model new methods of communication.

Entire books have been written on couples' communication, and a thorough discussion of strategies is beyond the scope of this chapter. However, we will share a few highlights that helped us communicate without attacking and defending. Take time to decide who will talk first and who will listen first. We cannot listen and talk at the same time. Two sayings help us remember this: When the mouth opens, the ears close, and there is a reason we are created with one mouth and two ears. Also, we remind ourselves that we are communicating to know our partner better. That means listening to the other's reality and talking to share our reality. Functional couples' communication is not about blaming, defending, case-building, or getting your way. It is about being vulnerable enough to share our reality and being respectful enough to listen without judging or defending.

Can we ever have intimacy in our relationship?

We learned that we had not known emotional intimacy with each other even before sex addiction took over the relationship. We didn't need a new partner to have intimacy. Both of us needed to stop blaming the other and learn how to create intimacy. When we began doing the following behaviors, it helped heal our relationship as a couple and created emotional intimacy:

- stop blaming
- risk trusting
- earning and giving forgiveness
- reducing shame individually and as a couple
- grieving together
- communicating with boundaries—simply to know and be known

By going through this process, it required us to risk being vulnerable with one another. We learned to communicate in feelings-related language. One day we recognized that we had created a functional, emotionally intimate relationship as a couple—without the need to change partners. We still had more work to do, but we had the start of a new relationship.

Can we ever experience healthy sexuality together?

We began learning about healthy sexuality early in our healing process. However, we didn't experience true sexual intimacy until we achieved emotional intimacy that resulted from practicing all of the behaviors noted in the previous question. The sex addict needed to change the core belief that sex was the most important need. The partner needed to stop believing that being sexual to please the addict, or avoiding sex to punish the addict or to protect oneself would result in power and control over the chaos that resulted from living in sex addiction.

In early recovery, we both needed a time-out from sex. We achieved that by agreeing to a celibacy contract. Our therapist recommended ninety days of no sex together, alone (masturbation), or in any way. Since we were getting back together after a time apart without sex for about six months, we abstained from sex for about nine months total before we were ready to begin this extremely vulnerable and intimate step.

We needed to learn how to nurture ourselves and each other in non-genital ways. Our therapist instructed us to have "skin time" at least twice a week. That was a time of holding each other in bed while nude. We learned to enjoy this form of touch without progressing to intercourse or any form of genital stimulation. This assignment was especially difficult for the sex addict. Over time, even the addict learned to enjoy this form of nurturing and intimacy.

We both needed to admit that we did not know a lot about sex. We needed to learn about the human sexual response cycle. There is so much more to good sex than orgasm. We learned together to enjoy every stage of the cycle. We recommend Dr. Patrick Carnes's book *Sexual Anorexia* as a resource for couples desiring better sexual intimacy.[7] About two-thirds of the book is devoted to healthy sexuality. Reading through and discussing each of the chapters together will enhance both emotional and sexual intimacy. Other good references include *Sexual Re-integration,* by Bill and Ginger Bercaw, and *Erotic Intelligence* by Alex Katehakis. (See the Recommended Reading list on page 261 for more suggestions.)

Can we ever be on the same page spiritually?

Throughout this chapter we attempt to emphasize that we felt powerless over the disease, and we felt powerless to heal our relationship. Working the Twelve Step program for our individual recoveries gave us the hope that we could recover if we surrendered and accepted help. We applied that same principle to our relationship as a couple. With help, we could do what we could not do alone.

Neither of us thought of spirituality as a way of experiencing intimacy. We automatically thought of religion. Although we both grew up in similar denominations and raised our children in a faith community, we rarely talked about religion. In our individual recoveries we learned to differentiate religion and spirituality.

In Recovery Couples Anonymous, we learned that spirituality for our relationship as a couple was just as important as our individual spiritual progress. We learned that we could have different religious beliefs and still connect with each other spiritually. The key here is connection. Both addict and partner learned to live in isolation. Many addicts relate to the expression "feeling alone in a crowd." We experienced any form of connection, not just connection to God, as spiritual progress.

Individually, both of us spent time in prayer and meditation each morning. We began to do that spiritual practice together. We would take turns reading from a meditation book from our recovery program. We would discuss it together. Then we would pray out loud together. We sat facing close enough to hold hands. We prayed with eyes open looking into each others' eyes. We do not know whether this is an effective way to talk to God. However, we do know that it is a very powerful way to connect with each other.

Both of us love to spend time outside in nature. We learned that this, too, can be a spiritual practice. Everything that results in feeling connected, whether to the universe, the planet, the community, family, or to another person—all of this is spiritual. We spend time together in nature on a regular basis. We love beaches, mountains, rivers, and deserts. All of these places help us feel connected to the earth, to each other, and to the spiritual realm.

For us, finding a place we could both worship a Higher Power together was an important part of our spirituality as a couple. We no longer worship out of a sense of obligation, but rather as an expression of gratitude and as a way to experience spiritual intimacy together. We learned that there are two parts to spirituality—spiritual principles and spiritual practice. If it is true that one spiritual principle is love, then everything we do to grow in intimacy together is spiritual practice.

When will all this just come naturally?

For us, the answer is never. We will celebrate our forty-sixth wedding anniversary this year. We have been recovering together for about thirty years. We still have to work at having a great relationship with each other. The problem is time. In order to have intimacy together, we need time together. At every life stage, things get in the way. Many recovering sex addicts replace their sex addiction with work addiction.

Just like a precious child, our relationship with each other requires time, nurturing, and valuing. We still schedule a date night together. When we don't, a whole week can slip by without time for intimacy and fun. It seems like everybody is too busy. We do find time for the things that are really important to us. We set goals of how much time to spend together as a couple. For example, taking thirty minutes a day with each other, spending one day a week together, or setting aside one weekend a month to spend together are some of our goals. We rarely achieve the goal. However, by striving for the goal, we have much more quality couples' time than we would without a goal.

When will we stop hurting each other?

Even after many years of individual and couples' recovery, we are still imperfect human beings. We still make mistakes. One of our most useful tools comes from Recovery Couples Anonymous. Once a week (daily in the beginning) we review the week (day) together. The talker shares "one thing I did this week that was hurtful to our relationship as a couple…" and "your gift to me was…" Then we switch roles and the listener shares in the same way. Notice the taking of responsibility and validating of our partner. We have come full circle from blaming and defending.

A successful relationship as a couple is not about being lucky enough to find the right partner. It is about learning how to function respectfully in a relationship. Even when the betrayal cuts so deep, as in sex addiction, couples can choose to build something brand new together that is better than what they had in the first place. That is what is possible when both partners bring individual recovery to the relationship.

The Twelve Steps of Sex Addicts Anonymous

ℰↄ⊂ℛ

Step One: We admitted we were powerless over addictive sexual behavior—that our lives had become unmanageable.

Step Two: Came to believe that a Power greater than ourselves could restore us to sanity.

Step Three: Made a decision to turn our will and our lives over to the care of God as we understood God.

Step Four: Made a searching and fearless moral inventory of ourselves.

Step Five: Admitted to God, to ourselves, and to another human being the exact nature of our wrongs.

Step Six: Were entirely ready to have God remove all these defects of character.

Step Seven: Humbly asked God to remove our shortcomings.

Step Eight: Made a list of all persons we had harmed and became willing to make amends to them all.

Step Nine: Made direct amends to such people wherever possible, except when to do so would injure them or others.

Step Ten: Continued to take personal inventory and when we were wrong promptly admitted it.

Step Eleven: Sought through prayer and meditation to improve our conscious contact with God as we understood God, praying only for knowledge of God's will for us and the power to carry that out.

Step Twelve: Having had a spiritual awakening as the result of these steps, we tried to carry this message to other sex addicts and to practice these principles in our lives.

Reprinted from the International Service Organization of SAA, Inc., 2005.

Resource Guide

ℰℭ

The following is a list of recovery fellowships that will help you on your journey to healing.

Adult Children of Alcoholics
310-534-1815
www.adultchildren.org

Al-Anon
800-344-2666
www.al-anon-alateen.org

Alateen
(ages twelve to seventeen)
800-356-9996
www.al-anon-alateen.org

Alcoholics Anonymous
212-870-3400
www.aa.org

CoAnon
www.co-anon.org

Cocaine Anonymous
800-347-8998
www.ca.org

Co-Dependents Anonymous
602-277-7991
www.codependents.org

Co-Dependents of Sex Addicts (COSA)
612-537-6904
www.cosa-recovery.org

Debtors Anonymous
781-453-2743
www.debtorsanonymous.org

Emotions Anonymous
651-647-9712
www.emotionsanonymous.org

Families Anonymous
310-815-8010
www.familiesanonymous.org

Gamblers Anonymous
213-386-8789
www.gamblersanonymous.org

International Institute for Trauma and Addiction Professionals (IITAP)
480-575-6853
www.iitap.com

Marijuana Anonymous
212-459-4423
www.marijuana-anonymous.org

Narcotics Anonymous
818-773-9999
www.na.org

**National Council for Couple
and Family Recovery**
314-997-9808

Nicotine Anonymous
www.nicotine-anonymous.org

Overeaters Anonymous
www.oa.org

Recovering Couples Anonymous
314-997-9808
www.recovering-couples.org

Runaway and Suicide Hotline
800-RUN-AWAY
www.1800runaway.org

S-Anon
615-833-3152
www.sanon.org

Sex Addicts Anonymous
713-869-4902
www.sexaa.org

**Sex and Love Addicts
Anonymous**
210-828-7900
www.slaafws.org

Sexaholics Anonymous
866-424-8777
www.sa.org

Sexual Addiction Resources
Dr. Patrick Carnes
www.sexhelp.com

Sexual Compulsives Anonymous
310-859-5585
www.sca-recovery.org

**Society for the Advancement
of Sexual Health**
770-541-9912
www.sash.net

Survivors of Incest Anonymous
410-282-3400
www.siawso.org

Recommended Reading

ℰᏣᏟᎡ

Adult Children of Alcoholics

C. Black, *It Will Never Happen to Me: Growing Up With Addiction As Youngsters, Adolescents, Adults* (Center City, MN: Hazelden, 2002).

C. Black, *My Dad Loves Me, My Dad Has a Disease: A Child's View: Living with Addiction* (Bainbridge Island, WA: MAC Publishing, 1997).

A.W. Smith, *Grandchildren of Alcoholics: Another Generation of Co-dependency* (Deerfield Beach, FL: HCI, 1988).

J.G. Woititz, *Adult Children of Alcoholics* (Deerfield Beach, FL: HCI, 1990).

J.G. Woititz, *Marriage on the Rocks* (Deerfield Beach, FL: HCI, 1986).

J.G. Woititz, *Healthy Parenting: How Your Upbringing Influences the Way You Raise Your Children, and What You Can Do to Make It Better for Them* (New York: Simon & Schuster, 1990).

Co-Dependency

M., Ann. *Letting Go of the Need to Control* (Center City, MN: Hazelden, 1987).

M. Beattie, *Codependent No More: How to Stop Controlling Others and Start Caring for Yourself* (Center City, MN: Hazelden, 1986).

J. Friel, T. Gorski, J. Greenleaf et al. *Co-Dependency* (Delray Beach, FL: HCI, 1988).

M. Hunter, *Joyous Sexuality* (Minneapolis, MN: CompCare, 1992).

M. Hunter and Jem, a recovering codependent, *The First Step for People in Relationships with Sex Addicts* (Minneapolis, MN: CompCare, 1989).

A. Katherine, *Boundaries—Where You End and I Begin: How to Recognize and Set Healthy Boundaries* (Center City, MN: Hazelden, 1994).

A. Katherine, *Where to Draw the Line: How to Set Healthy Boundaries Every Day* (New York: Fireside Books, 2000).

B. Lair-Robinson and R. Lair-Robinson, *If My Dad's a Sexaholic, What Does That Make Me?* (Minneapolis, MN: CompCare, 1991).

R. Lerner, *Living in the Comfort Zone: The Gift of Boundaries in Relationships* (Deerfield Beach, FL: HCI, 1995).

P. Melody and A. Miller, *Facing Codependence: What It Is, Where It Comes from, How It Sabotages Our Lives* (New York: Harper & Row, 1989).

A. Miller, *The Drama of the Gifted Child* (New York: Basic Books, 1997).

C. Nakken, *The Addictive Personality: Understanding the Addictive Process and Compulsive Behavior* (Center City, MN: Hazelden, 1998).

C. Orange, *Emotional Maturity* (Center City, MN: Hazelden, 1985).

B. Schaeffer, *Is It Love or Is It Addiction?* (Center City, MN: Hazelden, 2009).

K. Thornton, *Learning to Live with Emotions* (Center City, MN: Hazelden, 1987).

W.E. Thornton, *Codependency, Sexuality, and Depression* (Summit, NJ: Pia Press, 1990).

S. Wegscheider-Cruse, *Choicemaking: For Spirituality Seekers, Co-Dependents and Adult Children* (Deerfield Beach, FL: HCI, 1985).

C.L. Whitfield, *Boundaries and Relationships: Knowing, Protecting, and Enjoying the Self* (Deerfield Beach, FL: HCI, 1993).

C. Wills-Brandon, *Learning to Say No* (Lincoln, NE: iUniverse, 2000).

A. Wilson Schaff, *Escape From Intimacy* (San Francisco, CA: Harper, 1989).

Couples Recovery from Sex Addiction

A. Katehakis, *Erotic Intelligence: Igniting Hot, Healthy Sex While in Recovery from Sex Addiction* (Deerfield Beach, FL: HCI, 2010).

P. Carnes, M. Laaser, and D. Laaser, *Open Hearts: Renewing Relationships with Recovery, Romance & Reality* (Center City, MN: Hazelden, 1999).

D. Corley and J. Schneider, *Disclosing Secrets* (Carefree, AZ: Gentle Path Press, 2002).

W. Kritsberg, *Healing Together: A Guide to Intimacy and Recovery for Co-Dependent Couples* (Deerfield Beach, FL: HCI, 1989).

E. Marlin, *Relationships in Recovery: Healing Strategies for Couples and Families* (San Francisco, CA: Harper, 1990).

J. Schneider and B. Schneider, *Rebuilding Trust* (Deerfield Beach, FL: HCI, 1990).

Family of Origin

C. Black, *It Will Never Happen to Me* (Center City, MN: Hazelden, 2002).

C. Black, *Changing Course: Healing from Loss, Abandonment and Fear* (Center City, MN: Hazelden, 2002).

J. Bradshaw, *Healing the Shame That Binds You* (Deerfield Beach, FL: HCI, 2005).

C. Whitfield, *Healing the Child Within* (Deerfield Beach, FL: HCI, 1987).

Men's Issues

K. Adams, *When He's Married to Mom* (New York: Simon & Schuster, 2007).

B. Erickson, *Longing for Dad: Father Loss and Its Impact* (Deerfield Beach, FL: HCI, 1998).

R. Fisher, *The Knight in Rusty Armor* (Chatsworth, CA: Wilshire Book Co., 1989).

S. Keen, *Fire in the Belly: On Being A Man* (New York: Bantam, 1992).

G. Smalley, *If Only He Knew* (Grand Rapids, MI: Zondervan, 1982).

Money Issues

M. Bryan and J. Cameron, *Money Drunk, Money Sober* (New York: Ballantine, 1999).

K. Estes and M. Brubaker, *Deadly Odds: Recovery from Compulsive Gambling* (New York: Simon & Schuster, 1994).

J. Needleman, *Money and the Meaning of Life* (New York: Doubleday, 1994).

Partners of Sex Addicts

B. Steffens and M. Means, *Your Sexually Addicted Spouse: How Partners Can Cope and Heal* (Far Hills, NJ: New Horizon Press, 2009).

J. Schneider, *Back from Betrayal* (Center City, MN: Hazelden, 1988).

J. Schneider and B. Schneider, *Sex, Lies and Forgiveness* (Center City, MN: Hazelden, 2001).

D. Weiss and D. DeBusk, *Women Who Love Sex Addicts* (Deerfield Beach, FL: HCI, 1993).

D. Laaser, *Shattered Vows* (Grand Rapids: MI: Zondervan, 2008).

Recovery and Twelve Step Books

Anonymous, *Alcoholics Anonymous* (New York: AA World Services).

Anonymous, *Al-Anon Faces Alcoholism* (New York: Al-Anon Family Group Head Inc.).

Anonymous, *Al-Anon's Twelve Steps and Twelve Traditions* (New York: Al-Anon Family Group Head Inc.).

Anonymous, *One Day at a Time in Al-Anon* (New York: Al-Anon Family Group Head Inc., 1978).

Anonymous, *The Dilemma of the Alcoholic Marriage* (New York: Al-Anon Family Group Head Inc., 1977).

Anonymous, *Courage to Change: One Day at a Time in Al-Anon* (New York: Al-Anon Family Group Head Inc., 1992).

Anonymous, *Hope for Today* (New York: Al-Anon Family Group Headquarters, 2007).

Anonymous, *Alateen—A Day at a Time* (New York: Al-Anon Family Group Headquarters, 1983).

Anonymous, *Alateen—Hope for Children of Alcoholics* (New York: Al-Anon Family Group Headquarters).

Anonymous, *Having Had a Spiritual Awakening* (New York: Al-Anon Family Group Headquarters, 1998).

Anonymous, *Sex and Love Addicts Anonymous* (San Antonio, TX: The Augustine Fellowship, 1986).

Anonymous, *Codependents Anonymous* (Denver, CO: CoDA Resource Publishing, 1995).

Anonymous, *Recovering Couples Anonymous Blue Book* (Oakland, CA: Recovering Couples Anonymous, 1996).

Bill P. and Lisa D., *The Twelve Step Prayer Book* (Center City, MN: Hazelden, 2004).

S. Covington, *A Woman's Way Through the Twelve Steps* (Center City, MN: Hazelden, 1994).

Elisabeth L., *Twelve Steps for Overeaters* (Center City, MN: Hazelden, 1993).

S. Mcniff, *Trust the Process* (Boston, MA: Shambhala, 1998).

Sex Addiction

P. Carnes, *Don't Call It Love* (Center City, MN: Hazelden, 1992).

P. Carnes, *Out of the Shadows* (Center City, MN: Hazelden, 2001).

P. Carnes, *Contrary to Love* (Center City, MN: Hazelden, 1994).

P. Carnes, *The Betrayal Bond* (Deerfield Beach, FL: HCI, 1997).

P. Carnes, *Facing the Shadow* (Carefree, AZ: Gentle Path Press, 2001).

P. Carnes, *A Gentle Path Through the Twelve Steps* (Center City, MN: Hazelden, 1994).

P. Carnes, *Sexual Anorexia* (Center City, MN: Hazelden, 1997).

P. Carnes, D. Delmonico, and E. Griffin, *In the Shadows of the Net* (Center City, MN: Hazelden, 2001).

P. Carnes and K. Adams, *The Clinical Management of Sex Addiction* (New York: Brunner-Routledge, 2002).

D. Delmonico and E. Griffin, *Cybersex Unhooked* (Carefree, AZ: Gentle Path Press, 2001).

C. Kasl, *Women, Sex, and Addiction* (New York: Harper, 1990).

R. Weiss and J. Schneider, *Untangling the Web: Sex, Porn, and Fantasy Obsession in the Internet Age* (New York: Alyson Publications, 2006).

R. Weiss, *Cruise Control: Understanding Sex Addiction in Gay Men* (New York: Alyson Publications, 2005).

Sexual Abuse

K. Adams, *Silently Seduced: When Parents Make Their Children Partners* (Deerfield Beach, FL: HCI, 1991).

L. Bass, *The Courage to Heal: A Guide for Women Survivors of Child Sexual Abuse* (New York: Harper, 2008).

S. Brownmiller, *Against Our Will: Men, Women, and Rape* (New York: Ballantine, 1993).

P. Fleming, S. Lauber-Fleming, and M.T. Matousek, *Broken Trust: Stories of Pain, Hope and Healing from Clerical Abuse Survivors and Abusers* (New York: The Crossroad Publishing Co., 2007).

M. Hunter, *Abused Boys* (New York: Ballantine, 1991).

M. Lew, *Victims No Longer: The Classic Guide for Men Recovering from Sexual Child Abuse* (New York: HarperCollins, 2004).

Spirituality and Meditation

Anonymous, *Answers in the Heart* (Center City, MN: Hazelden, 1989).

Anonymous, *The Courage to Change* (New York: Al-Anon Family Group, 1992).

M. Beattie, *Journey to the Heart* (Center City, MN: Hazelden, 1990).

M. Beattie, *The Language of Letting Go* (Center City, MN: Hazelden, 1990).

K. Casey, *Each Day a New Beginning* (Center City, MN: Hazelden, 1982).

E. Kurtz and S. Ketchum, *The Spirituality of Imperfection* (New York: Bantam, 1993).

Elisabeth L., *Food for Thought: Daily Meditations for Dieters and Overeaters* (Center City, MN: Hazelden, 1980).

E. Larsen. *Days of Healing, Days of Joy* (Center City, MN: Hazelden, 1987).

B. Longyear. *Yesterday's Tomorrow: Recovery Meditations for Hard Cases* (Center City, MN: Hazelden, 1997).

G.G. May, *Addiction and Grace* (New York: HarperOne, 2007).

Trauma

T. Dayton, *Heartwounds* (Deerfield Beach, FL: HCI, 1997).

T. Dayton, *Trauma and Addiction* (Deerfield Beach, FL: HCI, 2000).

P. Levine and A. Frederick, *Waking the Tiger* (Berkeley, CA: North Atlantic Books, 1997).

L. M. Najavits, *Seeking Safety: A Treatment Manual for PTSD and Substance Abuse* (New York: The Guilford Press, 2002).

Women's Issues

R. Ackerman, *Perfect Daughters* (Deerfield Beach, FL: HCI, 2002).

H. Edelman, *Motherless Daughters: The Legacy of Loss* (Cambridge, MA: Da Capo Press, 2006).

Lois Frankel, *Women, Anger, and Depression* (Deerfield Beach, FL: HCI, 1991).

N. Friday, *My Mother/Myself: The Daughter's Search for Identity* (New York: Delta, 1997).

M. Grad, *The Princess Who Believed in Fairy Tales* (Chatsworth, CA: Wilshire Book Co., 1995).

M. Maine, *Father Hunger* (Carlsbad, CA: Gurze Books, 2004).

D. Miller, *Women Who Hurt Themselves* (New York: Basic Books, 1994).

Notes

ℰ᠉ℭ

Chapter 1

1. P.J. Carnes, *Out of The Shadows* (Center City, MN: Hazelden, 2001), 66-67.

2. B. A. Steffens and R. L. Rennie, "The Traumatic Nature of Disclosure for Wives of Sexual Addicts," *Sexual Addiction & Compulsivity* 13:247–67.

Chapter 2

1. D. Corley and J. Schneider, *Disclosing Secrets: When, to Whom, and How Much to Reveal* (Carefree, AZ: Gentle Path Press, 2002), 118.

2. Ibid., 119.

3. J. P. Schneider, D. Corley, and R. Irons, "Surviving Disclosure of Infidelity: Results of an International Survey of 164 Recovering Sex Addicts and Partners," *Sexual Addiction & Compulsivity* 5 (1998): 189–217.

4. Ibid.

5. Ibid.

6. J. P. Schneider and B. Schneider, *Sex, Lies & Forgiveness: Couples Speaking Out on Healing from Sex Addictions,* 3rd ed. (Tucson, AZ: Recovery Resources Press, 2004), 103.

Chapter 3

1. P. J. Carnes, *Don't Call It Love: Recovery from Sexual Addiction* (New York: Bantam Books, 1991).

2. Alcoholics Anonymous World Services, *Alcoholics Anonymous,* 4th ed. (New York: Alcoholics Anonymous World Services, 2001).

Chapter 4

1. M. Beattie and P. Carnes, "Interview with Melody Beattie," in *Contrary to Love* (Carefree, AZ: Gentle Path Press, 1999).

2. E. D. Payson, *The Wizard of Oz and Other Narcissists: Coping with the One-Way Relationship in Work, Love, and Family* (Royal Oaks, MI: Julian Day Publications, 2002).

3. P. J. Carnes, *Don't Call It Love: Recovery from Sexual Addiction* (New York: Bantam Books, 1991).

4. L. Cozolino, *The Neuroscience of Psychotherapy: Building and Rebuilding the Human Brain* (New York: W. W. Norton and Company, 2002).

5. *Shall We Dance* (Miramax, 2004). http://www.miramax.com/shallwedance

Chapter 6

1. W. Maltz, *The Sexual Healing Journey: A Guide for Survivors of Sexual Abuse* (Harper Collins, 1991).

2. Ibid.

Chapter 7

1. Center for Alcohol Studies, Rutgers University, http://aaalcoholstudies.rutgers.edu/

2. Sexual Recovery Anonymous (SRA) Literature. http://www.sexualrecovery.org/SRA%20Literature.htm

3. ISO of COSA literature, www.cosa-recovery.org

4. Alcoholics Anonymous World Services, *Alcoholics Anonymous,* 3rd ed. (New York: Alcoholics Anonymous World Services, 1976).

5. Ibid.

6. Ibid.

7. Ibid.

8. Center for Alcohol Studies, Rutgers University, http://aaalcoholstudies.rutgers.edu/

Chapter 8

1. M. Scott Peck, *People of the Lie: The Hope for Healing Human Evil*, 2nd ed. (New York: Touchstone, Simon and Schuster, 1998), 62–75.

2. C. Brown, "I've Got a Feeling..." quoting Dr. Emeran A. Mayer, *Oprah Magazine,* March 2007, 224–69.

3. M. Gladwell, *Blink: The Power of Thinking without Thinking* (New York: Little, Brown and Company, Time Warner Book Group, 2005).

4. Maslow and the Hierarchy of Needs from P. Carnes, & J. Bradshaw, "The Two Faces of Sexual Shame: Ecstasy and Agony," April 2001 presentation, Seattle.

5. G.R. Schiraldi, *The Self-Esteem Workbook* (Oakland, CA: New Harbinger, 2001).

6. Ibid.

7. P. Boss quotes T. H. Rainbolt, "Building Resilience," quote on handout, April 2007.

8. J. Carter, *The Virtues of Aging* (New York: Ballantine Books, 1998).

9. M. Beattie, *The Language of Letting Go: Daily Meditations for Codependents* (Center City, MN: Hazelden, 1990).

10. G.R. Schiraldi, *Facts to Relax By: A Guide to Relaxation and Stress Reduction* (Utah Valley Medical Center, 1982, 1987, 1996).

11. U. Schnyder, "Psychotherapies pour les PTSD—une vue d' ensemble [Psychotherapies for PTSD—An Overview]," *Psychotherapies* 25, no. 1 (2005): 39.

12. A. Bardin, "EMDR Within a Family System Perspective," *Journal of Family Psychotherapy* 15, no. 3 (2004): 47–61.

13. R. J. Taylor, "Therapeutic Intervention of Trauma and Stress Brought on by Divorce," *Journal of Divorce and Remarriage* 41, nos. 1–2 (2004): 129–35.

14. A. Siebert, *The Resiliency Advantage: Master Change, Thrive Under Pressure, and Bounce Back from Setbacks* (San Francisco: Berrett-Koehler, 2005).

15. M.E. Seligman, *Authentic Happiness: Using the New Positive Psychology to Realize Your Potential for Lasting Fulfillment* (New York: The Free Press, 2002), 160, 168, 266.

16. A. Siebert, *The Resiliency Advantage: Master Change, Thrive Under Pressure, and Bounce Back from Setbacks* (San Francisco: Berrett-Koehler, 2005).

17. Ibid.

Chapter 9

1. C. Black, D. Dillon, and S. Carnes, "Disclosure to Children: Hearing the Child's Experience," *Sexual Addiction and Compulsivity* 10: 67–78.

2. J. Piaget and B. Inhelder, *The Psychology of the Child* (New York: Basic Books, 1969).

3. C. Jung, *The Structure and Dynamics of the Psyche, Collected Works* (Princeton, NJ: Princeton University Press, 1969).

4. D. Corley and J. Schneider, *Disclosing Secrets: When, to Whom, and How Much to Reveal* (Carefree, AZ: Gentle Path Press, 2002).

5. Ibid.

6. C. Black, D. Dillon, and S. Carnes, "Disclosure to Children: Hearing the Child's Experience," *Sexual Addiction and Compulsivity* 10: 67–78.

7. Ibid.

Chapter 10

1. American Psychiatric Association, *Diagnostic and Statistical Manual of Mental Disorders*, 4th ed. (Washington, DC: American Psychiatric Association, 2000).

2. M. C. Seto and M. L. Lalumiere, "A Brief Screening Scale to Identify Pedophilic Interests among Child Molesters," *Sexual Abuse: A Journal of Research and Treatment* 13, (2001): 15–25.

3. American Psychiatric Association, *Diagnostic and Statistical Manual.*

4. Ibid.

5. M. C. Seto, J. M. Cantor, and R. Blanchard, "Child Pornography Offenses Are a Valid Diagnostic Indicator of Pedophilia," *Journal of Abnormal Psychology* 115 (2006): 610–15.

6. 18 United States Criminal Code 2252A.

7. T. Krone, "A Typology of Online Child Pornography Offending," *Trends and Issues in Crime and Criminal Justice,* no. 279 (2004).

8. 18 United States Criminal Code 2256.

9. E. Quayle and M. Taylor, *Child Pornography: An Internet Crime* (New York: Brunner-Routledge, 2003).

10. Ibid.

11. P. J. Carnes, "The Arousal Template" in *Facing the Shadow* (Carefree, AZ: Gentle Path Press, 2005), 227–230.

12. Ibid.

13. P. J. Carnes, D. L. Delmonico, E. Griffin, and J. M. Moriarity, *In the Shadows of the Net: Breaking Free of Compulsive Online Sexual Behavior* (Center City, MN: Hazelden, 2001).

Chapter 11

1. R. Weiss, *Cruise Control: Understanding Sex Addiction in Gay Men* (Los Angeles: Alyson Books, 2005).

Chapter 12

1. Center for Disease Control, revised, June 2007.

2. www.straightspouse.org

3. www.familypride.org

4. Pathela et al., "Discordance between Sexual Behavior and Self-Reported Sexual Identity: A Population-Based Survey of New York City Men," *Annals of Internal Medicine* 145 (2006): 416–25.

5. J. M. Preble and A. N. Groth, "Male Victims of Same-Sex Abuse: Addressing Their Sexual Response." 2002.

6. P. J. Carnes, *Don't Call It Love: Recovery from Sexual Addiction* (New York: Bantam Books, 1991).

Chapter 14

1. P. J. Carnes, *Don't Call It Love: Recovery from Sexual Addiction* (New York: Bantam Books, 1991).

2. Ibid.

3. D. M. Ruiz, *The Four Agreements: A Toltec Wisdom Book* (San Rafael, CA: Amber-Allen, 2001).

4. J. A. Spring, *How Can I Forgive You? The Courage to Forgive, the Freedom Not To* (New York: HarperCollins, 2004).

5. Presentation by Dr. Joe Cruse.

6. J. W. James, *The Grief Recovery Handbook* (New York: HarperCollins, 1998).

7. P. J. Carnes, *Sexual Anorexia: Overcoming Sexual Self-Hatred* (Center City, MN: Hazelden, 1997).

About the Authors

$\mathcal{SOCR}$

Stefanie Carnes, PhD, CSAT-S, has led numerous research projects on addiction and authored many publications including *Facing Addiction.* She is a licensed marriage and family therapist, and an AAMFT clinical member and approved supervisor. She is also certified through IITAP (International Institute for Trauma and Addiction Professionals) as a sex addiction therapist and supervisor. She is the former director of family services, research and intensive workshops at Pine Grove Behavioral Health & Addiction Services in Hattiesburg, MS. Dr. Carnes presents regularly at conferences at both the state and national levels.

Patrick Carnes, PhD, CAS, CSAT, is a nationally known speaker on addiction and recovery issues. He is the author of numerous books, including *Out of the Shadows: Understanding Sexual Addiction (1992), Contrary to Love: Helping the Sexual Addict (1989), The Betrayal Bond: Breaking Free of Exploitive Relationships (1997), Facing the Shadow (2001), In the Shadows of the Net (2001), The Clinical Management of Sex Addiction (2002), Facing Addiction (2011),* and *The Recovery Start Kit* (2007). Dr. Carnes is currently the Executive Director of the Gentle Path program at Pine Grove Behavioral Center in Hattiesburg, Miss. He is the primary architect of Gentle Path treatment programs for the treatment of sexual and addictive disorders. He also pioneered the founding of the Certified Sex Addiction Therapist (CSAT) program and the International Institute for Trauma and Addiction Professionals (IITAP).

Paul Hartman, MS, LMFT began a second career in counseling after graduating from Fuller Theological Seminary where he attended both the School of Theology and School of Psychology. Upon earning his license in marriage and family therapy, Mr. Hartman and his wife, Virginia, went into private practice together, opening The Healing Center. The couple specialized in treating addiction, co-addiction, couples and families. Mr. Hartman trained with Dr. Patrick Carnes to become a certified sex addiction therapist. He retired from his Michigan practice in 2005 but continues to work with Carnes and the International Institute for Trauma and Addiction Professionals (IITAP).

Virginia Hartman, MA, LPC began her professional career as an elementary school teacher before earning a MA in counseling psychology from Western Michigan University and becoming a Licensed Professional Counselor. After becoming certified as a substance abuse interventionist by the Johnson Institute, she gained experience in intervention, after-care, family treatment and primary treatment. She worked with several leaders in the field of addiction, then went into private practice with her husband Paul in Michigan. She trained with Dr. Patrick Carnes, using the task-based approach to treat trauma. She became a certified sex addiction therapist, specializing in treating sexually anorexic women. Although now retired, Ms. Hartman continues to teach, consult and conduct workshops for women and couples.

Mavis Humes Baird, CSAT-S, has developed several intervention and treatment programs in various modalities for addicts, family members and whole families. She consults with providers for their own program development. She is a CSAT Supervisor and an original member of Dr. Patrick Carnes' Practice Improvement Program. She worked in central and eastern Pennsylvania first as a drug and alcohol therapist, educator and interventionist, and then as a codependency and trauma therapist, treating eating disorders, sexual abuse and family systems issues. She also developed an effective treatment model for multiply-diagnosed clients. She has been working with sex addicts and co-addicts since 1988. With the help of a national rights organization, she is launching a legislative initiative to help educate society and aid sex addicts who want to find help.

Joe Kort, MA, MSW, CSAT, has specialized since 1985 in Gay Affirmative Psychotherapy, Marital Affairs, Mixed-Orientation Marriages, Sexual Addiction, Sexual Abuse and Imago Relationship Therapy through weekend workshops for singles and couples. He provides trainings to straight clinicians about Gay Affirmative Therapy around the country. Mr. Kort is the author of two books on gay-male identity and relationships as well as journal articles on sexual addiction. His newest book is *Gay Affirmative Therapy for the Straight Clinician: The Essential Guide.* An adjunct professor teaching Gay and Lesbian Studies at Wayne State University's School of Social Work, Mr. Kort maintains a regularly updated website at www.joekort.com.

Barbara S. Levinson, PhD, CSAT-S, is the Director of the Center for Healthy Sexuality in Houston. She offers specialized programs for the treatment of sex addicts and sex offenders and their partners. She also specializes in the treatment of Internet addictions. Dr. Levinson provides individual and couples therapy for persons who have intimacy and relationship problems. As a Certified Sex Therapist Diplomat for the American Association of Sexuality Educators, Counselors and Therapists, she deals with sexual issues of individuals and couples. At the Center for Healthy Sexuality, Dr. Levinson provides group therapy in many specialty areas. She is also a Licensed Marriage & Family Therapist, a Licensed Sex Offender Treatment Provider and a Therapist Supervisor for the International Institute for Trauma and Addiction Professionals Certified Sex Addiction Therapists.

Omar Minwalla, PhD, is a Licensed Psychologist and Clinical Sexologist, and the Clinical Director of the Sexual Recovery Institute in Los Angeles. Dr. Minwalla earned his doctorate in Clinical Psychology from the Illinois School of Professional Psychology in Chicago and completed his post-doctoral fellowship at the University of Minnesota Medical School's Program in Human Sexuality. His specializations include sexual compulsivity/sex addiction, sexual offending, sexual dysfunction, transgender populations, sexual orientation, BDSM and paraphilias. He also has a private practice specializing in marginalized sexuality and gender concerns.

Sonja Rudie, MA, LMHC, CSAT, C-EMDR, specializes in the treatment of trauma healing and recovery. Ms. Rudie is a Licensed Mental Health Counselor, Certified EMDR clinician, Certified Equine Assisted Therapist and a Certified Sex Addiction Therapist. She provides innovative and interesting treatment options for clients suffering from trauma in addition to the standard primary treatment protocol of Cognitive Behavioral Therapy. Ms. Rudie has provided therapy groups in resiliency skill-building, self-esteem, reality testing and creating mastery. She is the president and founder of La Perla Counseling and Trauma Response Services, Inc., which provides counseling for individuals, couples, families, youth and groups.

Jennifer Schneider, MD, PhD is a physician in Tucson, Ariz., specializing in addiction medicine and pain management. For 20 years she has been a researcher, speaker and author in the field of sex addiction, with a particular interest in the effects of sex addiction on the family. Dr. Schneider is the author of *Back From Betrayal: Recovering From his Affairs* (3rd Edition, 2005), *Sex, Lies, and Forgiveness: Couples Speak on Healing From Sex Addiction* (3rd Edition, 2004); *The Wounded Healer: Addiction-sensitive Approach to the Sexually Exploitative Professional* (with Dr. Richard Irons, 1998); *Disclosing Secrets: What, to Whom, and How Much to Reveal* (with Dr. Deborah Corley, 2002); and *Untangling the Web: Breaking Free from Sex, Porn, and Fantasy Addiction in the Internet Age* (with Robert Weiss, 2006).

Caroline Smith, MA, LPC, CSAT-S, CMAT is the director of family services and intensive workshops at Pine Grove Behavioral Healthin Hattiesburg, Mississippi. Her specialties are trauma, disordered attachment, sex addiction and eating disorders. Ms. Smith is an international trainer for interventionists who work with clients with chemical and process addictions. She frequently lectures on topics including trauma resolution, addiction interaction, food and sex, attachment style dynamics, and family systems legacy. Ms. Smith has published articles on family dynamics and strategies for resolving intimacy for couples. She is a passionate force in support of healing, hope and sustainable recovery.

Cara W. Tripodi, LCSW, MSS, CSAT-S, is the Executive Director and owner of S.T.A.R., Inc. (Sexual Trauma & Recovery) an outpatient practice in Wynnewood, Penn., devoted to the identification and treatment of sexual addiction, sexual anorexia and sexual codependency. She graduated from Bryn Mawr College in 1991 where she received her Master's in Social Science Degree. She has been treating sex addicts and their partners in both individual and group settings since 1991. She is a member of the Society for the Advancement of Sexual Health and is a certified sex addiction therapist. She is also a Level II trained EMDR therapist. Her previous experiences include service as a medical social worker where she developed an expertise in the area of traumatic and chronic illness and loss. Today, Ms. Tripoldi maintains a private practice as well as educating the behavioral healthcare community through workshops and lectures.

Robert Weiss, LCSW, CSAT-S, is founding Director of The Sexual Recovery Institute (SRI), Los Angeles and Director of Sexual Disorders Services for Elements Behavioral Health, which includes The Ranch in Nunnelly, TN, Promises Treatment Centers, and The Sexual Recovery Institute. A UCLA MSW graduate and trainee of Dr. Patrick Carnes, Mr. Weiss is author of *Cruise Control: Understanding Sex Addiction in Gay Men* (2005) and co-author (with Dr. Jennifer Schneider) of both *Untangling the Web: Sex, Porn and Fantasy Addiction in the Internet Age* (2006) and *Cybersex Exposed: Simple Fantasy to Obsession* (2001) along with numerous peer reviewed articles and chapters. He is a media expert to CNN, *The Oprah Winfrey Network, ESPN, Dr. Drew* and *The Today Show* among many others. Mr. Weiss also has provided clinical training in the assessment and treatment of sexual addiction for the National Institutes of Health (NIH), the US military, and behavioral treatment centers throughout the United States, Europe, and Asia.